HALLIDAY'S
NEW ENGLAND
FOOD EXPLORER

Novels by Fred Halliday

Ambler
A Slight Case of Champagne
The Raspberry Tart Affair
The Chocolate Mousse Murders

HALLIDAY'S NEW ENGLAND FOOD EXPLORER

Tours for Food Lovers

BY FRED HALLIDAY

Fodor's Travel Publications, Inc.
New York • Toronto • London • Sydney • Auckland

Fodor's is a registered trademark of Fodor's Travel Publications, Inc. All rights reserved under International and Pan-American Copyright Conventions. Published in the United States by Fodor's Travel Publications, Inc., a subsidiary of Random House, Inc., New York, and simultaneously in Canada by Random House of Canada Limited, Toronto. Distributed by Random House, Inc., New York.

No maps, illustrations, or other portions of this book may be reproduced in any form without written permission from the publisher.

Illustration of snail on page 7 from *The Random House Dictionary of the English Language,* 2nd Edition, Unabridged. Copyright © 1987 by Random House, Inc. Reprinted by permission of Random House, Inc.

Illustrations on pages 93 and 95 courtesy of Hancock Shaker Village, Pittsfield, MA.

Maple tree design on page 127 courtesy of Perception, Inc., Charlotte, VT.

Library of Congress Cataloging-in-Publication Data

Halliday, Fred, 1939–
    Halliday's New England food explorer: tours for food lovers / by Fred Halliday.
        p.   cm.
    Includes index.
    ISBN 0-679-02413-1
    1. Restaurants—New England—Guidebooks. 2. Markets—New England—Guidebooks. 3. Cookery, American—New England style. 4. New England—Guidebooks. I. Title. II. Title: New England food explorer.
    TX907.3.N35H35   1993
    647.9574—dc20   93-27060
                                            CIP

Text design: Fabrizio La Rocca
Cartographer: David Lindroth
Cover design: Fabrizio La Rocca, Tigist Getachew
Cover photograph: Steve Chenn/Westlight

Manufactured in the United States of America
10 9 8 7 6 5 4 3 2 1

Contents

NEW ENGLAND

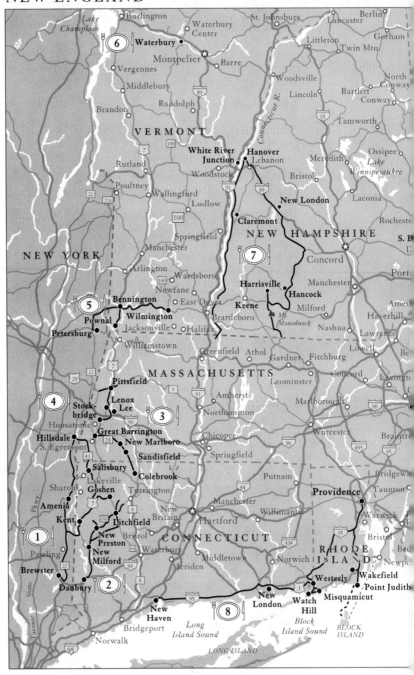

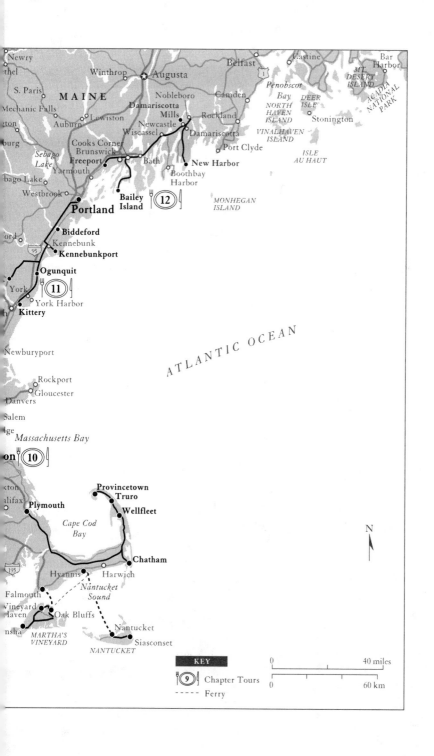

SETTING THE
TABLE

By the time I came to New England, I had already con-
tracted what was known to the Spanish and Christopher
Columbus as the Southern Complex. I believed there was
nothing in the world worth discovering in the north; if there
was anything good in the world, it must be to the south.

"But haven't you visited Maine?" my incredulous
neighbors would ask me. "And what about the Green
Mountains of Vermont?" I told them I liked my lobsters
Newburg, and as for skiing, it left me cold.

There was much to unlearn. No food can be as good as
food at the source. And it is surprising how much our national diet owes to New England for its start. Chowder, scrod,
cod, Boston baked beans—this much is familiar to most. But
lobster and its rolls, steamer clams, Jonah crabs, fiddleheads,
certain mustard greens, corncob smoked ham, red flannel
hash, hornpout in a pie, and, of course, maple syrup all hail
from New England, which is where you must go to get their
original taste in the mouth. (Maine's best lobsters are never
shipped south, but sold and eaten on its wharves.)

This is a book about food, and, more precisely, the food
that can be found if we get off the beaten track and search
out the rare, the primitive, and the exotic tastes of a region; so
let us call it food exploration. This is what I was doing in a
professional way when I was tracking down food stories,
usually in France, for American magazines and newspapers.
It was in this occupational setting that the idea of food exploration began to take shape. I learned to drive the French way,
with one eye peeled for mushrooms on the roadside and an
open guidebook on my lap. I began to see things as the

French did, through food. Returning to live in America, where food sources are mostly uncharted, I thought I would do the same thing in my own country.

Consider this. Would you like to go to a real New England clambake tonight? A place by the sea where there are layers of lobsters, clams, corn, and potatoes steaming in seawater and seaweed, while waves from the sea roll over a beach? "But hold it," you say—"there are only two of us, and a real New England clambake takes serious resources—clams by the hundreds, mountains of people to cook for, and songs and softball, too." Even so, between the covers of this book lie the routes to such adventures, where you can find such a clambake. The way to real organic beef, and what it is, is mapped out, too. There is an apple orchard with a stunning variety of apples to pick; and ways to Cheddar cheese, Christmas dinners in the country, plantations that serve what the Pilgrims ate in sites where they ate it, and inns to dine and sleep in. A hierarchy of beers is shown, a digest of fishes and mollusks, and ovensful of pizza. In short, there is everything to taste about New England geography, gastronomy, and history.

As for the food, the gastronomy, the exploration, I have tried to focus on the good things. There is so much. Except to warn the reader of occasional examples of kitchen incompetence and fraud, what is cited is the worthwhile and surprising: a plate maker in the woods, an unsuspected oyster farm at the end of a pier, the village teahouse where you can eat tomato pie, the dock at Cape Cod where the freshest fish come in; this is more than a book about restaurants.

One last thing. When Dr. Catherine Ward taught me English at the University of Maryland in the '60s, she left me with the most valuable advice of my life, and it is as applicable to food exploration as to wading through the folios of Shakespeare: "Go to the source."

This is the advice I now pass on to you.

HALLIDAY'S
NEW ENGLAND
FOOD EXPLORER

CHAPTER 1

AT THE GATES OF NEW ENGLAND

Hillsdale, New York, to Kent, Connecticut

In southern New England, forests still laze on hillsides liberally sprinkled with white houses and steeples. Fifty-four miles north of midtown Manhattan, where Interstate 684 ends at the top of a gradual rise, most of the traffic shoots off to the right onto Interstate 84; if you continue straight on to Route 22 north, you enter the delightful green grip of the Taconics, the western hills of the Berkshires, the principal mountains of southern New England. Here the highway narrows to a two-lane blacktop, the speed lessens, and worthwhile stops can stretch an hour's drive into a whole afternoon.

HIGHLIGHTS:
- The Taconic hills
- A mountaintop vineyard
- A French hostelry
- An inn in Salisbury
- A genuine tearoom
- A Shaker workshop
- A covered bridge
- Smoked alligator
- Berry picking
- Hamburgers

LENGTH OF LOOP: 127 miles
LENGTH OF STAY: One overnight, minimum

Three miles north of the town of Amenia's one traffic light, signs on the left side of Route 22 point out the turn for Cascade Mountain Vineyards. The lovely ramble of road passes up and down over rolling hills that overlook farmlands, school playing fields, and myriad pastoral perspectives. The trail unwinding upward toward the winery is whimsically marked only by triangles of grapes painted on boards nailed to the trees. Almost too soon, in 4 miles from Route 22, it runs out, the winery appears on a rounded summit, and the vineyards spread out on all sides.

Wine is a drink that is slipping. In recent years, the sales figures telling its story have dropped consistently, the curve of growth flattening out after the wine boom of the 1960s and '70s. In the early 1930s bad whiskey was called factory liquor. Now we've got factory wine. Steaming clouds of additives come together in chemical processes that leave less and less to nature. What is missing is the taste of the grape, and the public is not foolish.

For any lover of wine, this trend toward overprocessing is reason enough to take your taste on the road. Visiting little wineries out in the country like this one is what the wine distributors and owners of large wine shops used to do, looking for the natural, and tasting perhaps of the grape.

CASCADE MOUNTAIN VINEYARDS
Flint Hill Rd.
Amenia, NY 12501
Tel. 914/373-9021

We can taste wine at **Cascade Mountain Vineyards** from six kinds of grapes: three for white wine, three for red. It matters less what the grapes are than what they do. What they are supposed to do is allow us to taste the surroundings from which they come. The wines here fulfill that requirement. All the hills that we have seen—the soil, the temperature, the oxides and tannins, the elements of the earth—come out in the fruit, taken in through the hundreds of feet of the vine's roots. All this is washed into the earth and nurtured (not obfuscated) by the wine maker so that it comes out in the wine, whatever that taste may be. This is why no wine, if honestly made, will, or should, taste like a wine from any other place on earth, no matter what the grape, because no place on earth is exactly like any other.

The best time to arrive at Cascade is for lunch (till 2:30 PM); you can take a moment beforehand for a tasting of the wines. The tasting—sips from any of Cascade's wines in current production, lined up at the counter as you go into the restaurant (closed dinner and Jan.–Mar., weekdays Apr.–June and Nov.–Dec.)—is free. You can also order them by the glass ($1.50–$2) at your table with lunch.

At a fall tasting the three white wines in the lineup were flowery to nutty in taste. Among them the Private Reserve White was outstanding. Summertide offered the taste of a Gewürztraminer without the hardship of German prices. The reds, as a whole, were a little behind the whites. The Private Reserve Red, unmistakably a cabernet, nevertheless maintained its own sense of style. A single quality came through the vines we drank, and this was freshness. These are wines with a light, supple touch, and we are reminded of the taste of wines past.

Spiraling through as if in the frames of a film comes the black-and-white image of an Englishman, holding up a glass of wine and declaring it "a rare, fragile beauty." Of course it did not "travel." Now all wines do; they're made to. Because of a combination of entrepreneurship, rising operating costs, and taxes in countries where they are made, wines have to travel to boost export earnings. The fragile beauties of yesteryear are no more. They're loaded up with sulfur and bulked with alcohol to survive trips overseas and storage en route—110° in a Miami warehouse or minus 20° on a Chicago loading platform. To find the rare, the fragile, and the beautiful of the world today you must travel the wine regions, tasting as you go, to places where the wine makers are too stubborn, or too proud, or the villagers too wine literate, to swallow a product stabilized with excessive amounts of sulfur and alcohol.

Look at the labels of these wines from Cascade: 9½% alcohol, 10½%. The bottles of table wine in the wine shop or in your home range from 13½% to 14½%. Sulfur, too, deserves to be compared. Many people have low sulfur dioxide tolerance; it gives them headaches. Most people can taste sulfur in wine at around 150 parts per million. It's used in production to slow down or stop further development, or deterioration, of wine in the bottle. Excessive sulfur dioxide can be used to prevent wine from fermenting a second time in the bottle, a process the customer would find distasteful. U.S. law allows 350 parts per million to be used; most wine—foreign and domestic—carries 200 to 250 parts per million. Excessive alcohol, in the form of highly alcoholic wines, is then added to hide the taste.

One of the reds at the Cascade tasting was a total failure. It showed up dark and lugubrious in the bottle, tasted like old olive oil, and demonstrated exactly what a producer hazards in making (and the consumer risks in buying) pure, delicate wines that don't travel: spoilage. Still, one bad bottle in a lot of 9 or 12, plus a little unevenness among individuals, does not seem too high a price to pay for fresh, natural results.

Cascade's wines do travel, however, but gingerly shipped. Some go all the way to Japan (Summertide); others go down to New York City, to the U.S. Mission to the United Nations, where they represent our country at official recep-

tions and dinners. A production total of 4,000 cases a year, however, hardly makes Cascade a candidate for the big-time wine distributors, which deal in big-time numbers, but it does make the winery a welcome goal for food exploration. The product can be tasted and enjoyed at a leisurely pace before purchase, by the bottle or the case, for the home.

The restaurant, a bistro really, is a wood-timbered little place where the sun peeks past curtains; its touches of atmosphere all tend toward the cozy. The tables are rough-hewn wood; the chairs, showing studs, suggest Spain. Flowers decorate the tables and a wood-burning stove warms days when the temperature drops and clouds darken the sky. Lunch, very reasonably priced ($34 for two, with wine), should be kept straightforward. The duck liver pâté, for example, was more of a mousse, the angel-hair pasta too soft; but the tomato-based soup struck a better note. The tomatoes were from the winery garden, as were the oregano and basil. The heavy cream was fresh. The salad was excellent and the apple pie hearty. This is the niche that Cascade and its wine have carved out in our industrial world: a high-quality artisanal product.

Northward, Route 22 passes through several valley-huddled villages before climbing up the heights of Columbia County to the Berkshires at Hillsdale. Imperious Victorian houses look down along the high street from furrows of hills. Route 22 leads directly to the door of **L'Hostellerie Bressane.** The two-story brick mansion on its own knoll seems an unusual example of Georgian architecture so far north. But there is more to it than that. L'Hostellerie Bressane is an attempt to duplicate on American soil that authentic marvel of the French highway, the *restaurant-hôtel*.

L'HOSTELLERIE BRESSANE
Hillsdale, NY 12529
Tel. 518/325-3412

A restaurant-hôtel is more than an inn, or an auberge. It is usually presided over and owned by a famous chef. Here he holds forth, following his particular genius, and generally doing anything he wants. Restaurant-hôtels are usually found out in the country and on pages of national magazines, where they appear with mouth-watering photos of what they have to eat. They also take on the ambience of their locale, becoming a forest hunting lodge, for example, or a Provençal *mas* (farmhouse), or a Mediterranean villa, to a clientele who also come to enjoy the forest, the skiing, or the sun.

There are six rooms at L'Hostellerie Bressane, starting at $75 a night, but it is the restaurant we focus on. The chef-owner, Jean Morel, is from Bresse, northeast of Lyon in

France, a region famous for its chickens. Morel worked through the usual echelons of culinary skill in France and Paris before installing himself in his Hillsdale kitchen, where awards have come to him for doing exactly what he pleases.

Inside L'Hostellerie Bressane the nose fills with that most pleasing of all French fragrances, melting butter. Chef Morel has earned his spurs with classical, not nouvelle, cuisine. There are no vegetable roux or pots of purées, but full-blown sauces. These are delicately seasoned, however, with

chives or other herbs or mushrooms, and never contain even the slightest touch of flour.

The two drawing rooms, an inner and an outer, joined by a gentle arch, both have fireplaces. The inner room is done in oak paneling, with one 18th-century brick wall exposed. A pewter chandelier hangs above the fireplace, which is outlined in pictorial Breton tiles. The floor is wide wood plank, polished to show off the grain. The outer room has an upholstered look, with light-blue floral wallpaper and red carpeting. The tables have fresh flowers and stiff, white linen tablecloths. The chairs are padded Louis XV style. On the walls hang country scenes painted in the manner of Corot.

The menu is constantly kept fresh with interesting offbeat items, including game, but the prix-fixe dinner, only $21, comes in four courses; it allows choices, one of which is chicken, and you wonder how you could do better than ordering chicken from a man from Bresse. During the meal, Chef Morel comes out in his immaculate whites and does a little parade, hobnobbing with the regulars, and offering a confident nod to the rest before disappearing inside his kitchen.

Choosing escargots for the first course on the prix-fixe menu, I get surprises. These are not Provençal. There are no forceps, no little tines: The snails are out of their shells—you eat them with a knife and fork. They are Escargots de Bourgogne. This is a legal term for the highest quality of French snails and these come under guarantee of the French department of agriculture, which rules on the authenticity of French food products. The snails at the Hostellerie Bressane were, until very recently, sucking on a blade of grass on the Côte d'Or or some other Burgundian greenwood. Now they are under an exquisitely subtle sauce of chives, heavy cream, and butter. Topped with a flaky cap of *pâte feuilletée* (puff pastry), the snails are tender and tasty. The bread, from 40 miles away, has the proper lightness and crunch of real French bread.

The appeal of the bar wine, a Bergerac, is another surprise. It is an appealing white, Chateau Puch, that chef Morel has selected. To test a staple, I order pâté de campagne; the pork fat has been rendered (melted and strained), and the two large slices are plenty for four at the table. The prix-fixe chicken, chewy in texture but moist, comes with wild mushrooms—*trompettes de la mort* (horns of plenty) and morels, no relation to the chef. How can he get them fresh, I ask, and receive an interesting revelation: Of morels (*morilles* in French) there are two varieties, the white and the black, and it is the black you want. (American morels are white and lack the pungency of the French variety.) But the question of flavor goes deeper than that. Black morels from China or Thailand offer a confusion, not a solution, to marketplace prices. Deliberately copied from the European morel, they are cultivated and come with as bland a taste as the American even though they are black. The seeker of authentic wild morel taste, therefore, must pay the price for European. Current market value? $115 a pound in New York City. On the side of the chicken dish is salsify, an antique root vegetable, used extensively in the 19th century when it was called the oyster vegetable. To us it tastes more like a subtle graft of the flavors of leeks and endive.

A lover of game at our table hovers between the mignonettes of venison entrée ($24) and the smoked goose breast appetizer ($7.35), before he settles on the goose breast. It comes to the table thin-sliced like carpaccio, white and enticing.

Here and there throughout the evening are nouvelle touches, such as the raspberry-sauce decoration on the dessert plate of chocolate cake, but the mainstay of the restaurant's repertoire remains the classical approach to French food. The portions are generous: No tired asparagus draped over a radish here; the Villeroy & Boch plates overflow.

If your mother always said, "Breakfast should be your most important meal," I can think of no better place to eat it than **Mom's,** the country café just down the road (Route 23) from Hillsdale in South Egremont, Massachusetts. Mom's is one of those places that people from the cities come to the Berkshires to discover. It's painted just the right shade of funky gray; its bulletin board and wood-plank floors and Singer sewing-machine-stand tables strike an instant homey note. The little brook and terrace out back are fern shaded in summer; the falling snowflakes show through the windows in winter. The pancakes are buttermilk, buckwheat, or blueberry; the bagel–lox–cream-cheese platter wouldn't be better from the Carnegie Deli. The turkey club sandwich, on marbled rye bread from Pittsfield, is the hands-down winner in the American club sandwich category for $5.25, but it's the better part of wisdom to hold off serious sieges of appetite, like lunch, for points farther south.

On Route 41 south, only 19 miles down the road, is Salisbury, among the most picturesque New England towns in Connecticut. The Berkshires, tumbling down to earth behind straight streets of white clapboard houses, have left enough room for flowers to bloom. Two main routes (41 and 44) go through here, and at the fork where they meet stands the **White Hart Inn.**

THE WHITE HART INN
The Village Green
Salisbury, CT 06068
Tel. 203/435–0030

The White Hart has been at the center of things in Salisbury since it opened its doors in the early part of the 19th century. The inn underwent renovation recently and stands to face the 21st century as it did the 19th; spacious, accommodating, and meticulously managed.

The first thing you notice on entering the White Hart, aside from the fine state of the building, is the clientele. The people look as comfortable as the furniture they are on; it is as if frowns and formal attire are contraband. The only person wearing a tie near the reception desk may be Terry Moore, the owner, and he has his hair tied in a ponytail. The lean man from Brighton in England has put style back into the White Hart.

The west room is a lovely sitting room, with green Chesterfield lounges and an oak bar that runs its length. Big, leafy plants give shade from the light that streams through the windows at sundown.

The guest rooms are in simple Colonial style, with immaculate new fixtures in the bathrooms; cable TV and air-conditioning means you won't have to sleep with the doors open when the heat wave comes through every July. The nightly rate runs from $95 to $125 on weekends; weekdays are about 20% lower.

There are two entrances to the Tap Room, one from the street, one from inside. This is the one place where you can lunch at the White Hart, and it draws many locals and their guests on weekends. The atmosphere is cheerful and easy. The regulars know each other, but no one at the bar stays a stranger for long. Shellacked wood tables are wedged under mullioned windows that ring the inner space. The bar draws Double Diamond ale, Guinness, and Samuel Adams. More tables are angled around the three steps leading down from the lobby. Humming waiters pass in and out; the service is as warm as the soup. The onion soup ($3.50) is classic: The cheeses are Gruyère and Parmesan, and there are oodles of sliced onions and a taste of cognac, too. The house pâté ($4), made with rendered pork fat, pork, and veal, comes with a red-lettuce salad, croutons from the kitchen, and a horserad-ish mustard that is strong on personality. There is smoked salmon and crème fraîche (really) for $6.75, and a meal could be made on just these three. But the grilled sliced steak on garlic toast ($8.50) comes with long, lacy French fries that are cut *allumette*-style, like matchsticks (I have seen them being cut in the kitchen). The red bar wine is a Washington State 1988 Allison Combs, Columbia Valley—very nice and giving, with hints of vanilla, but not oaky.

The White Hart's elegant Sea Grill Restaurant serves dinner only. In consonance with its name, the room is deco-rated in subtle maritime accents enhanced by paintings of fresh, local fruit by an artist up the road, done in oils so painterly they seem just plucked from the orchard.

The lounge at the entrance to the restaurant is the only place where smoking is permitted in the Sea Grill, and the Grill is the place at the inn to go should you be of a mind for peace and quiet with dinner.

Main courses run from about $16 (the shrimp-and-pasta combination), and you should know the kitchen makes its own foccacia. For $19 to $22 you can have grilled tuna, with lime, and bouillabaisse (one of the cooks served an apprenticeship in Cannes). There are salads and swordfish on this interesting menu, as well as one thing that shouldn't be: sole. This is not a fish found in American waters; according to *American Wildlife,* "Food substitutes are common and the layman in many instances does not know what animal or fish may be disguised under an exotic or innocuous designation. When one eats 'fillet of sole,' one is really eating winter flounder and not sole at all." Genuine sole is a European fish. Gray or lemon sole is really flounder, and where it exists on the same market as real sole (in Paris, for instance, where no claim of sole is made for it at all) it sells at considerably less than half the market price of true sole. So-called Dover sole must arrive frozen (from England or France) except for Concorde (very rare) point-of-entry deliveries. The Maine lobsters ($24), however, are the McCoy, and the Sea Grill has oysters and mussels according to market availability.

Like the Tap Room, the Sea Grill provides a dining experience that is long on atmosphere and feeling. Is it gastronomic? Perhaps not. The test? The same dishes, in a humdrum environment, would come up empty. That said, the White Hart is a very comfortable inn for a weekend with a good book or a companion you might care to read it to.

Walk into the **Salisbury Package Store** (19 Main St., Salisbury, CT, tel. 203/435-2717) and you'll know it's not for nothing that this region is called New England. Vintage port is owner Joe Mulligan's specialty, and the offerings of Warre's, Sandeman, Graham, and Croft can be found over a spread of more than 35 specific vintage years. There is a heavy selection of table wines, too, Bordeaux being particularly well represented among the French; and the Allison Combs we liked so well with lunch at the White Hart shows up here for $6.75 a bottle.

Well, are you in the mood for a tearoom? Not a Japanese place with sliding shoji screens and geishas, but a warm place nonetheless where the atmosphere is friendly, the food delicious and light, and the tea hot and fragrant?

In the heart of Salisbury, set back from the road and its traffic, there is such a spot. It's ideal for refreshing fare with flair, and the heady liquors from the East that are poured here are pungent, laden with spice, and nonalcoholic. It is called **Chaiwalla.**

CHAIWALLA
1 Main St.
Salisbury, CT 06068
Tel. 203/435–9758

Chaiwalla is a Hindi word that refers to the person who makes tea. The maker in this case is the personable owner of Chaiwalla, Mary O'Brien. For a relaxing, light lunch and libation of teas you could not do better than put yourself in the hands of Mary and her staff.

Mary O'Brien is a tall, dark-haired young woman with blue eyes who believes in what she does, and whatever she's doing, it puts her in connection with something beautiful on this earth. You get the impression that, were she not continually searching out excellence at the source for her tearoom, she could be selling antiques at Sotheby's (which she has done). She has also selected artwork for the publications of the Museum of Modern Art, so she brings to her work the hunt for perfection. But there is nothing academic or stuffy about the tearoom where she welcomes you (open from mid-morning to 6 PM, closed in winter).

Chaiwalla is comfortably appointed with round and square wood tables, sofas with layers of throws, banquettes and window seats overlooking the town, and big, stuffed pillows that tuck around you; light spills over everything. In the center of this soft-edged decor is a workmanlike kitchen without walls, so you can see inside. It's set off by a counter where you can sit down to be close to the action or simply smell the teas and chat with Mary O'Brien. The tea maker makes good things to eat, too, but it is the teas that are a must; they draw people here from all over the countryside.

"We've got to import the best teas in the world," says a determined O'Brien as if it were her mission in life. She has felt this way since she first went to India in 1986 and tasted them. Her menu lists about 16, and the young woman bursts with a proselytizing zeal in promoting and describing them.

Chai is the Hindi word for tea; Chaiwalla sells it by the pot. Each one is brewed fresh for the customer in good Salisbury spring water. The Salisbury spring comes bubbling from a source two blocks down the road (marked by the spot where people line up with containers); its water is part of what makes Chaiwalla's tea so good. Boiling water is passed through a wide-lipped strainer, laden with leaves, that straddles the pot. The water saturates the leaves as it falls into the pot in a cloud of steam. No tea bag or ball is suspended in the glass pot. The tea is served, Indian style, in a glass mug with a clear glass handle, to let the color of the brew show through. "Teas can be seen and shown like bottles of wine," says O'Brien. Because she believes this, she buys her teas in single estate lots like the better wines. Her favorite variety, and mine, in stunning pale, yellow glints like Montrachet, is

Banarachi. Lightly flavored with vanilla and cardamom, it will put you in tea heaven.

A word about the liquorlike quality of some teas, which I have often read about, mostly in 19th-century accounts, but never before tasted. That quality is there. I am not especially recommending tea to anyone looking for a substitute for alcohol, but to call this tea a liquor is not too strong a description.

There are more teas here, including ones you've heard of but possibly never tasted under Chaiwalla's exacting conditions. Darjeeling, oolong, Russian, white, Keemun, silver tip, and Niligiri are on the list. Both teapots and loose teas are for sale. You should note that these last have been as carefully packed at the source as they were selected for their quality. After fermentation, tea leaves are dry-heated to remove moisture, but the water content remaining can amount to as much as 3% to 4%; it may increase to 6% to 8% during shipping; this is the problem that pursues the taste of teas.

The appropriate light things to eat with the tea range far beyond the expected scones and cakes to 10-bean soup, sausage pie, and onion tart. O'Brien's tomato pie has won accolades nationally, but what made the most sumptuous lunch for me were her eggs Italia: three shirred eggs, with ham and pesto, cooked under mozzarella.

Chaiwalla offers several desserts, but the whiskey cake, concocted by Mary O'Brien's "mither," is delicious with cranberries and hints of other fruits as well as lashings of spirits.

For a dessert drink, try the Indian chai. Drink it down as you would at a railroad station in India: with spices, milk, and ginger. It is the cappuccino of teas.

Call for a schedule of events at Chaiwalla. The shop is a center for tea tastings, lectures on tea, and tea readings. These last are not what you think; they are dramatic readings given over tea. Writers and actors read from plays and books, some of which refer to foods and teas.

After the little bridge on Route 41 south from Chaiwalla, take a scenic left turn onto Salmon Kill Road. This will set you rolling through some of the prettiest scenery in Connecticut. Another left onto Route 112 (in Lime Rock) and then south (right) on Route 7 will put you on the banks of the liveliest stretch of the bubbling Housatonic River. For the next 8 miles the circuitous route is overshadowed by old-growth spruce and fir trees, and the air feels as if it were scrubbed with pine tar. Across the race of the river and the conifers is West Cornwall, Connecticut's prettiest town, at the end of a covered bridge. Immediately beyond the one-lane bridge is parking, a ceramics shop, a Shaker furniture shop, and two restaurants. The Shaker store (just a few yards on the left after the bridge) sells ready-made objects plus custom-order products at quite classic prices, but anyone with an eye for the line of these pieces will surely be tempted. The ceramics store has many gift items; the pottery comes from a local kiln a few miles down the road on Route 7, in Cornwall. Of the two restaurants, **Freshfield's** is a place that sometimes shows imagination, style, and wit with a food approach that used to be called American Nouvelle. Weather permitting, sitting on the restaurant's deck while contemplating the shallow stream sliding by underneath may make you forget what is being served.

What they are fishing for up to the tops of their waders along the Housatonic is trout. If you do the same successfully, you are warned not to eat your catch. The fishing here, in waters polluted by dioxin from upriver, is termed "recreational," meaning throw it back. That state governors permit factories to operate in ways that spoil our waterways and natural resources is a fact sadly not yet historical.

Route 4 east from the Cornwall stop sign (a few miles south) leads up past Mohawk Mountain and on to Goshen, Connecticut (about 9 miles from the stop sign). Going north on Route 63, around the Goshen circle, and cruising very slowly down a wide street, you reach one of Connecticut's most authentic, and certainly most obscure, food miracles— **Nodine's** (rhymes with I dine) **Smokehouse.**

NODINE'S SMOKEHOUSE
Rte. 63N
Goshen, CT 06756
Tel. 203/491–4009

You will see that it's well hidden; Nodine's old smokehouse (the new one is in Torrington) sits demurely in the back yard of a house. Only a sign at the roadside points down the driveway that leads to an unsuspected larder of menu ideas. There are whole smoked fish, some boneless; and the hatchery trout are a tempting, ready-to-serve bargain at less than $5 per fish. The smoked, cured beef is hand rubbed with brown sugar. Also smoked are hams—country cured and New England dinner, to name two. Their differences can be judged best on ham sandwiches at $4 each to go. Buffalo meat is something of a health food with the statistics now in front of us: 50% less cholesterol and 70% less fat than most beef. It comes in steaks, or buffalo-burger packages of four patties each, $6.75 for a taste at home of the range. There are whole smoked birds: Chicken, turkey, and duck are all very satisfying with the tang of wood added to the taste; pheasant and quail are less so. American game birds, raised on the farm, are too tame in taste and much too fat to merit a premium price. The venison at Nodine's comes from far-off New Zealand. American game laws quite properly protect our own game from slaughter for mass consumption. It can never legally be purchased for sale by a restaurant or meat packer. Trout is from a hatchery, never wild. The buffalo is excepted, however, because it is penned to encourage its propagation for profit, a technique that is working as the herds are increasing. These animals are, in the end, what they eat, which is why nothing raised on a farm (on dry feed) or in a hatchery (on pellets) will ever approach the taste of animals that have grown up in the wild, feeding on living grasses and grains or insects.

If it is no-nitrite bacon you want, Nodine's has it, in Canadian style and juniper-smoked flavors, too. There are many other items—cheeses, hot dogs (again, no nitrites), rattlesnake and alligator steaks—to taste your way through. Today, as a meat-processing plant, the old Goshen place is finished, in favor of Nodine's new facility 9 miles away, where the public isn't welcome. But the old smokehouse continues as a selling space, a cheerful cedar-sided relic of the past, with candy sticks in kid-tempting colors in open jars on the counter and dried beef jerky as tasty in the car as it is on the trail. Neither requires refrigeration and both are good for either the sweet tooth or more substantial cravings.

ELLSWORTH HILL FARM
Rte. 4
Sharon, CT 06069
Tel. 203/364-0249

Should it be apple-blossom time (usually May 8–15), go back down Route 4 past the stop sign at Route 7 to pay a visit to **Ellsworth Hill Farm.** Two miles west of the intersection, on top of a hill on Route 4, 5,500 apple trees are in bloom. In

the fall, when their branches are laden with fruit, isn't a bad time to stop either: The harvest provides a lot to pick from, to taste, or to buy in larger quantities.

At the top of a rounded hill, the farm occupies both sides of the road. Broad swaths of strawberry and raspberry patches offer their fruit in summer, and virtually endless varieties of apple ripen in fall. There are apples for baking pies—Cortlands and Jonathans—and apples for making sauces—Northern Spy—apples, to be brief, of 11 specialized varieties. Three different kinds alone are called red: Paula, Ida, and Delicious (red and golden both). Macoun and McIntosh are traditionally the best for eating, but even in apples Japanese imports are pushing the local crop for a share of the orchard. Farm owner Jim March now offers the

Mutsu, a large, yellow-green apple. At first crunch it is a hard, crisp, and juicy fruit leaving an elusive, almost pear-ish taste on the palate. Try using that in your chutney.

At Ellsworth Hill you can buy any or all of the above by the basket ($4–$5) or the bushel ($15–$20). A bushel adds up to 42 pounds of apples—a savings of 60% to 70% off supermarket prices without even mentioning the superior variety, freshness, or taste of the farm. For 50¢ a pound, however, you can join the cast of *The Grapes of Wrath* and see what it's like to go picking your own.

Jim March's hilltop farm is more than a palate-pleaser: It's an educational experience. Busloads of senior citizens come up from Manhattan's 92nd Street Y every summer. Kindergartens and primary grades send their youngsters to Ellsworth Hill Farm. Both types of group take regular tours of the cider mill, orchards, and berry patches. What March gets from the kids are the charming, crayon-art thank-you notes hanging in his cider mill. The second-floor gallery of the building houses an observatory where the youngsters can look down through transparent plastic walls and see the onrushing horde of apples crushed to a flow of juices and pulp. The program includes an afternoon or morning of picking.

It isn't necessary to schedule a visit exclusively for the spring or fall, as something is ready for picking most any time in between. By May the greenhouse offers plants and herbs. The flowering of the 5,500 apple trees starts a little later. Strawberry season comes in early June and goes to the first raspberry season in mid-July. Early varieties of apples are ready around mid-August, and then in September comes the second raspberry season. With the large number of varieties and staggered ripening times, apple picking at Ellsworth Hill goes on well into November. In October you can pick pumpkins, which sit, fat and orange, on the grass and cost 35¢ a pound for the taking away. Near the end of the month comes the big flow of cider. March puts no potassium sorbate (a chemical used in wine and supermarket cider production as a stabilizer) in his cider. As a result, Ellsworth Hill Farm cider must be handled gently when packed in the car. In the home it must be refrigerated to slow down its fermentation. If you want the cider to go hard, let it warm up a few degrees. The sugars will naturally change to alcohol, you will have paid no tax for the privilege of making alcohol, and you'll have a nice hard drink to go along with your dinner on Thanksgiving. Call or write ahead for ripening schedules, picking times, and seasonal forecasts.

Finally turning south at the intersection of Routes 4 and 7, we go south on Route 7, pass the **Cornwall Package Store** (a nice selection of wines, and pleasant owners) and head for Kent. Along the way to Kent (about 9 miles), there's the **Kenko Grocery,** a health food store with a juice bar and an organic vegetable stand. The **Flanders Bed and Breakfast** (tel. 203/927–3040) is just north of Kent, where Cobble Road joins Route 7, should you want a bed-and-breakfast.

THE VILLAGER
Rte. 7
Kent, CT 06757
Tel. 203/927–3945

There is one more thing that it would be a shame to leave out about Kent. **The Villager.** Sometimes you don't want a fancy restaurant, but you do want something nice, a clean and pleasant place either for a cup of coffee over breakfast or for fish and chips; and you surely don't want to pay for failed sauces, long waits in line, uncertain service or nosebleed prices for what were essentially four bowls of rice. Then, the cozy country atmosphere and counter democracy of The Villager are for you. Eat among the local contractors, Kent School kids, airline pilots, ex-models, and farmers who make up the backbone of this bucolic community. Order the Mom's Meat Loaf, slurp the Swampwater (sic), munch a slice of apple pie, graze on a blueberry muffin. It's food that tastes like what it is—a good example of the art of short-order cooking, if not haute cuisine. Feel the relief when you pay the bill. Specials start at under $4 for a complete lunch. Dinner is double the enjoyment as the menu becomes more ambitious (Cajun shrimp), and you can bring in a bottle of wine from the **Kent Wine Merchant** next door; half-bottles are convenient and Sancerre is on hand. The Villager provides the glasses and the corkage at no extra charge.

Homeward bound on the southern leg of your journey, you come to a place where the pickings are so good that you just have to stop: **Henry Dykeman's Farm Stand** over on Route 22 south.

HENRY DYKEMAN'S FARM STAND
Rte. 22
Pawling, NY 12564
Tel. 914/855-5166

To get there from Kent, proceed south down Route 7 to Bull's Bridge (first traffic light after the Kent light), turn right, and go over the covered bridge. Keep to the left at all turns and follow the main road through the craft village of Webatuck (about 3 miles). Leaving the village, turn right onto Route 55, and then left (south) onto Route 22. Just past the Grand Union shopping center, Dykeman's Farm Stand comes up on the right. Why go to all this trouble to get here?

Because nearly everything comes from their own fields and, year in and year out, Dykeman's has the best selection of vegetables on this loop. If you come by early enough (before 5 PM in summer), they will provide you with a map to their fields on a back country road in the hills. The odds are good

you will get a tan along with your pickings, and good pickings they are.

On Dykeman's strawberry hill the water runs off all
sides of the knoll, so what you get is pure fruit. Sparkle and
Honey Eyes (strawberry varieties) are so sweet they melt in
your hands, and so delicate that their flavor vanishes within
hours of picking. Raspberries and blueberries have their seasons, too. Marvelous sweet peas come in May, so sugary that
they taste best when eaten raw in the pod. Their sugar

changes to starch once they are picked, and they're never as
sweet in the shops. Pick them yourself once and know why
they're called sweet peas. All these are for sale ready picked,
at the stand, but at considerably higher prices. There are garden tomatoes, too, that taste the way you once knew tomatoes
to taste; Italian eggplants; potatoes new enough to eat raw;
and those tiny, tiny 'taters, red and white—some as small as
marbles to sauté in the pan, others as big as golf balls to put
around the meat in the oven. The hot house is stocked with
flowers, vegetable plants, and herbs. The pantry has a whole
array of bottled local things. The chutney is wonderful, the
onion relish made from Vidalia onions. But most worthwhile, from about the end of June through fall, is the double

bin of sweet corn, the native American crop without which there would have been no New England.

Summer brings the sweetest varieties to harvest: Candy Store, Sweet Sue, Silver Queen, and Sundance. Sundance is the great local favorite, with big, crunchy yellow kernels. The ears come into the stand twice a day, morning and afternoon. Like the sweet pea's, corn's sugar starts to turn to starch as soon as it is picked. Dykeman's doesn't keep corn overnight, so you are bound to get something fresh for your pot. Call or write for harvesting information and a free mailer.

Well, is it late?

Feel like singing your way home and munching something in the car? Join the throng at the **Red Rooster** on Route 22, south of Dykeman's and 1 mile after the police barracks in Brewster. They have the best hamburgers north of Jackson Hole. Guaranteed.

CHAPTER 2

A NEW ENGLAND TASTING

Litchfield to New Preston, Connecticut

Litchfield is a town and a county. Both are well known to the New Englander—the former for its architectural ensemble of homes, churches, and spacious green mall, where everything goes on that should revolve around a New England town; the latter for its enticing landscapes of villages, hills, and ponds that fit so nicely into niches of what outdoor New England should look like. To Litchfield then; for both town and county offer enticing prospects for dining.

HIGHLIGHTS:
- The Litchfields
- A grill in black and white
- A toll house of burgundies
- A company for food and for wine
- White pizza and deep-fried atmosphere
- A flower farm
- The tale of the chicken
- A cooking school behind a barn door
- A boom town of taste
- A winery over a mountain lake
- A Florentine bistro

LENGTH OF LOOP: 47 miles

LENGTH OF STAY: One overnight, but plan for two

To get to the town of Litchfield, follow directions in Chapter 1 as far as the intersection of Interstate 84; take I–84 east to Connecticut exit 7 and follow Route 202 north.

At Litchfield town you are in the heart of Connecticut, New England. It is too far (96 miles) to commute to New York, and nobody does. Litchfield is one of those rare places in pastoral Connecticut where the weekenders don't wear running shoes and warmup suits to walk around the mall. Although a fair share of shopping centers have nibbled away at the town, the nibblings are bite-size (particularly confined to Route 202 south); the damage is light and at the edges. The heart of the town and its justly celebrated historical perspectives are to be found around its unspoiled hilltop common.

Many towns were constructed around a central grassy space lined with trees called the mall, the village green, or the common, in much of New England. But few greens in Connecticut remain so intact within their original lines. The buildings that front the Litchfield green have yet to be refaced. Storefronts don't scream out 1950s, the shade trees are a respectable two centuries old, the corner courthouse remains in its old weathered brick, and there are no department stores. The First Congregational Church on North Street (the northern edge of the green) is the most photographed church in Connecticut and rewards a long look inside. Erected in 1721 on the green itself, it was moved to the present site so its steeple could be seen as a beacon over the surrounding landscape and serve to guide travelers. Inside, the three-sided balcony has a triple-tiered seating arrangement dating from when the Congregational church was Puritan. The folk-art masterpiece of the church's interior is a massive mahogany pulpit with staircases leading up both sides. Although Litchfield is far from the sea, the Puritans brought their history with them, and the pulpit platform resembles the cockpit of a sailing ship, with yardarms, as well as ratlines running up each side.

From the steps outside the church, the division of the town into compass quadrants of north, south, east, and west streets is plain. Across the street and the wide divide of green is West Street, where a row of federal buildings contains the courthouse and several more earthy areas for contemplation. One of them is the **West Street Grill**. On any given night, it can be the finest restaurant in Connecticut.

THE WEST STREET GRILL
43 West St. (on the green)
Litchfield, CT 06759
Tel. 203/567–3885

Step through the heavy curtain across the inside of the door and you enter a world of *Dinner at Eight*: It is like walking into the frame of a black-and-white movie. (The decor is Bauhaus, or modern Art Deco.) A row of black tables and easy chairs holds the center of the floor, and black booths and black mirrors line white walls. The lighting is subdued with expert use of shades and sconces; the only touches of color are the people and the food. The tables are close enough together for everybody to be neighbors but not family. The customers are the food crowd, people who, with an infallible radar, manage to turn up in a restaurant the moment the word is out that it is good. Here you are confronted with a new proposal: The food is so new, its preparation so atypical, that you are likely to have no idea of what it is until you see it, and even then its taste will come as a surprise. The food at the West Street Grill thrives on the concentration of tastes. And the tastes come singly or in pairs, so what is concentrated is also illuminated through contrasts. Glance at the menu if you must, but here you can break my cardinal rule of never asking the advice of the maître d'hôtel.

27

Go ahead, ask; the maître d' is also part-owner James O'Shea. The advice he gives is based on the market selection of the moment, primarily fish, unless you demand steak. For openers there are interesting breads, in a wide assortment. For example, anchovies in an oil-based sauce on a piece of flat Tuscan bread may lead off, the oils fragrant, the bread spicy and making us crave more. Next there might be a mantislike creation of red codfish roe, perfumed in a contrasting oil and perched on a crisp of potato bread with wings, not quite thin enough to be a wafer. Layers of Arab bread with purées of salmon and tomato may follow, and others just as exotic and tasty.

The wine to accompany this could be a white Côte de Nuits Villages, Domaine du Château Puligny Montrachet, which is far from your usual Louis Latour, though costing no more. The West Street Grill is the kind of restaurant where part of what you pay for is the taste and enterprising spirit of the owners (Charles Kafferman is the other part-owner with O'Shea), not the opinion of the wine salesman who walks through the door because the restaurant happens to be in his territory. Owners who buy according to their own taste (they are rarer than you think) buy according to market value within that taste. They deliver their allegiance to their customer and not to the wine sales rep, and they don't chain themselves to any single wine importer. Such diligence in searching out values is to be rewarded, because it results not only in lower prices but also in constantly changing products that keep tastes fresh and visits exciting. Going to a restaurant like the West Street Grill is like going to a wine tasting where all you get to taste are the winners. The best course of action for the new customer is to describe what you like in general and then take each taste as it comes. Of course you can always change direction.

"James, we'd like a little red wine now," I tell O'Shea.

"What would you want to go with that?" he asks. We veto steaks and he proposes smoked scallops from Maine with

Gruyère. The wine is a very flexible red Loire, Menetou–Salon Morogues. It's what the French call *insolite* (unusual).

Then comes shrimp and chili peppers in olive oil. With it is a new bread topped with Parmesan aioli that has us panting. There are corn cakes, lighter than fritters, also sautéed in olive oil; and a chèvre cheese confection with the taste and look of ice cream. A salmon tartare, hand-minced and perfumed with Aquavit, proves that fish is an excellent agent for tasting other things as well. There is a lightness in

WEST
STREET
GRILL
LITCHFIELD

the cuisine that evokes the south of France. Working with chef Matthew Fahrner, O'Shea has pushed the kitchen toward using olive oil instead of butter. "I love Provence styles," O'Shea says. "And I love Provence."

There are pastas too—bowties with eggplant in tomato and basil—but crowd-pleasing bistro food makes the barest argument for coming to West Street. From March to early June there are sea urchins. West Street is the right address to acquaint yourself with how delectable these creatures can be, with their tops severed and served in a sauce of their roe; a vegetable wonton and ginger leaves the mouth feeling scrubbed and tingling. For after dinner the bar has an excellent Calvados.

Service and prices are worth mentioning; the restaurant is a training ground for locals. Nearly all the service personnel you'll see, 35 on a purely full-time basis, are from Litchfield. All have been trained by the current management. The result is a pleasant and competent staff who perform the restaurant's way.

You can manage a lunch or an evening's event for a moderate price here, but it may not be the best idea. Should O'Shea offer the unusual, be prepared to spend more. If he recommends a Maryvale chardonnay—and you have never tasted a Maryvale (which would be about $35)—by all means take it.

Finally, the West Street Grill represents an example of what seems to be a coming trend in restaurants. After generations of dominance by the chefs, we are entering the Age of the Restaurant Impresario. As with the opera impresario, the restaurant impresario assembles a cast and selects a repertoire. The impresario finds a place to play and stays on hand through rehearsals, continually fixing and fine-tuning. Then his or her job is to keep everything fresh and everybody happy. The West Street Grill has found its impresario in James O'Shea.

Once outside the restaurant, should you have arrived without parking your bags, you may want to find an inn for the night. The idyllic **Toll Gate Hill Inn,** in its own forested park, is the first choice and not 3 miles from the green. Follow North Street (Route 202 north) past the Congregational Church in the direction of Torrington. Keeping to the main highway, ignore the signs for other Toll Gates (there is a Toll Gate Motel, and so on). The sign for the Toll Gate Hill Inn itself comes up on the left side of the road. The drive goes up a steep grade. Make sure you have it in sight before you turn in.

THE TOLL GATE HILL INN
Rt. 202
Litchfield, CT 06759
Tel. 203/567–4545

The Toll Gate Hill is an 18th-century house restored as an inn. Not a whisper of traffic noise penetrates the sturdy needles of its pines. The building is floodlit at night so that its terra-cotta color glows within a deep cocoon of trees. A long, canopied walk leads out from the front door in case of rain. For daytime strolls there are cloistered walks with hidden cul-de-sacs in the woods; of course, there is also a hill to look down from. The inn is just five minutes from the Litchfield green.

Immediately through the doors there's a warm, friendly bar. Warm? Candles flicker on tables with wood benches set around the crackling logs on a stone hearth. Even on April nights a fireside is cozy. It is the place in Litchfield where people come for drinks before or after dinner, or for dinner in a Colonial atmosphere. The bar is particularly well stocked with single-malt scotches (it has an even dozen), and English ale is on tap.

The suites are lavished with a mixture of 18th-century antiques and reproductions and country French–style appointments; it's like stepping back in time and visiting a relative who is the military governor of Litchfield. The rooms evoke a country farmhouse except the conveniences are not down the hall, and yes, all accommodations have cable TV. There are Empire sofas in the suites, and enough room for a family of four to romp around. The inn, dating from 1745, is listed in the National Register of Historic Places, but it hardly creaks with antiquity. The rooms have been soundproofed, so you are not likely to hear any neighbors moving around or running water in the night. There are 15 rooms and five suites at the Toll Gate.

Three of the four timbered dining rooms have fire-places. At lunchtime in any of them the sun burnishes the wood paneling; the food is adventurous; and whatever you order, they put plenty of it on your plate.

Navy bean soup with scallions and *andouille* (Cajun sausage) is a tangy treat, thick and laced with flavor and meat. In general, chef Gregory Galuska avoids the mistake of cooking ethnic foods timidly, for people who do not like them—though the sautéed Maryland crabcakes, a staple on the menu, could crackle with more black pepper and mustard. The blue claws come from Nodine's (see Chapter 1) Torrington smokehouse, which is almost in sight down the hill. The meats (Cajun sausage, steaks, ducks, and so on) likewise come from Nodine's, and the beef gets this interesting fillip at the Toll Gate: The steak is cured and lightly smoked first at Nodine's before it is marinated and placed in the Toll Gate oven. The result is a New York sirloin plump in its juices and enhanced with the additional fragrances of maple (sugar) and hickory. Beef frequently needs something to leaven its taste a bit (the French and Italians use pork), but the presmoking is a different and interesting technique. When neighboring chefs come to dine at Toll Gate on their days off—some from as far away as New York—what they often eat is steak.

Pasta dishes have the explosion of the garden about them, even in winter. The fettuccine is folded into ample heapings of escarole, tomatoes, mushrooms, and Canadian bacon (again Nodine's, and thankfully without nitrites). The onion florette, too, goes marvelously with pasta and steak, and is fun to eat because it is so simple and gorgeous on the table. This is something you can do at home: peel a large Bermuda onion and crosshatch it across the top, but do not separate the sections. Pull them so that they start to open up, like a flower (think of a chrysanthemum); the bigger the onion, the more fun. Dip the whole flower in batter (the kind used for squash blossoms) and French fry it; the "flower" opens still more during cooking. Drain it dry, crisp it in the oven, and serve it on its own. It is frequently eaten with chopsticks. This is not high cuisine but the kind of invention the Toll Gate does so well.

In its choice of wines the old inn shows an iron orthodoxy. The owner, Fritz Zivic, son of a former welterweight champion, has a knockout collection of rare old burgundies. A mention that you share the same inclination in wine will

get you his special treat list. You can taste, for example, Puligny Montrachets from Sauzet, Chambolle Musignys from Hudelot, and, stretching to the seldom-seen, Charmes–Chambertin 1966 and Bonnes Mares 1970.

Suites, with wood-burning fireplaces and canopy beds, are reasonably priced, at under $200; rooms are more reasonable still, starting at slightly over $100. All prices are lower on weekdays. With three major routes funneling through Litchfield just 3 miles away, it's a good place to headquarter a food foray into the county.

Within 3 to 30 miles of the inn are a host of worthwhile destinations. In the town, on the green, are **Spinell's Litchfield Food Company** (203/567–3113) and the **Litchfield**

Wine Merchant (203/567–5289). Both are on West Street along the same block as the Grill. The buildings are old and their walls exude a Greenwich Village atmosphere.

Walk into the Food Company and find owner Rick Spinell, a former New York City pastry chef, who took over the business in 1992. He spends most of his time in the kitchen creating baked goods for the café and bakery that are part of the store. Down the aisles are shelves crammed with jumbles of good things to eat. For example, the Food Company is the indispensable coffee bean source in the center of Litchfield. Sixteen different varieties of bean rise up in their bins from the white-tile floor. Bentwood chairs and tables in windows overlook the green, so you can watch the life of a real New England town parading by as you munch on sandwiches from the deli counter or pastries from the bakery.

Just two doors down from the Food Company, past an art gallery, is the Wine Merchant. As you step in from the street onto its wooden floors, the cozy little store projects the hodgepodge appeal and smell of an antiques shop. Not that the vintages are excessively moldy or disorganized, but the place is jam-packed and invites the inveterate rummager to creak and poke around, nosing into dim mahogany bins richly crammed with tony Californians, offbeat French appellations, and Eastern European bargains. Each bottle is annotated, by hand, with curious inscriptions. A California Côtes du Rhône, for example, bears the following legend: "Le Cigare Volant. The great Randall Graham strikes terror in the hearts of all Frenchmen with this California Château Neuf du Pape" (only if hit over the head with the bottle, I judge)—Wine Merchant's owner Hans Bauer's noteworthy effort to replace the expensive with the accessible.

Before leaving Litchfield for points farther south, take a turn northward to Torrington. It is a town without pinstripes; a town with a wide blue-collar stripe to it. The restaurant is

Anthony's. If you want to know what an Italian restaurant in Brooklyn is like without going to Brooklyn, try this.

Reach Torrington down Route 202 from the Toll Gate, then turn left onto Main Street and go on and on. At the edge of town, next to a maker of tombstones, you will see a sign reading FISH—PIZZA. This is Anthony's.

ANTHONY'S
258 Main St.
Torrington, CT 06790
Tel. 203/489-6656

There were places like this out in Brooklyn, near Marine Park and the potato fields—places where the slate sidewalks were sunk in the earth, where weeds grew in the lots between the buildings and the stores always had gardens and new paint. Everyone would be fixing and planting, and what they put on your plate was the pure taste of Sorrento. In Anthony's it's the same; the tables have Formica tops and the fish come in golden crescent-shape crisps, and on pasta. The calamari is deep-fried and golden, but it is the white pizza, sweeping inland from New Haven, that everyone comes in for and that you must try.

Some Italians (mostly Romans) claim that pizza in America is too "gummy," but pizza is an Italian, and especially Neapolitan, specialty, something that the Romans don't always like to remember. Many Italians like it thick, crusted, and "gummy," and not those dainty doilies they snap up like water wafers in Paris, Florence, and Rome.

Torrington is an ethnic town, so it is no wonder that the best pizza around is found here. John Giansanti lived in Italy for six years. The best pizzas he tasted there came out of a brick oven, so it is a brick oven he has for himself at Anthony's. His white pizza topping, as in "just white, no red," is made of clams, Parmesan cheese, and bacon. He makes his own dough, and his own bread, too, 30 to 60 loaves daily, from just water, flour, yeast, and oil. Check that against the ingredients in a supermarket loaf.

After the pizza, try any of the veal, clams, mussels, calamari, or fish and seafood dishes. They appear on the menu in various forms, but only as suggestions. Giansanti will cook them almost any way you want them.

Back in Litchfield, it's impossible not to linger a little longer around a town that is so good. **Haight Vineyards** (203/567–4045), out on Route 118 to the east, on Chestnut Hill, is a little less than a mile from the green. Here a shed for tasting and buying what they make is surrounded by views of vineyards. Although considerable effort and investment have been made over a number of years to produce wines of a higher quality at Haight, the vineyard has not consistently delivered the hoped-for results. The wine business is like baseball: every season brings new hope. The tasting at Haight is free, and the chardonnay is appealing, though not necessarily its price.

From Litchfield, follow South Street, Route 63, southward. This wide, handsome thoroughfare passes a lineup of what must have been some of the most prepossessing examples of residential architecture in 19th-century New England. The Puritans dropped the architectural fig leaf after the 18th century, and severity in building styles diminished during the 19th. All the houses are set back as if to be admired from the road. Come no farther, they seem to say, look and ogle, and keep going. Arresting forms of gingerbread Victorian, Greek revival, and obvious kitsch design slip by. Some houses provoke admiration, others gasps, and some laughs; this was how the affluent in wealthy towns lived in the 19th century, and some still do.

About a mile from the green, the wide street narrows into a country highway. If you keep to the main road, without taking a turn or a fork, in another 3 miles the grounds of **White Flower Farm** appear on both sides. If you've ever ordered bulbs and plants through the mail, the odds are quite good that this is the place where some of them came from.

WHITE FLOWER FARM
Rte. 63S
Litchfield, CT 06759
Tel. 203/567–0801

There is visitor's parking at the first turn on the right. The slot in front of the store is mainly for picking up orders and is also the spot where the venerable David Smith begins the free tours he leads through some 14 greenhouses and 30 to 50 beds, depending on the season. Be prepared to walk; the tours pass through some 30 acres of flowering banks of plants such as azaleas, begonias, tulips, and roses of many varieties and colors; English strains are quite popular here. The tours are well attended by local residents, and it's a good way to meet them. If you are planning to tour White Flower Farm (and why not?), call ahead, as the timing of the tours depends on the season and the weather. If you plan to buy, bring enough money. My father once paid $25 here for a single bulb, a tuberous begonia.

It is quite possible you may have already admired these flowers; the farm is the source for the arrangements at the West Street Grill. But something else comes to the Grill by way of White Flower Farm's greenhouses and is especially germane to the topic of these travels: produce from **Shepherd's Seeds.** Shepherd's Seeds is an importer, adapter, and distributor of mostly European herbs and seeds that are used for cooking. The plants that grow from these seeds, mostly native to the south of France and Italy, bring the flower and smell of the garden to food. They are often the Oh-I-wish-we-had-that-here sort of herb, savored in the Midi or the Tuscan hills, without which forever after salads in America seem a banal disaster. Shepherd's Seeds also distributes seeds for tomato plants, garlics, and eggplants.

But first, the herbs. Shepherd's offers an assortment of seeds for 10 different basils—five Italian, five scented, such as lemon and cinnamon—and these are wonderful and what they should be. But Shepherd's seeds for mesclun, a green that we have loved draped over a chèvre, and mâche (lamb's lettuce), a delicate, French salad green, produce leaves that are too grassy, too laden with chlorophyll. Like so many things from California, where Shepherd's products are developed, plants grown from their seeds are cosmetically correct and look wonderful, but the taste is just not there. Shepherd's other salad greens are somewhat more successful—French *roquette* (red and bronze lettuce) and *frisée* (curly endive)—but they are still too strong and not leaf-tender enough to reward the finicky—still a far cry from the produce of the greengrocer in Paris. People who take time to grow them may justly wonder what all the trouble is for.

Not so Shepherd's seeds for several varieties of French tomatoes, as sweet as they should be; and real *haricots vert* (green beans). There are also edible flowers—squash blossoms and nasturtiums—to decorate a salad or turn into *beignets* (fritters). Herbs grown from Sheperd's Seeds (in season) and a complete Shepherd's Seeds catalogue are available at White Flower Farm.

Proceeding south from the farm is a lovely drive down Route 63 to Morris and then south on Route 109. You can make it last about an hour. It passes through forests, along rushing streams past grasslands and bog, as it heads down to the town of Washington. En route the rolling hills of the countryside are flecked with barns and farms, some with names suggestive of chickens, but there's not a range-fed bird to be had for sale.

The way the farmer tells it, local laws governing poultry farms have been rewritten over the last 20 years to favor agribusinesses. These producers, often from out of state, ship chickens in great bulk over great distances to local supermarkets, which are far more numerous than they were 20 years ago. As a result, it's almost impossible today to buy a range-fed chicken in a countryside where there are literally thou-

sands of chickens walking around, especially at egg farms.

I once took this up with a former egg farmer who said he would have liked to continue selling chickens, as he had at one time as an adjunct to his egg business. But state regulations had required that any chicken sold to the public have its innards removed, packaged in paper, iced, and stuffed back inside the same chicken. The chicken in turn had to be wrapped in plastic and refrigerated, even if it had been fresh killed in front of the customer and sold on site.

Furthermore, the egg man said, because of a shortage of inspectors, they had been trying to put small producers out of business (they couldn't be bothered with small inspections); they would descend on his farm just after a rain to give him citations for a puddle of water.

The state inspectors got their way; eventually the egg man became so disgusted he quit the egg business too. Now Connecticut gets masses of its eggs shipped in from Chicago. The wastefulness of all this transportation and fuel use should not be lost on the public. Perhaps if more people stalked into restaurants raving, "Where do you get your eggs (or your chickens)?" before they ordered them, improvements in the taste of the eggs (or chicken) on their plate might be forthcoming.

Farther along is New Milford, home to **The Silo,** a rare thing in a ready-made world. It is a cooking school and store where there once was a farm, but what makes it rare is the pastoral plot it's on, and the flocks of ceramic geese and ducks that populate its barns.

The Silo: the Store, and the School
Upland Rd.
New Milford, CT 06776
Tel. 203/355-0300

Coming from Route 109, turn right onto Route 202, and find Upland Road and a sign for the Silo 3 miles ahead on the right. Take Upland Road to the pasture on top of the hill. For perhaps 20 years, Ruth and Skitch Henderson—the former bandleader on "The Tonight Show," and current conductor of the New York Pops—have been turning this collection of barns, houses, open pasture, and, of course, silo, into a food lovers' paradise. While the musician practices in his studio among his fabulous menagerie of carousel animals (on certain occasions this is viewable), Ruth gathers in kitchenware from around the United States, Mexico, and Europe, keeping up on trends for the store.

The first floor of the barn is stocked to the rafters, from which more stock is hung. Here is where much of Litchfield comes to furnish its kitchens. There are glasses, both stemmed and clunky, some made with finesse and others strictly for service. There is flatware for all kinds of tables and prices, bizarre hot mitts (some of the interesting things that hang from the rafters), tea kettles and cozies, terra-cotta, stoneware and china bowls, and an almost religious convocation of mugs.

On the other side of a wide-open portal (and across a yawning chasm in price) are cooking utensils that are almost indispensable for the serious and well-heeled chef. Le

Creuset is for sale in a great range of shapes and sizes, including those irreplaceable #28 *poêles* (frying pans) with fitted cast-iron lids that can break your arm to lift (but what else can you use?). The adjoining silo itself contains things on sale, frequently closeout items marked down 50%, and is also a very good source for gifts.

On the second floor the Silo demonstrates the personality that keeps it from being just another food-related store with an interesting range of upscale stock. The gallery upstairs holds forth in every season (the Christmas parties are sumptuous) with arts and crafts shows under its wood-timbered ceilings. It presents the work of local artists and artisans (this takes in all of New England), ranging from painters to ceramicists to furniture makers, giving them all a taste of recognition.

Most of the work is well wrought, and the Silo is the place in Litchfield to be on any "gallery Sunday." The events are catered with music—wine and cheese plus local musicians in cello recitals—and peopled by local celebrities. "Shake a tree around here and a writer falls out," said Theodore White to me as Arthur Miller walked in one Sunday.

How to be invited? Drop in during the early afternoon most any Sunday, especially in the height of summer, go up to the gallery, and shake hands with Skitch and Ruth; or you can improve your luck by calling or writing the Silo ahead. They'll send you a schedule that might match your interest with an event.

The second floor also has a food shop, where autographed copies of cookbooks are sold, and the Silo's school, where some of the major names in the food trade come to give cooking classes in its state-of-the-art kitchen. Jacques Pepin and Giuliano Bugialli are among the international personalities who hold forth. There are classes, say, on lasagna, on bread alone—French and focaccia—on low-fat Chinese food, or on food from coastal Maine.

Locally, James O'Shea and Matthew Fahrner come down to shed light on what they do at the West Street Grill, and Skitch shares his love for the barbecue with outdoor classes at the pit. All classes are given in self-contained three-hour units and start in the early spring. They go on every weekend to Christmas, when Bugialli gives his celebrated *Buon Natale* class and there is a gingerbread house-raising. All in all, the Silo is more than a shop and a diverting gallery with cooking classes thrown in; it is a continuous feast.

There are yet a few more places close by. It might be worth making a run to the north on Route 202 for a few miles and then turning left onto Route 45. There can be found the interesting frontier town of taste known as New Preston.

In one precious little strip, barely 400 yards long, beginning about 100 yards after the turn from Route 202, is an ensemble of gentrified little stores that are not part of a theme park but see themselves as a sort of Taste City. Rooted on just the slightest little dimple of ground, and behind a veneer of newly painted clapboard, are a housewares and fashion shop, a package store, a barbershop, two bookshops, and seven antiques shops, all clustered around an old Grange turned meeting hall with a stream running down the back. It's all so cute you'd expect Laurel and Hardy and the Wooden Soldiers to march out. The best value in town? The barbershop. A haircut costs $8.

The antiques shops are expensive, but go into **Jonathan Peters;** it has nice dry and fresh flower arrangements, and its assorted linens and bedding are artfully done. The housewares and fashion shop, **J. Seitz,** has for men what could be called artist's and writer's workshirts; for women there are southwestern T-shirts with chic Native American motifs. Tim Mawson's bookshop has garden books and rustic herb planters that are as charming as old toys.

Back in your car, if you continue about a half-mile, you'll reach a big lake, a vineyard to tour, a very good bistro, and a charming bed-and-breakfast. Because there's wine to buy, and later a place to drink it, and then to sleep, take in the vineyard first.

Follow Route 45 as it curves around Lake Waramaug (a likely spot for lake trout and trophy-size pickerel; in the winter the lake supports troops of ice fishermen in their little booths). On the way to the vineyard you will see restaurants, some set in the mountains, with expansive pavilions above the waters, but their offerings do not merit a stop.

HOPKINS WINERY AND VINEYARD
Lake Waramaug, CT 06777
Tel. 203/868-7954

On a hill with a perfect southern exposure is **Hopkins Winery and Vineyard.** The whole Hopkins family has been farming here for generations, and they'll tell you frankly they got into wine making because it paid better than dairy farming. Never mind the fancy tastings and dinners; much of wine making is backbreaking farm labor. That a family of farmers can make a success of it shouldn't come as much of a surprise. Planting, pruning, and turning a spade come naturally to farmers, and so do harvesting and loading a truck and bringing in a crop; the Hopkinses don't have to hire help because they're a family of five.

The winery and tasting room are well marked, with white lettering on a red barn; there's a place to park and lovely views down verdant slopes to Lake Waramaug. Barely audible whispers of motorboats drift upward through channels of leaves.

Follow the flow of the wine, coming down the hill from the vines in the back of the winery. A short walk or a drive will get you up there, and much of what is behind the idea of vine pruning can be viewed from the road. Vines are pruned in such a way as to maximize growth on one (sometimes more) new shoot each year. Each summer's growth bears flowers in late spring, produces ripe fruit in the fall, and is lopped off in January. Then the whole process begins again with the new year.

In September the grapes that develop from the vine flowers are taken down to the winery. Back down the hill, Hopkins winery has a balcony over its working space of stainless-steel vats, tubing, and barrels. You follow the process of vinification through a series of detailed wall-mounted charts and photos above each step (vatting, fermentation, aging, and racking) until the wine is in the bottle.

In the tasting room the bottles are opened, and one of the Hopkinses gives a tasting over the range of eight vineyard wines. It's not like judging an international event, where you know what to expect, but it's not giving blue ribbons to cows either. The wines come from good stock (most are French–American hybrids), are full of surprises, and are realistically priced. The tasting is free, and together with the winery tour and vineyard walk, is quite an enjoyable way to see how wine is made and what it should be (a natural farm product). While you are not pressured to buy, it might be wise to keep an eye open for a dinner accompaniment. The restaurant down the hill (*see below*) has divine antipasto, but no liquor license. You are invited to bring your own wine.

Retracing our path briefly on Route 45 brings us back to the end of the lake and a stop sign. Directly across from the beach, in an unpretentious clapboard building, is **Doc's,** as in the doctor gave the money (yes, to start up this restaurant).

D O C ' S

Rte. 45
New Preston, CT 06777
Tel. 203/868–9415

Reservations on weekends are an absolute must, sometimes for weeks in advance. Success follows the unique, and Doc's is the only Florentine bistro along the shores of Lake Waramaug. It has become home to a fanatically loyal freewheeling band of Italian food partisans. The reasons for this are: one, its prices—bringing their own wine, a couple can get out the door for under $24. Two, for those low prices you eat very well: Doc's understands seasoning—bottles of crushed red peppers in oil are available and liter bottles of excellent olive oil are on every table; the pizzas come with lamb sausage, as does the bean casserole; and the antipasto is a Tuscan smörgåsbord of fresh delights. Three, there is no quiche; and four, partisans step into the relaxed atmosphere in any clothes they want to wear. Even if you have a reservation for Doc's, you must be slavishly punctual. Show up 10 minutes late, and your table is gone. The need is pressing, as the table is only one out of nine and Doc's doesn't kick people out who are dawdling over coffee.

Do not think that this is going to be a horrible experience with people dining on top of you; among the delights of going to Doc's are exactly the people who wind up next to you. Hidden as they are in rural homes carefully secreted at the ends of long driveways, or from where they can't see another human soul, they come to Doc's—most of them gregarious ex-New Yorkers—craving the human touch and conviviality, and they communicate through what they know about food. Going to Doc's is like going to a movie where everyone knows all the lines.

Not to your taste? Not so fast; a demanding audience does keep (as it does in Italy and France) a kitchen on its toes. Doc's is an example of cuisine through peer pressure; the food is good, in part, because the customers are demanding.

Try especially Doc's antipasto. It comes on a platter surrounding a crisp, flowery centerpiece, which I have heard variously described as an artichoke, which it does resemble, and an edible marigold. What it is is garlic. A whole bulb, roasted on its hips until it is soft, sweet, and the skin charred. It's surrounded with a host of tidbits of whatever the season brings: roasted vegetables (little crinkly potent peppers, eggplant, sun-dried tomatoes, baby squash) and assorted cheeses (fresh and smoked mozzarella, ricotta, and many more). Chef Riad Aamar goes down to Arthur Avenue in the Bronx on his days off and it's from that source that his breads come, and all of his sausages. Sample the aforementioned lamb-sausage pizza, or have the sausage in the white bean (great Northern) casserole with tomatoes and sage, which comes out as a sort of thick native cassoulet by way of the Bronx.

They love to linger with coffee on the shores of the Connecticut lake with the sun going down. If you have a room for the night, try biding your time with Doc's specialty of *tiramisu*—soft Italian cheese (mascarpone), rum, ladyfingers and espresso powder. There will be just 3 miles to drive before you sleep.

The **Constitutional Oak Farms** (Beardsly Rd., Kent, CT 06757, tel. 203/354–6495) is an old farmhouse, dating from the 18th century. It has a lovely site on an old road where the night is dark as pitch. On a veranda outside the kitchen, breakfast is served from the crack of dawn until any time you want. The nice people who run it are as authentic as the floorboards, and they charge only $65 for two with private bath. It is the ideal spot to anchor around Lake Waramaug.

CHAPTER 3

THE HUB OF THE BERKSHIRES

Great Barrington and New Marlborough, Massachusetts

Great Barrington is the big town in the heart of the Berkshire hills. If you come to these mountains from the west, or the south, you are sure to pass through Great Barrington. It would be a shame not to stop, a crime to miss this picturesque center of these most admired hills. In their sheltering folds some of America's household names of the arts have made their homes. Great Barrington is the place most of them come to when they come to town.

HIGHLIGHTS:
- A bread and cupcake window
- French wines and hard-boiled eggs
- A sandwich workshop
- A jewel box in a gingerbread house
- Ladybugs, vegetables, chicken potpies, and tin cabins for sweet teeth
- A locker of cheeses, butter, and oil in the soap
- A teahouse in a pottery
- An inn on a village green

LENGTH OF LOOP: 9½ miles, with the inn
LENGTH OF STAY: Two days

To get to Great Barrington take Route 23 east from the Taconic Parkway, the Thruway, or Albany, as far as Route 7; take Route 7 north into Main Street. From the south follow Chapter 1's directions to Hillsdale, where you will pick up Route 23.

Great Barrington is not one of those ugly or dumpy little towns that sometimes pop up to poke you in the eye and ruin a fine day or some scenic masterpiece of nature. Great Barrington is a place of high, wide, and handsome streets, where the art of leisure is practiced; it is both a vacation spot and a 9-to-5 workplace town where much of its product is pleasing people. There are art theaters and art supply houses (try **Shelly's,** out on Route 7 South if you're looking for bargains in prints, canvas, or paint).

But the princely passion of Great Barrington is noshing. A word about noshing; we might as well jump into the subject right here. Noshing is a word coming directly from the Yiddish into the American—where it fits so nicely—which means to chew, to nibble, and to taste. Nowhere does it suggest to digest, or swallow; that's where the seltzer comes in. It is a form of eating that has an ambulatory quality about it. The moving mouth tastes, and having bitten, moves on. There is nothing studious or serious about it. Noshing means having fun with food.

Great Barrington is a great place to do this because the pleasures of its streets are equal to the foods. This is not a dollhouse of a town, with cute little cupboardlike traps of stores for tourists to stroll into; you will never be taken to one of those in this book. Great Barrington's pavement is full of atmosphere because its streets are full of unexpected and original offbeat things.

Park your car in the center of town, on Main Street (which is Route 7); but wait until you pass the first of three handsome stone churches—St. John's, on the left—and its adjoining Town Hall before you park, or you will have too far to walk without compensation.

Almost to whet your appetite for the feast to come, drop in on **Memories** (310 Main St., tel. 413/528–6380), which has nothing to put in your mouth unless you still put your toys there. It is a shop chock-full of real old-time things, not facsimiles: wind-up and electric trains, cast-iron trucks, flat boxes of old British redcoats, ship models of Revolutionary War frigates, and things that tend to the naïve and technically primitive. Do you have a place for old, upright radios with green electric eyes or oscillating fans? There is also usually a stock of old movie cameras and projectors, circa 1950–'60s, sound and silent, in 8, super-8, and 16 millimeter, featuring makes like Kodak and Bell & Howell for those who were never captured by the mushy quality of video. Memories has just what you wished for before you had money.

Around the corner and up Railroad Street, walk into the **Daily Bread** (17 Railroad St., tel. 413/528–9610). It's not only the best in bread, but in shortbread and cupcakes, too. You could not do better in Devon, Glasgow, or Montmartre. Inside it's just a shoebox of a place with two seats by the window at a counter that faces the street. You can watch what goes up and down outside and turn around to snap up coffee and snacks from the store counter.

Make sure to start with the blackbottom cupcakes. They must be downed first because, no matter where you're looking once you sink in your teeth, you'll swear you're in Chocolate City. Order coffee then; all you've got to do is turn around. This is the meaning of noshing. The sticky buns (I once thought this was a name given by a friend with a very limited vocabulary) are impossibly rich and gross, with real honey and real cinnamon. The Devonshire scones are buttery and wonderful; and for those who have been to Scotland, and despaired of ever tasting their like again, the shortbread cakes are the equivalent of what they serve at the hospitality lounge of the Glenfiddich distilleries in Dufftown itself. In this region of western Massachusetts, and especially in Connecticut, good bread (as in a decent baguette) is almost unknown to the general public, which still buys those supermarket loaves best used as down pillows. Good bread must be mentioned wherever it is found, as a public service. If you are new in the area and have rented a house, you are advised to do as so many others do: Buy your bread in advance and freeze it. The Daily Bread (they've opened an annex in

Stockbridge, the demand is so great) processes orders for baguettes by phone, and the orders come in by the hundreds on weekends.

You are not expected to eat all you've piled up to taste, but take a nice selection with you for walking (holding onto a bit of baguette is a good idea, for the cheese to come), or later when driving. The Daily Bread provides napkins and bags to wrap the excess.

In case you should want a sit-down, traditional lunch, or a place where you can spread out in a wonderful bar, under a painted tin ceiling, try the restaurant behind the old brick facade across the street that you have been staring at from the window of the Daily Bread—if you sat to eat where you were told.

20 Railroad Street (tel. 413/528–9345) is the epitome of the cozy restaurant for people who hunger and thirst after nostalgia. It is exactly the sort of restaurant you have been in before, but you can't exactly say where. Maybe it was on television, or in a very old neighborhood. Good hamburgers, good bar, the tin ceiling, wooden tables, time-stained dark walls, a big blackboard chalked with the menu. A big, comfortable crowd is always, day or night, in an unbroken undercurrent of conversation, and in daytime it's too dark inside for sunglasses. It's the place in the Berkshires to sit back in an old bentwood chair and order whatever they have—hamburger, or better, broccoli gratinée, grilled bluefish, and a bottle of Beaujolais. It's a warm place, and a warm feeling will come over you—especially if you ever liked P.J.'s in Manhattan.

Farther up Railroad Street, at no. 49, is **Martin's** (tel. 413/528–5455). It's a place for breakfast and brunch, and with its white walls and bleached tables it makes me think of eggs. It will also remind you of the time when the most chic sentence in the English language when ordering was, "A glass of white wine, please." Now it's just a sentence.

Railroad Street is almost a pedestrian zone. Some of the shops have some of what's regional in fashion as well as food and are a distillation of what you might find if you went down to the end of every little road that winds through the hills. **Gatsby's** (25 Railroad St., tel. 413/528–9455) likes to call itself the Bloomie's of the North. They even have dining room displays of rattan and wicker chairs up on the second floor. **Leather Woods** (9 Railroad St., tel. 413/528–4884) will dress you in deerskin and silver baubles and bracelets, as well as sandals, shearling slippers, and leather hats.

Around the corner is Main Street again and some excellent values in food that might be overlooked if you race by on the way to Tanglewood or to your house. If you haven't time or the makings to pack your picnic basket at home, the place to make one up is in Great Barrington.

Gorham and Norton (278 Main St., tel. 413/528–0900) can be a good place to go for more than the cheese for your bread. It is a combination vegetable stand, delicatessen, and wine shop. In the former two categories they have a good grasp on what is local; in the latter category the excellent is on hand. Here is a place to buy Massachusetts goat cheese. The chèvre is made in nearby Monterey and is buttery with a succulence that is unusual for goat cheese. Come to think of it, where can you buy rock candy? Here is where, in both white and mahogany varieties. There are all manner of vegetables, brands of cookies and crackers (for kids or the car), and chips, some in exotic (eggplant) styles. There are imported as well as domestic cheeses. Most of the well-known varieties are here—Roquefort, Port Salut, Vermont Cheddars, and so on. There are sandwich meats and rye breads, and of particular note is High Lawn milk. This local dairy (Lenox) bottles milk in a nonhomogenized form; it separates, so you can make your own *crème fraîche* and Devonshire cream.

When it comes to wine, a big French selection is unusual in any deli. Gorham and Norton must be the source for at least some of the fancy picnics that spread out on the Tanglewood lawn. What can be drawn from their stocks to accompany the Boston Symphony are many strands of Beaujolais, Loire wines featuring Vouvray, and name-brand Bordeaux. Brane-Cantenac was the best buy in the store with offerings of its 1985 vintage at a reasonable $35. Of the many champagnes that go so well with Mozart, Veuve Clicquot is especially recommended and well represented.

There is still one place where you must drop in and sit down even if you are not tired from all this walking.

The Berkshire Coffee Roasting Company (286 Main St., tel. 413/528–5505) imports, roasts, grinds, and sells beans— and serves such marvelous cups of steamed coffee that gradually its dark and warm interior has become one of the most fashionable places in the Berkshires. Everybody comes to this coffeehouse; even in the dead of February it is packed with its fragrance and denizens who are free to rummage through stacks of old butter-yellow *National Geographic*s and circa-Diana-Vreeland copies of *Vogue*. Sixty cents will get you an excellent coffee made with live steam and hours of library privileges. There are copies of local newspapers and the Sunday *New York Times*, plus marvelous machines to watch.

Hero of the shop is the giant coffee roaster, a Dietrich from California, taking up the space of two tables. Beans are roasted once a week, in small batches to ensure freshness and flavor; phone for a schedule of feeding times. But it is in the selection of its beans that the café especially shines. Don't look for flavor fads of Old Dutch Cinnamon or Lemon Gingerbread here, but old classic beans that were precious cargo in the epic sailing days: Celebes, Sumatra, Java—jewels of the spice islands. Berkshire Coffee has about 20 varieties of bean. One is herbal, none are flavored, the argument being that flavored beans (the perfume is so strong) would contaminate the grinder. For those who want tea, the coffee company exerts its same demanding preferences over a range of herbal and black teas, such as Darjeeling, Earl Grey, and Ceylon. There are no mail orders here and that's too bad, but the take-out business is brisk, and there are some delicious cakes, croissants, and the like, to hit whatever quick hunger you aim at.

Great Barrington, with all its sturdy New England character—the three churches on Main Street are made of stone—might seem an ideal spot for a sunny, Provençal restaurant, with the fragrance of olive oil, fresh herbs, and garlic. Unfortunately that's not what's presented at **La Tomate** (293 Main St., tel. 413/528–3003). The painted tomato on the sign outside was the only one in sight on one visit. This is a restaurant that looks better from the outside than it does from within. The olive oil was of everyday grocery-store ilk and the people inside seemed to care less about whether you had the taste of Provence in the mouth than about coaxing you into ordering a lobster, which you're better off having in Maine. Much better off.

How about a sandwich then? If you are in the mood, or are packing for the car, you couldn't do better than at the sandwich-and-soup city known as **The Deli** (343 Main St., tel. 413/528–1482). They will even make up your order ahead. The place is a funky sort of masterpiece, with a crayon-colored list of sandwich varieties and other specialties papered on the wall. The atmosphere is like eating in a comic strip: highly entertaining and with prices to laugh at. Sandwiches come in full and half sizes. You can design your own or order from the Deli Hall of Fame—a list of sandwiches (roast beef, salami, corned beef, pastrami, ham, turkey, seafood, cheese, and their combos) named for famous persons from Captain Jacques Cousteau, shrimp; to actor Oscar Homolka, tuna (but it should have been ham). There are daily soups, a selection of surprisingly fresh salads, and gross dressings like creamy dill. The place has bagels, a counterculture bulletin board, and the authentic taste of a good downtown deli in the country.

Next, there is something for those who take their architectural gingerbread in jewel boxes. The **Mahaiwe Theatre**
(14 Castle St., tel. 413/528–0100) is worth the investment of a
50-yard walk up from Main. The corner of its marquee is
visible from down the street, and it is not the simple little
movie house you might think it. This kind of theater, once
popular, has become invisible over much of the American
landscape. It is a neo-Renaissance gem, a theater built in 1905
for pre-Broadway runs of legitimate plays and musical enter-
tainments, the kind of classical jewel box that Hollywood so
often set down in films set in antique Paris. The Mahaiwe
could be patterned after the little theater in Versailles,
although Louis XIV showed less interest in Pennsylvania
brick. But the Mahaiwe's generous use of marble trim, its
painted loges and boxes, the lavish sets still in the flies, add a
sense of drama and musical conviviality in tune with 19th-
century comic opera and lost in our strident times. The utter
cleanliness of everything—the floors and the fresh smell, the
rugs and the upholstery—makes the final impression that
you are not standing in a monument of France, but a gilt-
edged echo of our recent past, unhappily gone.

Happily, there do remain performances to be attended.
You can dress up in your best and have somewhere to go
before or after dinner. L'Orchestra (tel. 413/528–1872), a
Baroque-Classical ensemble, often appears on the stage; the
Berkshire Film Society (tel. 413/528–5120) screens films of a
classical interest; and the theater has a regular schedule of current box-office hits. There is an exhibition of mint-condition
publicity stills and movie posters in the Belle-Epoque lobby,
where it would be quite appropriate to stride up to the ticket
window in a cape and demand, "Two on the aisle!" Or,
"(gasp) I must see (choke) Miss Langtree!"

Next door to the Mahaiwe, there's an Oriental rug shop
with an honest man inside. If you have an interest in either, go
in to **Donald McGrory Oriental Rugs** (12 Castle St., tel.

413/528–9594). The stock is quite fine and mixes Eastern European with the usual Iranian; McGrory keeps his prices competitive with most city outlets. Rug stocks roll through the Berkshires in trucks driven by itinerant salesmen, and you can profit. McGrory's is the kind of place where you can drop in during a shower and just talk rugs, and it's a good place to go.

THE CASTLE STREET CAFE
10 Castle St.
Great Barrington, MA 01230
Tel. 413/528–5244

The **Castle Street Café** next door is a lot of fun and full of surprises. Chef-owner Michael Ballon worked at Lavin's and Sofi in New York City and was a great hit with nouvelle tastes in those places, but in his haven in the Berkshires he is his own master and profferer of tastes that run to the eclectic.

This is as good an address as you will find in town for dinner, and it is open for dinner only. The restaurant offers options in styles that are as welcome as a breath of fresh air, difficult to classify but a joy to sit down to. In trying times it can be easy on the wallet, or you may find it just as suitable for a splurge of proven elegance. On the economical side are the festive pasta dishes that are always on the menu; then there is a range of bistro dishes at bistro prices ranging from coq au vin to steak au poivre and cassoulet (great Northern beans, a whole lamb shank, and garlic sausage), which is served all winter long. There are hamburgers, too, half-pounders coming with real straw potatoes cut fresh, a thick bun, a serving of salad, too, and a measly price of $8. Where else can you get that with a tablecloth thrown in?

There are excellent wines at a range of prices, but with the burger Ballon opts for beer. He has several excellent micro brews (*see* Chapter 7).

From this point, rejuvenated by the walking tour, it's time once more to get behind the wheel of a car. As you drive north on Route 7, do not take the right turn at the bridge over the Housatonic River; instead, head straight north on Route 41 toward the town of Housatonic, a distance of 3½ miles. Here is a nice stretch of road that can't make up its mind whether it's suburban or rural, in a forest or parkside. It's edged with neat bungalow houses surrounded with dogwood and laurel and interlaced with running streams flowing toward the Housatonic and crossed by nasty intersections, so watch out.

GREAT BARRINGTON POTTERY
Rte. 41
Housatonic, MA 01236
Tel. 413/274–6259

The foliage cover on the left will fall suddenly away, and in its own peculiar site **Great Barrington Pottery** stands out. Peculiar? There is a Japanese garden, falling water, a teahouse, and a studio. The parking lot is signposted from the road, the drive takes a little curl behind a stand of spruce, and you walk up pine-shaded steps leading to the Japanese garden. The teahouse is straight ahead, and the studio is to the left. You have entered the ceramic and ceremonial world of Richard Bennett.

"I don't do lamps," the artist, who looks like an Irish attorney in a sweatshirt, says decidedly. "No, I'm a dish maker. I make dishes for dining." So there you have it. Richard Bennett is an artist who happens to make things that people can use, and use three times a day. That he should live and work in the Berkshires is part of the story of Great Barrington and of the Berkshires today. There is space to spread out a studio; it is close to the great markets of New York and Boston. If you have an interest in ceramics, as well as in serviceable dishes for everyday use, you cannot do better than to go to this combination art gallery/bargain basement.

Too good to be true? Listen.

Richard Bennett learned his art from a master potter in Japan while studying with a Zen priest. Correspondingly, his aim became to make objects that are as beautiful as they are because they are what they are. He would rather have one of his tea bowls, for example, used every day of its life for the enjoyment of tea than see it in a museum. Yet his works *are* displayed in museums, from the Hancock Shaker Museum in Lebanon nearby, to the Chase Manhattan Bank in New York City, and to the Shimane Museum near Matsue, Japan.

In the other direction, from Japan to the Berkshires, comes the design of Bennett's main kiln. It was built by his Japanese master as Bennett handed him its 7,000 bricks. The stoneware that it fires (Great Barrington was always a pottery center because of clay deposits nearby, as is every pottery center) is heated to a temperature of 2,300°. So of course it can go into the oven and into a dishwasher at home.

Bennett's work comes in colors ranging from natural clay earth tones to multicolored (cobalt streaked with black), and most of his pieces (plates, mugs, cups) that make up a dining set run from $10 to $100; $100 per place setting seems to strike an average. These are the bulk, the great mass, of what the artist sells; their sale helps finance the rest of his life, the fabrication of his museum-quality serving pieces and vases , his tea-service exhibitions, and frequent trips to Ireland and Japan.

His collection of serving pieces is large and stunning. The singular vases are done with angular sides in swirls of colors, cobalts and blacks, and run from $100 to $500 and sometimes higher. Larger, exhibit-size serving pieces cost much more. The highest price paid on site for a single piece of Bennett's work was $15,000. It doesn't happen every day, but the crowds that pour in from New York (whose proximity and relationship with the Berkshires is very much like that of Paris with Normandy) are dense; Tanglewood, spring's flowers, summer's coolness, and the fall colors do their share to keep the folks coming; the artist who perseveres can have the work he wants on his plate.

This one also does his share to attract the folks who come up. Bennett imports a Japanese tea mistress from a tea school in Kyoto, for example. Within the paper and wood walls of his 75-year-old teahouse, a dwarf maple outside, demonstrations of the patient art of the tea ceremony are given. Visitors then love to take in the scents of a wildflower garden and to poke around a real ceramics studio. Each year 50,000 come to do that, and some also buy Bennett's distinctive dishes; the West Street Grill in Litchfield, Connecticut (*see* Chapter 2), uses them as place settings, the Umeda restaurant in New York City has 2,000 of them in daily use, which must hit the spiritual jackpot in Zen dish making.

Perfect sets of dishes and dishes that are a perfect dream have been coming out of Bennett's converted barn studio in Housatonic, Massachusetts, since 1967. A visit to the studio and the grounds offers not only a contemporary insight into the life of a Berkshire artist, but a glimpse into the extended cultural experience of food.

Moving out from Bennett's digs, you can still catch two interesting markets before you dine. Turn south back down Route 41. In about a half-mile, at the flashing light, turn left. This is Division Street, and you are in the legal limits of Great Barrington again. After a few hundred yards, on the left, will appear a former church (I can't say it's old), once the home of Alice Brock, who gave us the original Alice's Restaurant; and now the office of Arlo Guthrie, also of *Alice's Restaurant* fame. On the right, at the next large intersection, which is Route 183, is **Taft Farms**. It's hard to miss because it's the only thing that's there. Pull into the parking lot, where it is time for a story.

TAFT FARMS

Rte. 183 and Division St.
Great Barrington, MA 01230
Tel. 413/528–1515

Of course you have heard about pesticides and what they do, and of organic farming. Taft Farms offers a program that is somewhere in between, and it is interesting because it works. Anyone who has ever gardened vegetables can tell you that raising them without pesticides is very difficult. To raise vegetables commercially that way is nearly impossible. You can pick off all the white mealybugs, and spray with all the soapy water you want, but if the gypsy moth caterpillar ever lights, it's either the heavy-duty stuff or you are doomed. Never mind the praying for rain, high winds, or wild flocks of starlings. Aboriginal farming techniques won't put the veg on the nation's table.

Taft Farms is not Aboriginal Farms. It's 200 acres of crops raised to be sold for market at their Division Street stand where you are, and here's how they do it. None of the broccoli, carrots, sweet corn, cabbage, cauliflower, lettuce, spinach, beets, squash, cucumbers, melons, and potatoes that you'll find inside Taft's wooden buildings have been sprayed. They are from fields that have not been sprayed for several years. They meet all the qualifications for "organically grown" produce by any definition. The strawberries have been grown using the same techniques since 1987, without chemical insecticides or fungicides.

What are these techniques, then? Taft Farms, like many other such small farms and food cooperatives in the Berkshires, uses Integrated Pest Management (I.P.M.), a farming method that was developed at the University of

Massachusetts at Amherst. I.P.M. starts with natural predators—killer bugs, ladybugs, our friends the birds (certain birds that eat insects do not eat seed at all—robins, for example). This is augmented with vigilant field patrols and the use of biological controls—certain bacteria will kill certain pests. Finally, sprays are used as a last resort, not as a first defense. Practical results show that, in some places, the need to spray can be eliminated with certain vegetables, though it is a much less reliable technique in raising fruits—apples, for instance.

Inside the cool shed of the farm stand there is a nice pick of fresh vegetables up and down the aisles as well as specialty items—fiddleheads, for example. Especially attractive for gifts is maple syrup in little tin houses. The gift will be particularly appreciated by foreign friends, as there are no sugar maples outside North America. Taft has also chicken potpies from Otis Poultry Farm, which are frozen and can be kept for gastronomic emergencies, such as the arrival of the aforementioned friends, or taken to the city. There is a big plant selection in the greenhouse, where the jades and huge ferns reach extravagant heights. Aside from home-baked products, pastas, sauces, eggs, and fresh milk (High Lawn Farms again), decent baguettes can also be found here.

Leaving the Taft parking lot, proceed east on Route 183 to Route 7 south, back toward Great Barrington. Before you get to the intersection with Route 23, you will come upon a most appealing health and specialty food store. Slow down and keep your eyes peeled on the right for **Locke, Stock and Barrel.**

LOCKE, STOCK AND BARREL
Rte. 7
Great Barrington, MA 01230
Tel. 413/528–0800

This is a food shop, but there is one thing on its shelves that you wouldn't want to put in your mouth. The Marseillaise is a great big cube of soap from the south of France, and the luxury is so appealing: the scents of the south of France—the lavender, the wild thyme, and tarragon are all there, but especially the olive oil. Put one of these in your tub, and you'll feel like you are bathing on the Riviera, perhaps like a movie star. It's like smoking a Gauloise, without the harm. Unfortunately, the big cube costs $16, which might be quite reasonable for all of the above. If you feel that $16 is a steep price to pay for what is still a bar of soap, more reasonably sized cakes come at less than $1. They will give your bath the same fruity sensation, but not the opulence of stardom.

Rarely is a shop so well stocked and so neat, with merchandise so well chosen. It seems, as with the soap, that everything we can't find, or find hard to get, is here. Even if you're on your way to Timbuktu, or opening your house for the summer, or live next to Zabar's in Manhattan, this is a place to stop. There is not only smoked salmon, but fresh salmon steaks. The very full array of good olive oil suggests that somebody here knew what a hard item it is to find in America. Hain products are sold here, as well as those from France. And, speaking of France, when it comes to butter, here is the nutty and luscious *beurre de Charante*—try that on your hot blueberry muffins or *tartine de baguette*. A lineup of honey, some unprocessed and raw, some crystallized and unheated and not filtered, and from Champlain Valley Apiaries, is sold at real bargain prices; as they say, compare, when you can find comparisons. There are grains—in wonderful condition, I might add—such as rolled oats, to make your own cereals. The cereals themselves—Familia Swiss products—are sold here. Locke, Stock and Barrel is a place to stop for a hostess gift if you're on your way to a visit.

Proceed south on Route 7 for less than a half-mile until you reach the junction of Route 23, where you turn left onto Route 23 East. You are on your way to the mountains. Pass the ski area of Butternut, unless you're going in, and veer off Route 23 onto Route 57 (about 3 miles), heading for New Marlborough.

Be sure to make this drive in daylight. Eastward from the turn you climb upward to find yourself in the most glorious tract of Berkshires we know. There are no more invigorating mountains than these. Their breath lies on your face like a cool compress. Scent layers come in as you climb. Laurel, pine, cedar: It's pure mountain air. Try that for an energizing appetizer.

New Marlborough is not a town, certainly not a city; it's just a dimple of a green patch on this earth, white houses on a mountaintop. On the way there, you pass some important sights.

The Red Bird Bed and Breakfast (Rte. 57, Great Barrington 01230, tel. 413/229–2433) is just down to the right in a little dell; you can see it from the road, a pleasant wood frame house, bathed in a pool of light. Try to catch it in the midmorning. Swinging screen doors, screened-in porch—it's a good spot to stay if you don't want anything too complicated or intend to be out a long time on the road and want to save a little money to let your time last longer. The Red Bird is like going to the country and staying with grandma, or folks that you like. In no time, you feel at home. There are two swimming lakes nearby and a place to catch trout (more about that later), so it's worth it to bring your fishing gear and get yourself a license (a stop at the Great Barrington Town Hall will fix up the latter and is on the way here).

Meanwhile, the hills ahead form the sort of picture you can take for a postcard; on your left, just as you pass the limits of New Marlborough, is a place with a big deck called **The Hillside Restaurant** (Rte. 57, Great Barrington, tel. 413/528–3123). It's due to one of those tricks in the way the road cuts that the Hillside has a Great Barrington address, but it's out there, notched into New Marlborough's landscape and a pretty place to watch the sun go down or contemplate a mountain; they're sometimes blue, sometimes purple, sometimes green from here.

Joseph Chighine is from Rome, "Roma," he says; he has run this place for 20 years, but he has no pasta on his menu. You ask him what kind of food he does, and he says, "Continental." This used to be shorthand for quite awful when I was growing up, but you cannot call a restaurant that has no pasta Italian. So "Continental" it is.

He calls his best veal dish "Veal Napoli"; another is Veal Picatta; and his veal is Provini brand. But no pasta, he says. Yet his olive oil is Martinelli, from Italy; he gets Italian olives for his salads; and his I.P.M.-grown greens come from the best local producers. Still, no pasta. You can't go into an "American" restaurant anymore without getting pasta, I say. How about pasta for the tourists? He has paid his bills for 20 years, so the best meat and bread purveyors come from Springfield and Pittsfield up the mountain road, even in winter. So do his customers; he has never advertised in 20 years, and still they keep coming. That must count for something. Besides, American pasta is "sloppy and runny," and his sister is coming from Italy in September. She will see the fall foliage, and then she will do the pasta. Then the Hillside will have pasta.

How about wine? I ask. We have a nice "California burgundy," Chighine says. Suffice it to say, if you order carefully, and if you let Chighine think you've been to Italy, or at least Brooklyn—lie if you haven't—he can do what's right. The bill averages about $27 per person, and if you're not just passing through, and are going to be in the region for a few days or a week, the Hillside is a good place to visit. Pick a nice day and get there before sundown.

OLD INN ON THE GREEN
Star Rte. 70
New Marlborough, MA 01230
Tel. 413/229-3131

After the Hillside you still have a way to go before reaching the community of buildings around New Marlborough's **Old Inn on the Green.** You would find it hard to miss, however, because Route 57 East goes right by the inn. Continue straight on as far as the curves in the road will permit. The inn looks like a white Colonial mansion from the road, and the Congregational Church, next door, seems a part of its grounds. The spacious sweep of sand and lawn that stands between them must be the way all village greens looked before roads were paved. At any rate, angling off the pavement of Route 57, we go back in time and arrive at the door of the Old Inn on the Green.

The sign over the portal reads 1760, and it could be just that. There are violets in a flower box by the steps, and we go up to the veranda hoping no bore will ruin our stay by mentioning the Stamp Act.

What? There is no television in the rooms. Owner Brad Wagstaff will put one in if you desire, but he says nobody does. There are telephones. The inn has the sort of guests who have the means to spend time. They walk—there is a forest out back and a long, long trail. Berries can be gathered in summer, mushrooms fill the bill in fall, and the rooms have good views and cheerful decor. This is an old inn firm in an old inn's ways. It didn't come in pieces from out of a set; no truck from Madison Avenue rolled up to its doors and unpacked it; I'm sure it never had a decorator. It is full of what it was full of when it started out—furniture. Over the passage of time pieces of the furniture have become what are called priceless antiques. After all, it has been in continuous operation, almost without interruption (except for a few years in the 1950s) since 1760. It wasn't "restored." It is what it grew up with. If you want to stay, it is as near as you can get to the 18th century. Everyone should have the experience of a time warp once.

There are soot marks on the ceilings, but these are made by the chandeliers, which are lit every evening. At night, the public rooms are lit only by candles. In one of the four dining rooms a tranquil mural wraps the room with the security of a cocoon; it is green and hilly in the style of Grandma Moses, showing much of New Marlborough and the rolling landscape around the inn.

Upstairs in the inn the rooms are all quite different; each has its own dimensions. The corner rooms are large, with all the space you could want for a few days' stay. Their appointments include big, ages-old four-posters, heirloom patchwork quilts, fine old chests of drawers, and Queen Anne wing chairs. The floors are wide-board, and there is a fireplace in most guest rooms. They overlook the lawn, mustard yellow in the sunset, and the trail into the forest. The prices for the rooms run from about $95 to $125. This is a place you should come to with a bottle or two of champagne and somebody you'd like to share your meals and maybe the rest of your life with.

Speaking of meals, they are hardly an incidental attraction. An aperitif on the Summertime terrace isn't hard to take first; the waiter knows what a Negroni is. Then it's into the mural room for dinner. The flickering candelabra are suggestive of the light from a fireside, but it's useful to read the menu before going in, or have it recited by the waiter. The lighting is the last concession made to ambience; the food is dynamite. It is an adventure into modernism in these parts.

Chef Hanan Braunstein and his wife Marta, the pastry chef, are refugees from the pressures of New York. They met in the kitchens of Marta's native Basque country of Spain. Their food is loaded with excitement, drama, and taste. It may be modern, as far as that definition can be pushed. But that doesn't mean skimpy or lame. It means plates that are pretty to look at—some, works of art—but laced with tastes of Spanish panache.

The starting dish can be a spring garden soup. This is principally green on the surface with purées of spinach and fava beans and has cosmic touches of milky crème fraîche arranged like radiating teardrops or comet tails from an op-art splash in the center. It is a soup that is breathtaking to look at, and the tangy taste balances the freshness of the greens and ease of the cream against a zippy background of forced radish oil.

The eggplant and roasted pepper terrine appetizer is a surprise. It is also tasty, which makes the surprise more delightful. It's square and comes on a flat plate looking for all the world like a dish of tricolor ice cream—raspberry, pistachio, and vanilla—and nothing more. But the raspberry layer is a purée of red pepper, the pistachio is the pulp of an eggplant, the vanilla on the end is a snappy and fresh goat cheese. Excitement and drama—an excellent food idea—you gobble and gobble, and soon it's all gone.

"What's a fava bean?" comes the question to a waiter at a nearby table. "Look. Can we substitute potatoes for rice because my husband doesn't like rice."

No restaurant can be better than its customers, just as it is true there is no good theater without a good audience. The place to which the Braunsteins have come can be counted among the most beautiful spots in America. Gastronomically, however, New Marlborough, Massachusetts, is no San Sebastian, Spain, or even West 46th Street, New York City, and that people have money is no guarantee they have taste. Things can get mighty discouraging in a small, hot kitchen, when what you have labored to create with art and finesse comes back to you because all they really want out there is mashed potatoes and a bowl of sweet-and-sour soup. But Wagstaff is determined to keep his couple working and his inn a drawing card to those who fill the mountains with weekend reservations and dollars even if, from time to time, the taste of frustration creeps in.

What comes next could be the centerpiece for any meal at the Café de Paris in Biarritz: a huge plate of artichoke bottoms stuffed with crabs, on a fire of red beets (and never mind saying you don't like beets), forced basil oil, forced chive oil, and a touch of balsamic vinegar.

Now is the time to talk about forced oils. This is something anyone can do. It is the idea that is important. All that is needed is excellent olive oil—not those cans of motor oil sold in supermarkets, but a specialty oil. One made from the Chianti maker Brolio, or Baena from Spain would be superb; there are several good ones from California, too. What is wanted is to put the taste (or the zing) of an herb, spice, or vegetable right into the oil, so its taste will flow over, saturate more strongly, the essence of the sauce or soup that is to be seasoned. Think of the red pepper grains that can sometimes be seen in bottles of oil. You shake out the oil, you get red pepper.

With certain vegetables and more delicate herbs, however, the desired taste must be forced. This is done in the following way: Say you want the oil of the radish, or chive, or basil; it's no difficult matter to make a purée of the vegetable or herb in question in the blender, then mix in olive oil and "force" the resulting mixture through a strainer. *Voilà,* forced oil, of whatever you choose. Note that you will always have the taste of the oil to deal with; you should add it to the sort of foods that would naturally take olive oil. Try it on your bean soup in the winter, for example, to add the snap and crackle of radishes or the springlike flavor of basil.

Here chive oil and basil oil are blended into the purée of beets that dresses the artichokes, and the resulting fragrance and surrounding color are a joy to behold and better to taste.

An opinion: Don't ask questions (as in substitutions) unless you are either disappointed or in a hash house. Take the chef (like the poet) with all his tricks. Afterward you can applaud or complain bitterly; come back or don't come again.

If there is one flaw at the Inn on the Green, it is that they could do better with wine. In these days when interesting wines come from all over the world, affording us the chance to learn something or share in a new experience, the list at the inn is loaded with very high-end name-brand material. The wines that turn up on the list are generally in the $35 range; what's offered as a bargain (California sauvignon blanc) does not attract a rush of tasters. Finally a Rhône wine strikes our fancy: The shipper is good and the price (around $20) is fair. The waiter comes back to report that the wine is out; what is then proposed as a substitute is a burgundy, at double the price.

That said, the inn is very comfortable, its site is a tonic, the rooms and public halls are original, and the food preparation is professional and elegant.

There is another food that should be mentioned in connection with the Old Inn on the Green. It inhabits York Lake, which is nearby. Go down the dirt road that parts from Route 57 at the end of the property. The sign indicates Colebrook, Connecticut, and Wagstaff will be happy to point the way. Almost as soon as you start down the road, you enter the

Sandisfield State Forest. In about a mile there is a sign for York Lake, a pristine and tranquil place suitable for bathing and fishing. In its blue depths you will find its most savory inhabitants, live trout. They are stocked by the state, but some are wild, with the taste not money, but only patience, can buy. Wild fish have to be caught, as only hatchery fish can be sold at a market or by a restaurant, and these are a far cry from the wild. But if you find a comfortable spot near the end of the dam, where the big trout are known to hunger and wait for

all good things to come, there is more than a chance to be lucky. Here is how: Put a night crawler on the end of your line, don't use a bobber; cast 40 feet out and let the bait be brought along the bottom toward the dam by the constant current. All you will need then is patience to have the best taste of fish you can bring home from these parts.

Here's how you can tell if the trout you caught is wild and not hatchery, and the degree of its wildness: When it is cut open to be cleaned—and this should be done as soon as you decide to keep the fish—the color of the flesh tells the tale. It is said that trout return to the natural state after three generations in the wild. White flesh is the sign of a hatchery fish. The taste is bound to be bland and unexciting, about what you get in a restaurant. The closer to pink, or salmon color, the flesh is (rainbow trout are what are found here), the closer the fish is to the wild; shades of near-red are the most delicious and desired. In-between shades are nothing to sneer at, light pink being about the color of a "holdover," a trout that was not planted by the state in the year it was caught but has wintered over, and the more seasons the better, feasting on natural food, not hatchery pellets. The closer to red the flesh, the less dressing the fish will need. A red trout is no candidate for butter, heavy cream, herbs, and sauces. They would get in the way of what you came trout fishing for in the first place, the taste of the wild.

One last thing. Go down the road to Colebrook. It's only 5 miles. See what everybody in America says they are yearning to see: an unspoiled town. It's almost pure 18th century. Colebrook was a stop on the old road that came from Boston over the top of the Berkshires, and the road is still unpaved. The town stopped growing but hasn't been deserted.

When you get there, the most modern building you will see is the general store. Greek Revival, it was built in 1812 and is a genuine piece of what our country came from. Most everyone who comes to this place feels the experience has done them some good and has an urge to stay. But you know where you are; to get back, you just make a U-turn.

CHAPTER 4

BERKSHIRE PASSAGES

Stockbridge to Pittsfield, Massachusetts

The Rockies are rugged, the Alps are alpine; why is it that the Berkshires around Stockbridge, with Lenox and Lee, have such cachet? They are the most elegant mountains in the world. The towns have charming settings without being resorts. Nowhere is there urban blight, but droll urbanity. The Berkshires are where The New Yorker magazine used to go on vacation.

The music festivals started here; so did the women's movement. People still send gifted children to summer camps on emerald-crusted hillsides where all the work is divided into string quartets. There is live theater, dance, elegant mansions, the Appalachian Trail, as well as the Appalachian Springs, but the most anticipated of evening projects is going out to dinner. The region supports a fine harvest of foods.

HIGHLIGHTS
- The Lion in clapboard
- Steaks and autumn soup
- Eat at Joe's
- Lenox, music, and caterers for picnics
- Jersey, Guernsey, and cheesecakes
- Shortbreads and bridies
- Guido's the great
- A Shaker food festival
- Elizabeth's

LENGTH OF LOOP: 27 miles
LENGTH OF STAY: Two days

To get to Stockbridge, follow Chapter 3's directions to
Great Barrington. From Great Barrington take Route 7 north 8
miles to the center of town.

So it is that you make a little right turn into Stockbridge. The town stands discovered all at once in most of its
details. It is so small. Think of Norman Rockwell: His hori-
zontal strip poster of Main Street was the street you are on.
This is his town, and these are his people.

There is his museum, the **Norman Rockwell Museum** (9
Glendale Rd., tel. 413/298–4100), just a few hundred yards
ahead on the right, in the most Norman Rockwell of quaint
white houses neat as a pin. Inside, it has the full-size paintings
from which some of his most typical *Saturday Evening Post* covers were reproduced—the boy getting his first haircut, the cop
eating a piece of pie—the faces once so cherished by most of
America. Some, in hyperrealism, wrap around the room like
movie screens, and you would not have guessed Rockwell had
done them. Unappreciated by the art mob in his own time
(aren't they all?), now, like Victorian houses, he is catching on.

The most arresting sight of all in Stockbridge, domi-
nating the street you came in on, is the **Red Lion Inn,** its
white clapboard sides dappled in the tree-filtered light. Here
you must stay. In all New England no inn so much defines
the town it is found in.

THE RED LION INN
Stockbridge, MA 01262
Tel. 413/298–5545

It is the center around which the rest of Stockbridge
revolves. The visitors who come to animate the town's streets
and buzz in its galleries are the guests who stay in the Red
Lion's rooms, or at least climb the steps to its wide, open

veranda where cold drinks are put out, as well as teas with hot scones, biscuits, spiced jams, and butter.

Inside are three dining rooms; they all serve more or less the same menu, with no concession to mode, fad, or fancy. Nobody cares what's in or nouvelle. What's in is what's always been in: long crusts of Yorkshire pudding dipped in gravy of marinated ribs of beef roasted till rosy.

The three restaurants are the Lion at the Inn, where the rugs are red and the table cloths very white. Farther back

The Red Lion Inn

is the cozy and hospitable Tavern; full of nooks and crannies, it is a re-creation of the time when the Red Lion was a stop on the stagecoach line between Albany and Boston. For more contemporary surroundings in the delightful days of spring through summer to autumn, there is the sun-splashed Courtyard, easily the most dazzling dining spot in Stockbridge, where you must eat at least once, the weather permitting. A little white picket fence follows the mews walk at the side of the building with its own private gate to the Courtyard. Boughs of sycamore and maple shade the tables: white furniture and white slacks; men in blue blazers on a cushion of white gravel. Three nights a week (the sun goes down late this far north in the summer), there are outdoor barbecues. "We could do them every night," says director

Dennis Barquinero, and maybe they will. What are the entrées most preferred and demanded at the Red Lion? Dennis rolls his tongue over his lips. "Our beefs," he says.

Certainly the most underrated dish in all New England is one of its popular favorites, and nowhere is it better done—steak and squash. It is the first meal I had in the region, and my senses still tingle from that taste. Steak and squash. Simply that and nothing more. I always hope to find it the same way, and this is how it is done at the Red Lion.

The squash is always butternut or acorn, simply prepared: cut in half along its length, scooped of seed, buttered, and doused in ground nutmeg. Face down, the halves are set in a baking pan, ¼-inch of water is added to the pan, and it goes into the oven. After 40 minutes the halves are turned over, butter and honey are added to their cavities, and they are then crisped for 10 minutes more at 500°. This is the squash of the farms of western New England. For steak they choose a simple boneless sirloin, porterhouse, or T-bone, not a mignon or part of a tenderloin; they broil or charbroil it, or, better, roast it over the coals of a spent maplewood fire. If that maple is sugar maple, the most succulent flavor I know rises to the beef; the fat drips and hisses in the coals, and the flames sprout up to be doused by water, producing volumes of maple smoke to flavor the meat. If you are concerned about fat in your diet, not only is beef bred leaner these days, but most of what fat there is drips off when it's cooked this way. This is steak and squash at the Red Lion: No bearnaise or other sauce or top knot of marrow is needed to go with it. If you think of ham and eggs, corned beef and cabbage, oysters and Chablis, to those pairs add steak and squash.

Squash is an undeniably versatile vegetable. It is not meant to be buttered and spiced for steak and nothing more. In the fall—squash harvest time in New England—the Red Lion turns the great American vegetable into squash soup. They call it Autumn Bisque, and what it tastes like is autumn leaves going down, fat and lazy. It's made from butternut squash along with apples, another fall crop. For dessert, stick to apple pie; they do it well, topped with Cheddar cheese, at the Red Lion. Cheddar came from the town of Cheddar, in England, but then they don't call this region New England for nothing.

The decor in the rooms might best be described as cheerful chintz. The Red Lion, with all its charms, is hardly what you'd describe as high gastronomy, or even gastronomy at all, but they are not trying for that, and what you pay is fair—which is not always the case in this part of the Berkshires.

Chesterwood (Box 827, Stockbridge, MA 01262, tel. 413/298–3579; closed Nov.–Apr. except Veterans Day weekend) is an estate just off Route 183 west of Stockbridge. It is the grounds, former studio, and home of Daniel Chester French, the American sculptor who created the statue of Abraham Lincoln in the Lincoln Memorial in Washington, DC, among other works. There is a place to picnic under the trees in the parking lot. For a small admission charge you can take a guided tour of French's summer estate behind the fence. It is a veritable woodland walk, with a park to stroll and a studio to visit, where among its prizes is a 6-foot marble model of his most famous statue, the seated Lincoln. A museum shop sells cards and souvenirs, but the buildings and grounds themselves contain quite a few architectural surprises; the most interesting is the dining room in the summer house, which brings the outdoors in. Of all the mansions in Stockbridge, where there seems to be an estate around every turn in the road, Chesterwood is the most rewarding to visit.

To answer the challenge of finding reasonable places to dine in these fashionable hills, and for the first price bonus on leaving Stockbridge, go past the **Berkshire Playhouse** on

Route 7 North and take the first turn to the right for the cozy confines of Lee.

JOE'S DINER
Center St.
Lee, MA 01238
Tel. 413/243–9756

Joe's Diner is a place that everybody who lives in the northern Berkshires knows. It is off the well-worn tourist track, the food is good—even delicious—and the welcome is hearty. Joe's is a place where you can bring your dented vacation budget in for repairs.

To get there, cruise down the main street of Lee, resisting all intervening temptations, and follow Route 20 heading for the bridge at the far end of town. You will find Lee just a little larger than a village and typical of New England, where the most imposing building in town is the library. Joe's Diner will appear on your right (if you come to Kentucky Fried Chicken you've gone a little too far). There is free parking along the curb. Joe himself is still going strong after 38 years in the place that still bears his name and still supports him and his sons, who work here, too. It also supports the waitress, who has been here 13 years; she inherited the job from her mother, so you see Joe's is a family sort of place. Everybody knows everybody else. The customers are all sorts of workers doing all sorts of things—real estate, contracting, sales. There are only three tables, so most sit at a long counter. How good is the food, you ask? People come from as far away as Pittsfield, two towns to the north, and even over to Hancock, another town after that to the west—and they are regulars who come in every day. In a tourist area, where everything tends to the expensive (for what it is) or closed, Joe's is one of the few games in town for people who have to be on the road and eat out all the time.

How cheap is it? The menu is more or less posted in witty sayings on colorful posters hanging over the back of the counter. Featured are things like McRibb sandwich (beef; I asked), McRibb complete dinner, broiled scallops, scrod, pork chop dinner; soft-shell crab dinner, leg of lamb and wild mint dinner, and nothing is more than $5.99.

This includes vegetable, mushrooms, a side of tartar sauce, and potatoes—boiled, browned, or fries. A young fellow in the center of the counter washes dishes; he hands out

JOE'S DINER

OPEN 24 HOURS · TRUCK STOP
TEL. 243-9756 · CENTER ST. · LEE, MASS.

WHERE THE ELITE MEET
TO SHOOT THE SHEET

regular menus, and the waitress is out from the back before you are ready to order. On one visit, the man sitting next to me asks if I mind that he's smoking his pipe. It is an attractive one: The bowl is held to the stem by a little silver circle of people holding hands. Pewter, he says. "If I had such a pipe, I'd still be smoking it," I say.

Then I am ready. Deep-fried mushrooms, broiled scallops in drawn butter, tartar sauce, boiled potatoes, and lemonade all come out quickly. I eat in the same style, and I am happy. I am so happy I have a strawberry shortcake. I see a can of Redi Whip come out, but I don't let it bother me. The bill comes. And the happiness increases. $8.49.

I leave a good tip, and the waitress calls Joe, who comes out from his ranges and bubbling cooking surfaces in the back to shake hands. "How come you're so good and cheap?" I ask.

"When you're doing something thirty-eight years, you learn how."

You walk out, and everybody along the line of the counter knows you and says good-bye, led by the dishwasher. You've become one of the regulars.

Joe's Diner. No wonder they come back. There's no one in the Berkshires who doesn't know about it. Very few will tell you where it is.

Taking the wheel, we keep on Route 20 to Lenox. If the respite at Joe's place was a promised land of happy prices, we next reach the Terra Incognita where the value of the dollar seems to fall off the edge of the earth.

Crossing over to Lenox takes only a few minutes; the road widens, and at the near edge of a golf course there is a sign that simply says **Blantyre.** This does not mean that you shouldn't go in. It only means that you should be prepared.

BLANTYRE

Rte. 20
Lenox, MA 01240
Tel. 413/637–3556, 413/298–3806 in winter
(closed Nov.–May)

Brick portals stand astride an open gate. There is a sort of guardhouse in one of the portals, but nobody is there to stamp your passport. A gravel drive winds upward through a very civilized forest of the kind frequently seen in Europe in which the trees have been thinned out and the leaves swept away. Through the branches presently a building comes into view. It is at the top of the hill and an outstanding example of what I would call Alfred Hitchcock Tudor American: many

gables and flying chimney pots rising like towers; red brick
and half-timbering with cornices like those on New York City
brownstones except here they're cleaner. It faces croquet gardens. You are greeted by a very thin woman in a long dress
with her hair back in a bun; she introduces herself as Dorinda.
Here the whole price of a dinner down the road wouldn't
cover the tax on a tip. At the entrance to the mansion there is a
bronze-looking plaque. "Relais & Châteaux" it reads.

Relais & Châteaux is an association of hotels found primarily in the French countryside. Blantyre is a place in
Scotland, and the name is as close as the place in Lenox comes
to a castle in France or in Scotland. It was built by a successful
import-export entrepreneur in 1903 to replicate his wife's family's house in Scotland and restored in 1980. I suppose if you
compared Blantyre with Culloden House (in Inverness),
Blantyre would be happy. Culloden House is one of the places
the Prince of Wales stays when he goes to Scotland. It is of
ages-old stone and has public rooms full of rare old books; the
restaurant is one of the glories of Scotland. In no way is it as
expensive as Blantyre. Relais & Châteaux in France can be
more pricey than Culloden House, but still don't compare
with Blantyre's rates. Here, rooms in the main house run to
$525 a day, from a start above $200. The menu is prix fixe, $65
per person, and nothing is astonishing (salmon, scallops, steak).
The wine list is all heady stuff, but the vintages are new (mostly 1980s) and average about $55 a bottle, although many run
from $65 to $90, with a top of over $200. Even the best-known
gastronomic restaurants in the world will consciously produce
a wine list that rewards the cognoscenti. A Moët & Chandon
Brut Imperial nonvintage, for example, will be sprinkled
among champagnes of a much higher price; and he who
knows champagne knows that Brut Imperial is a benchmark,
and that its taste will be just fine even though its price is less.
But Blantyre's list offers no such concessions in any category. It
may be that Blantyre is not interested in the customer who

looks for concessions; nevertheless choosy customers who know wine will demand better vintages. Two wine lovers will easily consume two bottles of wine over a good dinner; so with wine, taxes, and tip, it is painfully apparent what the bill can come to.

On the same grounds, the bar is an embarrassment to its category. The bartenders have been to cognac and Armagnac school, but to them things like Chartreuse and Marc, not to mention a full range of single-malt scotches, remain a mystery.

The rooms, grounds, furniture, decor, public rooms, and breakfast wing are all impeccable, and rarely is such a vast and stately place maintained with such a glow. There are tennis courts and a swimming pool and, of course, the previously mentioned croquet.

So, is it worth it?

Not if you've traveled. If you've ever been to a castle in Scotland, or dined in a château in France, and are looking to repeat the experience, Blantyre leaves a lot to be desired. If, however, you have not traveled to those places where the comparison is inevitable, and do not plan a trip across the seas, then Blantyre becomes a bargain at even $525 a night (and especially the room at $525, the Patterson Room), because these kinds of accommodations are rare in the world and becoming rarer. They should be experienced at least once in a lifetime.

About the prices you have been warned. One night should be enough to revive your interest in the road, if not in Joe's down the same.

This part of the Berkshires is heavily traveled by tourists, and many of the region's pleasures are taken outdoors, as is its arguably greatest attraction, the Boston Symphony Orchestra at **Tanglewood**. Follow the sign (left off Route 20) for the Lenox business district and continue west past the center of town to the tree-shaded lawns of the orchestra's summer quarters.

Tanglewood Music Festival
West St.
Lenox, MA 01240
Tel. 413/637–1940 (June–Aug.), 617/266–1492 (Sept.–May)

Ever since I was a camp counselor in the area, I have always thought that the best seats in Tanglewood were lawn

space, but so does most everyone else. The way to go to Tanglewood is to arrive early and picnic, and then ease back with a civilized drink. To spread a blanket on the grass, lie back and watch a summer sky go through a tantrum of clouds as it crosses from sunset to dusk . . . what can compare with it? Many people set out a festive dinner on their blankets, with candlelight or at least flashlights, to better mull the music.

There are those who make a business supplying these picnics, allowing you to call ahead and order your meal for pickup before the concert. In Lenox they are called picnic caterers. The principal of these is **Crosby's.**

CROSBY'S

62 Church St.

Lenox, MA 01240

Tel. 413/637-3396

The caterer is in a white frame house with on-premises cooking and ample parking on the side. Here's how it works: There is a choice of two picnics every week, each taken from a nine-menu list that is available from Crosby's by mail.

Menus may include boneless breast of lemon chicken, pasta primavera, broccoli and red pepper salad, cheese and a roll, and fruit and cookies to finish. And that's one menu. Another might be cheese tortellini salad, carrots vinaigrette, and sliced tomatoes and basil, followed by cheese and a roll and the fruit and cookies with which all menus end.

The cost is $15 per picnic; one picnic feeds one. All the courses are made from scratch using local products. Jeanette and Helen, who run the place, cater museum parties as well, and Crosby's is open all year. They have some fancy wines; including a Trefethen chardonnay and a Domaine de Pouilly Pouilly–Fuissé. Chardonnay and Pouilly–Fuissé must be the Harvard and Yale of picnic wines, and I ask if they're always on hand in Crosby's cooler. "Yes," says Jeanette, "it's a classy joint." Fifteen dollars for the picnic and $20 for the Pouilly–Fuissé does seem a reasonable tariff for a catered affair at the symphony.

But with all those salads and rolls you might want to pick up something sweet for encores. How about cheesecake? For that you can go on foot from Crosby's.

CHEESECAKE CHARLIE'S
72 Main St. (Village Shopping Center)
Lenox, MA 01240
Tel. 413/637–3411

Diagonally across the street, behind a little shopping area, in another shopping center opposite the Lenox Post Office, you will find **Cheesecake Charlie's.** Before you walk through the door, take heed; the cheesecake inside is fabulous—thick and creamy, while light and fluffy. Some people consider the Cheesecake Charlie's Key lime flavor the cutting edge of cheesecake art. There are 44 flavors to choose from at the store with the white floors and walls; if you call ahead, Ralph and Sophie Pettillo will have your favorite waiting. They make the cream cheese themselves with heavy whole milk from the Jersey herds of High Lawn Dairy Farm (*see* Chapter 3, Gorham and Norton). This is a story worth pointing out.

All over America and the world, black-and-white Holstein cows are taking over pasture space from the once-favored Jerseys and Guernseys. This is not because Holsteins give better milk. They are in favor (and this is true of France as well as the United States) because (1) their milk's butterfat content is low, and (2) the yield of milk per cow is much higher. The Holstein works out better on the cost-to-yield profit line. High Lawn Dairy Farms' herd is exclusively Jersey. I remember the comment of my uncle, who owned a dairy farm, when the local milk wholesaler had told him to change his Guernseys for Holsteins. "I won't use them," he said. "Holsteins give water." So you can imagine the kind of cheese and cream cheese their milk makes.

LAURA'S SCOTTISH TEA ROOM AND BAKERY
Pittsfield Rd. (Rte. 7)
Lenox, MA 01240
Tel. 413/637–1060

To the north along Route 20, **Laura's Scottish Tea Room and Bakery,** in the Lenox House Country Shops, makes a valiant effort with British foods and products. Their shortbreads are cooked on-premises and shipped in tins all over America. Here they are available hot and in bags as well. Also available are fresh scones, chocolate-chip cookies, and English jams and preserves. But the most interesting things are served at the table in the tearoom. Baked fresh in the ovens, they go no farther than the patio with umbrellas outside: Bridies, Scottish meat turnovers, are flavored with sage and onions. There are sausage rolls and bangers (English sausages), English pork pies, shepherd's pie, and steak and kidney pie. Of course English tea (Ty-phoo) is served and for sale. The teapots are from Boston.

Pittsfield is the town in the Berkshires north of Lenox; it is too often altogether missed. The pleasures of Pittsfield are many—of a different, less touristic, and more democratic nature. Pittsfield has handsome streets and old buildings unrivaled in this part of the Berkshires, as well as several major food surprises just as you get there.

On Route 7 just south of the Pittsfield line itself, at the unceremonious end of an everyday shopper's mall on the left, an unpretentious name announces a major surprise: **Guido's.**

GUIDO'S
Rte. 7
Lenox, MA 01240
Tel. 413/442–9912

Seen from the highway approaching Pittsfield, it looks like just another shopping-center Italian restaurant, not the sort of place where a food maven would stop. The facade is in faux bois brown. Certainly nothing fit for food exploration, it would seem. Well, Guido's is not a restaurant. It started from a simple fruit and vegetable stand just a few years ago and has become a specialty food supermarket in a style it seems to have invented for itself. It deserves more than a glance. As strange as it may seem, there was once a time when few people had heard of Balducci's in New York City, or the Haymarket in Boston. Someday Guido's may get the same respect, but one thing is certain, there are plenty of people in Pittsfield and this part of the Berkshires who already know this place. Even on a drizzly spring Sunday the parking lot is jammed, and as you get out of your car you come to the sudden realization that behind the whole blessed facade at the end of the lot there is only one shop in the mall and that shop is Guido's. What can they be selling inside?

You put your doubts aside and walk in. All the checkout lines are humming. For starters, a forest of baskets hangs from the ceiling of the enormous selling space. They are of rattan and wicker from China, priced so cheaply that you can just reach up and take one down for shopping. But there are also carts, to be pushed directly into the larder of Guido's.

First, what's fresh? There is every sort of fish and seafood product to go into a shore dinner: clams, mussels, oysters, all alive and all with a fresh, impeccable look. But a different starter could be the simmering smoked shrimp soup. And there are also fresh shrimp of all sizes, from the little pink and gray—to perhaps eat raw, or blanched a minute in hot water for those who insist—to the large and jumbo, reaching almost to the size of a lobster tail.

Speaking of lobsters, there are several swimming in a tank, but it is Sunday, and the herd looks a little tired and thin after the sieges of Saturday. Also in the crustacean department, which has several counters and display aquariums to itself, there are trays of soft-shell crabs that have the gray, glassy glow of health that provokes pangs of hunger, while for the finicky there are the precooked and plastic-wrapped kind that you can pop in the oven on the way to your mouth.

Of course, the big fish are at Guido's, the name-brand varieties: salmon, smoked, or cut for steaks; swordfish and mackerel (the whole fish or cut in fillets); whitefish, the buyers of which are divided into two camps, those who know how good it can be and those who buy it for sturgeon; chubb—any angler from Long Island Sound would tell you that its delicate and firm flesh comes with a zesty taste of the sea; and rows and rows of little silver smelts, which, dipped in batter, make an American (as in large, economy-size) *friture*.

If all that is too much work, there are two precooked and surefire items taste-tested to please: New England clam chowder, in pints, quarts, and what look like hot-tub sizes; and lobster bisque—what else do you expect them to do with the shells (yes, lobster shells are in fact puréed and included in bisque)? Either way, both are from Massachusetts seafaring traditions and recipes. They have a down-home taste and a homespun unevenness.

Next is the poultry selection, and this is not so exciting: chickens, turkeys, and their parts, sporting the usual name tags. Yes, there are ducks, some cooked and ready to go, but poultry is one place Guido's could do better; where are the game birds?

Meats—the steaks, chops, and fillets—are all there; but chops and roasts are not what bring the crowds to Guido's. They come for sausages, laid out in all shapes and stuffings, Italian and American, from little tiny breakfast links to giant oblongs. There is saucisson the way the French do it: It's meant to be eaten hard, whittled onto boiled slices of potato with a smear of mustard while the potato is still steaming.

Then there are "health sausages"; but who would want to eat them—chicken, chicken curry, and turkey? Sausage is supposed to be greasy, to get you through a cold winter night, the way the pioneers used to eat bear grease. If you want to duck grease in your diet, eat the white meat of chicken. Besides, most good sausages put the grease right back in, but rendered (liked goose fat), and that's where the taste comes from. The meat is just an incidental ornament to chew on.

CHEESE MIMOLETTE, the sign says. We have passed over to the cheese section and I have found an old friend, straight from my cheese shop on the avenue Victor Hugo. This is a semihard cheese that Parisians eat, in enormous quantities, and it's the first time I've seen it in the United States. Someone at Guido's has a sharp eye. Mimolette is a sort of French Cheddar. Orange under the rind, it requires a little more push with the knife but cuts up nicely on apples, canapés, crackers, and bread, to be eaten with a stout red wine, the same way as Cheddar. It has more personality, even, than Vermont sharp Cheddar, which compares with it most closely. Cheddar is a little paler and nuttier, while Mimolette is a little redder and tangier.

Another of the items they have that's hard to find are Turkish waters, such as orange-blossom water and rose water, which you sprinkle on desserts (think of macaroons and anything with almonds or dates). Prepared and ready to go from Guido's own kitchen are sesame tahini, tabbouleh, and hummus. As well as the Near Eastern foods, there is an

East Asian selection, featuring oils and sauces from Hong Kong and China. Olive oils are everywhere.

There are bins and bins of apples, fresh corn, produce, especially good melons, and something that's rare for here but we've noted before: mesclun and mâche (*see* Chapter 2, White Flower Farm). The French salad greens at Guido's, however, spring from a provenance that's altogether different. Five times a week Guido's owners, Chris and Matthew Massiero, go to Boston's New England Produce Center, a colossal wholesale selling space where fresh produce comes in not only from all over New England (and where it is said the best berries in all the world can be found) but from the whole Northeast. For instance, the mesclun and mâche come from the Lakeville Specialty Produce Company in Washingtonville, Pennsylvania. The greens make the trip in a day and a half from Washingtonville to Boston to Pittsfield. And how do they taste? Lakeville does not grow from California seeds or those "adapted" to American conditions. They grow from a French stock, inside greenhouses, as they do in the Midi. The result is the kind of mesclun and mâche you are likely to get were you shopping at a greengrocer in Paris.

Perhaps because the enormous G.E. plant in Pittsfield drew a strong working class into the community, and the Italians had willing hands, soon after their arrival every garden or lawn space that was not mulched or sprayed and weeded and watered to be looked at, or as a playing field for croquet, was staked with tomatoes. Of course, Italians knew what to do with these and with basil, and with pignole, which the Americans called pine nuts and left for the squirrels. As a result, they know what pesto is in Western Massachusetts, and Guido's has it to go.

One sour note, or at least a soggy one: Guido's makes its own pasta. There is a Plexiglas booth in the center of the store, and it's riveting to watch the whole process of pasta making, as the fettuccine, spaghetti, or linguine comes rolling through the mechanical teeth. It is taken up by a fetching young person, who does not let it dry. She plops it into a plastic bag and when you get home it is all stuck together. At its last stage of production a good thing is nearly ruined by lack of care and attention. It is saved as you and your guests sit around a bowl pulling the strands apart. It ends up remarkable, better than our guests say they can get at their standby Italian grocery in Manhattan, and that is our final report on things Guido's.

At the traffic light just south of Pittsfield's main business center, Route 20 takes a turn to the left to **Hancock Shaker Village,** which, as irony would have it, is more in Pittsfield than it is in Hancock.

HANCOCK SHAKER VILLAGE
Box 898
Pittsfield, MA 01202
Tel. 413/443–0188

The Shakers produced one of the earliest North American food traditions to come from European stock. Of course, Shaker furniture is well known, and the purity of its line much admired and copied. That Shaker foods and cooking were highly appreciated in their own time is perhaps not so well known.

The men and women of this religious sect lived and worked together on farms that produced not only elegant furniture but an abundance of food. It was frequently sold to people from "the World," as outsiders were called, and everyday citizens came rolling into Shaker farms and villages on wagons to buy canned applesauce, preserves, and such, as Shaker excellence in farming frequently afforded a surplus.

At the largest Shaker village left intact in America, operated as a non-profit museum since 1959 when it was last occupied by members if the sect, you can have a taste of that civilization. You can not only inspect the farm and its unique buildings, farm implements, animals, and furniture, but partake of a meal (from July to October) within the community, a meal just like one Shakers fixed more than 150 years ago, a mid-19th-century dinner complete with Shaker drinks, songs, costumes, and traditions.

The event is called An Evening at Hancock Shaker Village. You must have reservations. The foods chosen for the dinner are always in season or from stocks of preserves, which are also for sale at the village. It is advisable to get cleaned up and come in your best. After a welcoming tour of the village and the kitchen downstairs, you assemble in the Believers' Dining Room, in an 1830 building. The dining room has four long candlelit refectory tables divided by a center aisle. In Shaker times the sexes were separated for dinner; they came in through different entrances to opposite sides of the room, and they lived what was in many respects a monastic life. Now you can sit next to the person you came with.

The menu may be had three days before the event (always a Saturday night) by telephone, or at the Shaker village. Each dinner is different; each menu depends on the progress of the seasons. The herb soup that begins the meal after the lovely grace is sung has evolved in the same way: It starts with a beef stock and can then be prepared in two variations, one with cream, blended with marjoram, parsley, cumin, and celery seeds; the other, which appears to be older, with butter, chervil, and chives. Either brings a taste of the herb garden to the table in a society that didn't eat salads.

Next, the Shaker platters may bear creamed chicken or baked ham in cider. The village raises its own chickens, which scurry about on the farm. Tarragon is used for flavoring, as it

often is in France; the pepper-and-salt-colored birds themselves are an old French farm breed called Dominique. The pigs, too, are raised on the farm, as are the oxen and the Percheron horses that graze in the pastures; the last two are sold on the hoof. Complete recipes for the dinner are taken from the Shaker cookbook, which is available at the village store. The breads are rye, brown, and corn streaked with seeds and herbs from the herb garden. Loaves are passed around the table on plates. In fact everything is served family style; you break bread with and hand platters to people you have never met, and you seem part of one great, big family; there's something about eating in a group that makes food taste better.

The fixed price is reasonable, and you get all the wine you want. That, the experience, and the theater of the location, make the Shakers' one of the best food addresses in New England.

How about a bed nearby for the night? It's nice to stay in the county. So the **Heart of the Berkshires Motel** seems a good idea.

HEART OF THE BERKSHIRES MOTEL
970 W. Housatonic St., Rte. 20W
Pittsfield, MA 01201
Tel. 413/443–1255

It's nothing fancy and not typically New England— just a string of connected units on the road. But it's right along your path on Route 20; it's handy (only 2 miles away); and it's a quiet place in which to wake up.

There are further food experiences in Pittsfield. Joining Route 7 again, proceed north to Park Square, where the town's quadrants and happiest architectural perspectives meet. It is worth a stop here just to get out of the car and look; the Cottage is a nice gift shop on the corner. Of the several churches, the Congregational dates from 1832; the City Hall is Greek Revival, and the Victorian Berkshire Athenaeum is chocolate stone.

Next, you'll travel through a different sort of neighborhood: not up to some golden hillside where you sit squinting and dividing a lobster in the sunset; not a fancy location on a green riverbank. You cross into the nearest thing to an industrial zone in the Berkshires, factory-rich, but worker-poor. Rows of high buildings lined with staring windows loom in blocks over the horizon. But along the way the road whips around one of the unsung but most delightful bakeries in

New England. Slow down so you won't miss **Pittsfield Rye Bakery** on your right.

PITTSFIELD RYE BAKERY
East St.
Pittsfield, MA 01201
Tel. 413/443–9141

Their '50s-style building in turquoise and ivory with a tasting rotunda and a fleet of blue trucks marks the spot. This is the source of the marbled rye so highly prized earlier (*see* Mom's in Chapter 1). Here is Pittsfield Rye's home office, where you can pick some up to make your own club sandwiches or sit down and taste what else comes out of a tradition established here 60 years ago. What other bakery do you know that has a tasting bar? It serves coffee and doughnuts, Danishes, and bagels from right out of the oven in the very same building. Try the muffins—pumpkin muffins. These are unique, with a true pumpkin taste from a secret recipe that owner Arnold Robbins of Pittsfield Rye refuses to divulge; you must stop by to taste them. Besides these, this singular bread company has come up with an even more extraordinary item: Special Corn Rye. It comes from a recipe developed by Robbins's father more than 60 years ago, and even though he ships to various food purveyors throughout the country (to the trade only), chances are you have not tried it.

After the bakery East Street straightens out, and factory views crowd around us—G.E., Polymer; even in broad daylight on a weekend there is no one on the streets. You don't risk running into traffic because there is no traffic. You pass by these huge empty piles of granite and bricks that come right up to the road, and just when it seems that Pittsfield has petered out, a little two-story frame house, across the street from a towering behemoth, appears. There is plenty of parking at **Elizabeth's Borderline Café.**

ELIZABETH'S BORDERLINE CAFÉ

1264 East St.
Pittsfield, MA 01202
Tel. 413/448–8244

It seems to be more than on the borderline, it seems over the edge. But then you see that the paint is in excellent condition, the place has an air of prosperity, and the vents are certainly working, humming with the pure smell of oregano. The porch columns are pink, and as you step inside, a man in walking shorts is peeling great heaps of garlic into a bowl. The garlic bulbs are pink, the man is one of the owners, and you say to yourself, this is my kind of café.

A word about decor. Sometimes it strikes you and sometimes it does not. Elizabeth's Borderline Café is a master of the funky. Upstairs and downstairs, the modest space is so appealing you cannot take your eyes off its accents, so much has been done with so little. You are torn between sitting down and walking around. Mostly it's the little fish. They float on every table and dip from the ceiling: wood carvings—beautiful, very fanciful they seem, but are actually realistic—of tropical sea fish. Queen triggerfish, parrot fish, blue and gold angelfish, all in wood and in fresh, bright colors. There are flowers, too—tulips in trompe l'oeil arrangement on the table in wood and acrylics. Graceful curves of plastic used with wood conceal the upstairs bathroom entrances. In some places this would be awful; here it turns out just fine.

The peeler of garlic has been working this street since 1988. His name is Tom. His wife, who is Elizabeth, is stationed in the kitchen, which is open on all sides so she's right there in the center of things. He is the kind of person who, with any encouragement, sits down at your table to discuss the menu, which we throw away after a glance.

Tom pushes a Caesar salad from which Elizabeth has left out the egg. "Who needs it?" says Tom, tossing. The salad is delicious and has plenty of those tender, tiny, pale-edged leaves of romaine, luscious olive oil, Parmesan, garlic, some apple for crunch; it sets us up for what is to come.

A quick course of toasted Parmesan bread: simple Reggiano and garlic goes into the oven on a crusty slice of "old-world Italian loaf," developed especially for Elizabeth's by our friends Linda and Arnold Robbins of the Pittsfield Rye Bakery down the road. Its crust crackles, it has chewy textures inside, and seeds that pop alive with a tang in the mouth. It also makes us thirsty. We order Italian beer and wait for more.

The place used to do a mostly lunch order business, and there is still a good list of sandwiches on the menu—prosciutto and oregano; Genoa salami, provolone, and tomato; and more—and there used to be a line of people stacked outside the door so you couldn't get in.

Then came the bad times of recession. The G.E. plant went from 15,000 to 3,700 workers and is still counting down, and the crowds are gone from Elizabeth's door. "We used to have people from all over the world," says Tom. "Trainees," he describes them; "I'd see their faces and I'd know what they'd order." Now the business is different. It comes at night and from an average of 20 miles away, from Great Barrington, Stockbridge, New York State—people who travel to eat.

The Italian beer is a little light but okay. It's from Friuli, so it's almost Austrian. Then comes a bowl of Mexican cream of tomato soup. What makes it Mexican is, I suppose, the touch of cumin and jalapeño. With Parmesan cheese and wonderfully fresh tomatoes, it is delicate and delicious.

There is a polenta dish, and you must visit Elizabeth's to have this. It comes with tomato, sliced very thin and seared in the pan so it picks up the subtle vegetable sugars. This would be fine, as in enough, for dinner, and the next time I will choose white wine instead of the beer. But Elizabeth's is known for its pizza hereabouts and that is why we came; and so, while not really hungry, we order it, asking for the kind that most people prefer.

Sadly, we are disappointed. It comes laden with cut-up tomatoes and stacked in a shell with garden things, a veritable vegetable surprise pie. It is too laden, it is what they call "deep dish" pizza, or a pie, the kind they sell you from Domino's or Pizza Hut. Just bring us tomatoes and mozzarella on a flat circle of dough, something Neapolitan, something to pick up with our hands. For me it's like a visit to a Paris McDonald's where they eat hamburgers with a knife and fork. I am suspicious of people who eat pizza with a knife and fork. At Elizabeth's I am suspicious of myself; the wedge is so laden I have to eat it that way.

But it's often like that: The thing that has the reputation, that brought you, in the end leaves you cold. At least we have made a real find, and as we drive away we are already looking forward to a repeat of the succulent polenta, the hot and herbed bread, and new and different things when we come back.

CHAPTER 5

FIDDLEHEADS
AND HORSERADISH

Bennington to Newfane, Vermont

Vermont is the best place in the world to eat breakfast. The chickens come right up to the door. The eggs on the griddle are fresh from the coop. The French toast is slathered with butter and batter. The pancakes have raspberries in them, and there is always a cruet of maple syrup handy. After that comes bacon, sausages, and ham smoked on corn cob embers. We are interested in dining indigenously in Vermont: We are interested in fiddlehead greens and horseradish and Gil's feather turnips; in red-flannel hash and hornpout in a pie, and maybe a nice slice of bear thrown in.

HIGHLIGHTS:
- The view from Grandma's schoolhouse and the college of communities
- Steamed hot dogs on steamed rolls
- Smoked trout
- Trees on the horizon and the leaf-peeper drive
- A cup and saucer for breakfast: chocolate-chip flapjacks and Canadian oat French toast
- The formula: 2 eggs on 2 pancakes plus 2 bacons and 2 sausages
- A Vermonter's tale: Hornpouts and red flannel for the mouth
- A Hobson's choice of cheeses
- Swimming for free on a hot dog
- New England boiled dinner

- A circuit of ladies'-aid suppers: the Harvest Supper, the Hunter's Supper, the Strawberry Supper, the Sugaring-Off Supper

LENGTH OF LOOP: 78 miles

LENGTH OF STAY: Two nights

Bennington is served by Albany airport; Routes 7 and 22 also offer good access if you are driving.

The best way to come into Vermont is through Bennington. A rush of old Vermont rises up to greet you in the old town, a sudden and very green swell of hill with a traffic circle and white houses, a pristine Congregational church, and the stately **Four Chimneys Inn** (21 West Rd., Old Bennington, VT 05201, tel. 802/447–3500). This is Vermont (Bennington College is on the same hilltop) at its most stylish.

Before you go down into the center of town, Route 9 (which is what became of N.Y. Route 7) passes an absolutely indispensable stop: the **Bennington Museum.** Behind the Greek Revival facade of the building, past a collection of Tiffany glass, is the Little Schoolhouse of Mary Robertson Moses—Grandma Moses. Grandma Moses hailed from not far away (Hoosick Falls, New York), and if you took N.Y. Route 7, you came in that way. Now neighboring Bennington has her paintings, and an interesting and graphically revealing collection they are.

Moses paintings are so full of color and gaiety that you fill up with a perceptible joy on entering a room where they hang. Little scenes, 17 by 26 inches, are stretched with primitive story-telling flatness. In one a chain of figures dances around a country school; another shows a community around a footbridge and over a stream (to Grandma's house?). Then there is a community snuggled in winter, a community in summer. Mary Robertson Moses painted in a time (the 1950s) when America was on the verge of losing its sense of community. Maybe that is what we seek today in her pictures, and what is the greatest reward in visiting Vermont. In towns organized around single buildings—a town hall, a church, or a Grange Hall (where local farmers held meetings)—the sense of community still thrives.

As I leave the little museum, a headache strikes: A tour operator has his bus backed up to the door. He is reading a newspaper with the bus motor running. The noise of the diesel is as great as the stink in the face. I conclude that tour bus drivers in our country are not paid by the day or the hour but by the number of gallons of diesel fuel they burn in the face of the rest of us. The sooner the Bennington Museum gains control of its parking lot, the more its visitors will enjoy it.

Downtown Bennington is a small, neat jumble of shops, scrubbed family department stores, and a junior high school. The **Vermont Steak House** serves opulent steaks to town workers; the prices are low. A pushcart by the curb near the Bank of Vermont purveys that great New England delicacy you must try—steamed hot dogs on steamed rolls (*see* Chapter 11, Flo's). If you need to nurse your appetite, though, wait until you reach the other side of the Bennington hills.

Following the major road (Route 9) eastward across the gulch, before leaving the town you take a left fork and stay on Route 9. Here we come to a most interesting store: **De Marco's Sporting Goods.**

DE MARCO'S SPORTING GOODS
1001 E. Main St.
Bennington, VT 05201
Tel. 802/442–5300

The store is a curious triangle like a miniature of Manhattan's Flatiron Building. The stenciled paint signs on the building's clapboard sides would light up the eyes of an antiques collector. They advertise cob-smoked meats; a smokehouse once resided here.

Inside are gun and fishing-rod racks; browsers creak on wood floors as they examine the selection of weapons. They sniff waxed stocks and steel and get the feel of fly rod grips. There is a difference with this tackle shop: It also sells meat. Smoked ham, sausages, wursts, slabs of bacon, and pepperoni fly out of the store even faster than an antique Shakespeare rod, a Remington, or a Winchester.

Williams Smokehouse, now **Williams of Vermont Smokehouse,** got its start here and is typical of the independent smokehouses that are still to be found in many small Vermont cities and towns. The smokehouse operation moved on to larger quarters as the demand for its products grew. Now the meats are sold from behind a thick glass case in their own section of the sporting goods store, away from the Remingtons and rods, but with a smattering of other things from field and stream—like smoked brook trout.

A look over the meats and the cheeses soon draws other eyes inspecting you. Sandy Danfort, the woman behind them, is not much higher than the glass-and-wood case. Like many Vermonters, she does not say much until she is spoken to, and then it's well that you listen. A half butt of ham is about $30, and all this is still smoked on corn cobs, she explains. She has a particular liking for Canadian bacon in slabs.

There are wheels of cheeses, Vermont Cheddars; and Sandy says you absolutely must buy from a wheel to get the best from any cheese maker, Cabot included. She has Cheddars from other shippers, including Grafton's, but as I have noticed more than once, and this time, too, Vermont Cheddar from Cabot seems to be the Cheddar of choice for most of the people of Vermont.

The pepperoni is a hot item among the meats, and it is very spicy, but I have eyes for the trout. It's split down the center, filleted, and smoked whole. It's the right color, dark pink (*see* Chapter 3); so it must be wild, I say.

There comes only the slightest crease of smile from the woman, like a fold in a business letter—neat, but with wrinkles on its ends. "Trout," she says, as if letting escape a house secret; "once you smoke it, you'll never know if it's wild."

In other words, in the smoking all trout take on the dark color of wild fish. Smoking is the surefire way to disguise white-fleshed hatchery fish and sell them for wild.

A little farther on, Vermont Route 9 becomes a long (7-mile) incline, serrated with truck crash stops in the other direction on the way down (useful to note, especially should you travel down at night). For so long a pull uphill the road is fairly wide, and there are three lanes in most places. The highway is out in the open, not overhung with trees. What trees you will see along the way are priceless. They are the heritage and fortune of the Vermont forest. Vermont got its name from the French who explored it: *Ver(t) mont(s)* = Green Mountains. Big hemlocks, tamaracks, and bearded spruces break up the skyline of an otherwise deciduous curtain of maple and oak, and beyond the reaches of Bennington the Green Mountain National Forest beckons. Here are the clean air and restless foliage precincts that roll out a green carpet to upper Vermont. Here the wind is blowing and the scene is always changing, in color or—with a current of air—in light and shadow that falls with a cloud.

Some long-standing Vermonters, upon watching the migrations that accompany the autumnal and vernal equinoxes, of the leaf peepers, the-come-for-summer dwellers, and the skiers with racks on their cars, have a point of view on all this traffic and on those who make it. Flatlanders, they call them; air people. For the Vermonters, even in the mountains, are close to the ground. Air people live in towers in the sky, they go up and down to work in elevators, and rarely are their feet on the ground. In crossing streets and traversing towns they endure life on the ground as long as they must, and they don't feel well until they are up in the air again.

"When the air people and the ground people meet," the Vermonter says, "they don't see eye to eye." So the air people have gone off and established their own community, which they run like a theme park in Vermont as if they were Americans living within their own compound in another country. They bring up and establish their own food styles and restaurants named Jonathan's and tout them to each other and to national magazines as the true Vermont. But it is the non-theme-park Vermont that we seek here.

Seven miles before Wilmington Route 9 starts its descent. This is one of the great views of the Vermont forest and the favorite drive of the leaf peepers in the fall. The descent is gradual and tortuous (but safe) as the road aims down into the valley that feeds Lake Whitingham. The road reaches a streambed where, in October, flame reds, chrome yellows, browns, and greens mix as white stones stand out in the dry sides of the bed. The stream flows along the bottom, turning into a rushing torrent alongside the road and eventually swelling into Lake Whitingham.

The wide lake is about 11 miles long, with secretive coves and little inlets. On the far shore, to which there is only limited access, is a beach known as Nudie Beach. Lake Whitingham also has tour boats operated by the Green Mountain Flagship Company. On their turn around the lake the paddlewheelers swing close to Nudie Beach and come about while the tourists make a beeline to the rail with their shutters clicking and their video apparatuses whirring, their lenses pointed at the sunbathers in their altogether. These curse and offer up to the boats a stream of oaths and obscene gestures, and this is the Green Mountains, too.

In Wilmington traffic backs up from the light where you will make the turn north onto Route 100. On the right is a country store complex, with all kinds of things (mostly kitsch) in all kinds of little shops. On the left is a baseball card trading post. The Vermont House Tavern, in a Greek Revival build-ing on the left halfway to the light, serves food of indifferent quality; and a half-baked health food store sells coffee.

Turning left (onto Route 100 North) we drive only a few miles before the first breakfast treat shows up on the side of the road, across from the Deerfield Farm. This is the doughty **Cup and Saucer.**

THE CUP AND SAUCER
Rte. 100N
Wilmington, VT 05363
Tel. 802/464–8062

The Cup and Saucer really isn't much to look at from the outside: just a Wedgwood-blue sign on the road and a gritty pull-in. You walk across a cinder and gravel lot into a painted vestibule where there is a lot to read. The communi-ty bulletin board is pinned with the addresses of the contrac-tors and carpenters, developers, and day-care givers who frequent the restaurant.

Two aqua counters describe horseshoes. There's nothing at all grand about the place, but as you hear the sizzle of batter in the pan and smell the cream and fresh butter, you just know it's going to be good. The regulars are sitting around with their hats on, and they are as polite as pie. Cups of coffee sit in front of everyone; little thimble pitchers of maple syrup stand on the side. The thimbles are fat and generous at the bottom and hold about 2 ounces of syrup from local trees. You never taste the like outside Vermont, even if the label says the syrup is from Vermont. Here, poured from five-gallon jugs, it is indelibly sweet. Nobody takes seconds. The griddle and galley kitchen are only partially hidden behind the open end of the horseshoe and run the width of the room. As soon as you take a seat (those little stools kids spin, driving candy-store men mad), a waitress appears with menus and coffee and asks what you want. It being near noon, I ask if we can still have breakfast, and the lady with dark hair tied in a knot says, "We serve breakfast all day."

Good, then, so breakfast it is, and we'll have a big one. The menu and wall board are pinned with signs pushing special Vermont breakfasts that sing out to be tried. Raspberry pancakes, chocolate-chip ones, too; Canadian oat French toast, and a Hungry Man's Special: 2 eggs on 2 pancakes plus 2 bacon strips and 2 sausages: $2. The standard steak and eggs comes up with home fries and toast, and nothing in this whole menu costs more than $4.95.

The best thing about all of these, aside from the price, are the eggs. They are so exquisite—yes, that is the word for them—that you must try them, straight, scrambled, or sunny-side up. They deliver the same remarkable sweetness they do in France—so delicate, so light, like air, and yet so tender. How come? Are they beaten with milk, I ask, or just a little plain water, as is often done in France? No, the answer comes back simple: The eggs are laid at the door. Sunny-side up, the yolks stand up and stare from the plate; scrambled, they have a soft molten quality, yet are deliciously sweet. The freshness of the eggs matters in the batter, too. The flapjacks come out smooth and creamy. The French toast is light and puffy.

But there is more to this breakfast: outrageously rich, you might say, but certainly it seems worth taking where you can get it, to know the taste of the farm. Go to the source in all things and you will not go wrong. Places like The Cup and Saucer still exist, but they are becoming scarcer (although I must say this one is doing a brisk business and will not die if it doesn't get yours); come to a breakfast banquet here and learn what it is like to wake up in the country and smell the coffee.

The orange juice comes to you fresh and vigorous, with none of the bland uniformity or chemical background of blended concentrates. Breakfast is an underrated meal in America; everybody writes about dinner. A trip to a place like this can help redress the balance in diets and attitude.

Now to the sausages and the ham, which is as good as a Smithfield, but sweeter (remember the corn-cob smoking in Vermont). As for the sausage links, they come dry, but not brittle or cardboard-stiff. When they break apart, there is not a globule of fat visible, and they go into the mouth with just the right amount of snap and spice.

The hash browns are likewise not greasy—crisp, yes, and mahogany in color, but plump with the flesh of potato and the zing of onions. Potatoes as good as this can make you forget all about French fries and scalloping.

Yes, and the flapjacks: All three varieties, the two previously mentioned and the plain, are faultless. I could not find a lump or discern a burn hole in any of them, and I looked. The raspberries seem to have the sort of affinity for flapjacks and breakfast that blueberries do for muffins. The chocolate-chip variety could stand alone. All alone. The idea works as the chocolate melts (later stiffens), and what you are left with is a flapjack shaped like a cookie—a large tollhouse kind.

What maple syrup does to all of this (real maple syrup, not just anybody's syrup product, or anything fortified with corn syrup) must be tasted to be known. There is a clarity to maple syrup—and I do not speak of the color but of the taste—that stands alone in the world of sweets. It is often counterfeited, but the real New England product—and Vermont is the leader here—has a unique character that is light, never lugubrious, and does not leave you feeling sugared.

Our bill is $9 for two breakfasts like those described. We have dined very well, better than most lunches and dinners costing far more. Is there any dishonor, discomfort, or disorder that we have done so at the first meal of the day rather than the middle or the last? On this I will reflect.

As we have dined so well, for lunch there will be no lunch, but a food shopping spree, of vegetables, cheeses, fresh fruit, and greens.

HOBSON'S CHOICE

Rte. 100N
Wilmington, VT 05363
Tel. 802/464-2236

You cannot understand food in Vermont until you've been to **Hobson's Choice**. This garden and greengrocer with specialty foods and a wine shop stands beside the road. You drive into a long gravel parking lot that is likely to be full on any nice weekend day.

Especially sought after at Hobson's is the Vermont Cheddar. They have three kinds: sharp, mild, and Hobson's choice. Although they have Cheddars from other places, Hobson's prefers Cabot's. Their Hobson's choice is especially prepared for the store. It is somewhere between sharp and mild on the taste scale, aged a year and a half, and is not too creamy (which is what people hereabouts think is the fault with Grafton's). Vermonters like some backtalk from their Cheddar, even when it is mild.

Remembering the opinion that Cabot's seems to do better cut from a large wheel, you should also know they seem to send their best wheels to their best customers. You might stand to get a better Vermont Cheddar at Hobson's Choice than if you drive all the way up (147 miles farther) to Cabot, Vermont. But Cabot also ships by mail (although it's bending the rules of food exploration somewhat not to go the source, cheese keeps, especially Cheddar), and you can try charming your way to cheese greatness on the phone (**Cabot Creamery,** Cabot, VT 05647, tel. 802/563–2231).

In April and the first part of May the tender fiddle-heads come in for salads and for spring vegetable dishes. At apple gathering time at Hobson's Choice, which—for some varieties—coincides with leaf-peeping time, the baskets and paper satchels of Cortlands and McIntosh (the varieties that ripen in the second week of October) are lined up by the door. They are always from this year's crop, which isn't necessarily the case at the supermarket; for a taste twice as good you pay half city prices.

Fall is also winter squash time. This is a vegetable traditional to New England dinners that, like red wine, goes so well with meat, and especially with steak (*see* Chapter 4, The Red Lion Inn). Hobson's has an abundant harvest of squash, including (but not exclusively) acorn, butternut, and turban. The choice is yours. The squashes, especially the turban, are so colorful and exotic-looking you'll probably let them sit too long in a basket on the table as a centerpiece before you have the heart to eat them. Put them outside, or in the refrigerator at night; squash will last about a month kept cold but not frozen.

Among the fruit, the most interesting fall crop, and something I have rarely seen for sale in a shop, is Concord grapes. This grape, indigenous to America, is chiefly used in the production of wine and grape juice. Here they are for the mouth. Try a fresh royal blue one and it tastes like Welch's grape juice. Try it when it's older and it will taste like Manischewitz wine. In any case, the soft lusciousness of these grapes is seldom available in stores in this unprocessed shape, and a bunch or two set out for dessert will be the hit of a Vermont dinner—with Cheddar cheese they'd be marvelous—and leave your guests with a taste in the mouth for exactly what the Concord is, a grape like no other.

Because it is so far north, much of the produce of Vermont is told in the tale of the underground: root vegetables and tubers. The most haunting and original of all these, by far, is the Gil's feather turnip. Now there's a name we've hardly been beaten over the head with. Nor is it conjured with in fashionable food markets and restaurants. It seems long ago there was a man named Gil, from Dover, who developed an original Vermont turnip. It was a little fairer, a little whiter, with just a blush of light violet upon it, and it had the most delicate, yet enticing flavor. When it was cooked, it rocked the room like a musky perfume. It is a fully recognized food commodity in the area of Wilmington–Dover–Newfane, if still a little rare, and it is becoming known throughout the rest of the state, where it is eagerly snapped up when available. It is offered in season—it goes fabulously with game—at stands and stops like Hobson's Choice.

The opposite of the rare in Vermont is the horseradish. You know what they say about horseradish: Plant it once and you'll have it forever. Judging from the size and variety of Vermont horseradish, and the varying degree of its pungency, it seems everybody in Vermont has planted his or her own favorite strain. In the fall, little bouquets of straw-colored chrysanthemums and horseradish–maple-sugar mustard are popular gifts. The mustard is a must to sample and cry over. Rounding out tubers, Vermont potatoes come in six kinds, and all are good-looking in their bins.

Vermont is a leading honey-producing state; there are several offerings from the familiar and excellent Champlain Valley Apiaries (*see* Chapter 3, Locke, Stock and Barrel) in Middlebury, Vermont, as well as the homey honeys from Warren's Apiaries in Spring Lake.

This brings us to wine. Of course it is offered at Hobson's Choice, but none of it is from Vermont. Thank God. It seems every unlikely place in the world you go, someone is making wine. That it is of a very indifferent qual-

ity is disguised only by a designer label that offers no reputation and only local interest. Unless it has been married by years of dedication and expertise to its locale (*see* Chapter 1, Cascade), local wine is best left for locals to experience.

Hobson's Choice has a small group of very nice standard wines, Jadot Chardonnay and Beaujolais, with name-brand Bordeaux and California varietals in support—safe but not outstanding. It's as if someone a little unsure of the ground was interested in not making a mistake instead of making a killing and erred on the side of reliability over value and price. Not an irresponsible way to go, I suppose, but will those who are taken really enjoy the ride?

Likewise, there is the standard selection of pricey pastas usually found in food boutiques: DeCecco from Italy, for exam-

ple, which is made with American semolina. Muellers uses the
same stuff and is more reasonable. All in all, as in its restaurants, Vermont does much better when sticking to Vermont.

Leaving Hobson's, we continue up Route 100. Next
comes a break that is truly Vermont, and one the tired traveler in need of a little recreation will appreciate. Remember,
we did not lunch after so big a breakfast. Then there was
shopping. Now is the time to fill the growing vacancy in the
solar plexus region. Taking a turn to the right, nose off Route
100 in favor of the East Dover Road (about 5 miles from
Hobson's Choice). A few hundred yards after the intersection
you will reach the little bathing club and 9-hole golf course
known as **Sitzmark**. The golf course is off by itself and
charges a small admission; the rectangular pool does not. It is
a very nice pool—the kind you swam in when you were 16:
on a thick, plush green lawn, it's surrounded with a chain-
link fence and lounge chairs. The chairs are aluminum frame
and the backs are strung with gaily colored plastic cords. You
swim for free; all you have to do is buy a hot dog or a hamburger from the canteen, and you're in the sun. For only a
hot dog and a soft drink, you can swim all day; it's a great
place to take kids.

Now we are in the thick of where we are going.

> *Did you see flame*
> *dying in October leaves?*
> *Did you wake to frost,*
> *lie down in plenty,*
> *arise in want?*

These are undeniably the words of a New England
poet. They are more: They are those of the poet laureate of
Vermont. Mr. William Mundell, who comes from eight gen-

erations of Vermonters, lives along the path we have taken and knows more about the real local foods than anyone else. It is with him that we get down to the food essences of Vermont.

Following the road from Sitzmark, we find ourselves tumbling down a pleasant country blacktop on the way to Newfane. The road is hedged in with tree limbs making a canopy of fire, gold and mauve. We turn into the driveway of a pleasant white farmhouse with a red barn stuffed with tractors and a garden that has a picnic table overlooking the tranquil road. They give up on summer only reluctantly here. Two Cadillacs are parked near the house, for Mimi Andrews is with Mr. Mundell. Both Vermonters are in their eighties. It is Mundell who comes to the open door, and we enter through the side porch, which is painted the serviceable New England blue.

We sit down in a big, comfortable living room, in big, comfortable overstuffed chairs. There are no logs burning in the stone fireplace and no fire in the wood stove, but after we savor a nice moment of tea and remark in passing that the early part of Vermont winters has become quite mild, the conversation veers toward red-flannel hash and hornpout holiday pie.

Clearly these are words that make for magic. The poet's eyes twinkle, and his lips bow open in a smile. "The red flannel is easy," he says. "You just add beets."

Can he clear up the mystery of the hornpout so easily? I ask. First, what is one?

"A hornpout is a catfish."

All kinds of hash (there is one served at The Cup and Saucer) hail from Vermont, as potatoes come from the earth and they keep through the winter. This is the basic red-flannel hash according to the poet: The raw beef is hashed (some people have a little machine that they crank) and put in the pot, and then are added boiled potatoes, which are not mashed, nor are they quite cut up, either. Mundell shows off a bit of handiwork in his kitchen, a chopping device he made from a tin can long ago; it works like a very deep cookie cutter. For chopping potatoes for hash it's just the right thing. Onions are cooked and added to the mix steaming in the pot; finally another root vegetable, the beets (cooked separately first) are stirred in, and you have your red flannel. You also have your three-course dinner in one sweeping meat-and-potatoes dish, with a good vegetable, too—beets—and for seasoning, onions. The dish comes to the table hot and triumphant, and no one can tell what it is. But not to leave well enough alone, try stirring in a little horseradish for zing, or some horseradish–maple-sugar mustard to set the palate tingling.

This, from the ground up, is the taste of Vermont.

Next on the list comes the hornpout, and this is Mimi Andrews's dish. "Hornpout holiday pie is really a chowder made with catfish," she says, "and then put in a pie. There are bits of tails and solid things in it; there's a lot of good meat on a catfish, you know." Today's cooks who would use a frozen catfish from the supermarket or stoop to using fillets are to be sneered at. Nor should the creation ever be called catfish or bullhead pie, as Vermonters rightly insist their own term be used on the creature. Every part of America where the catfish crawls or swims gives it some horrid local name, but the hornpout belongs to the state that gave us the pie.

As in a chowder, potatoes and onions go into the pie, too. "Probably some black bass sneaks in," says Mundell, especially in winter—though it does little for the taste. Ice fishermen can get bass in winter, and, landlocked, Vermonters learned how to feed themselves from their lakes.

"Add apples to the pie," says Andrews, as these do nicely over winter, too. They also give a nice touch of crispness and a sauce to the hornpout.

"Only if they have the right amount of crunch," chips in her friend.

"Did you know the girl who won the apple pie contest this year used all the varieties of apples she could find to put in her pie instead of only one?" Mundell tells me.

"I think she used four," says Andrews.

With eight generations of Vermont firmness behind him, Mundell has the last word. "An apple should be solid," he says.

New England boiled dinner is something else Mundell encourages us to discover. It is not something vague or with

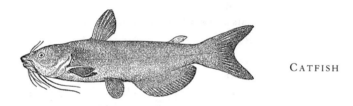

CATFISH

extra added attractions or options. It is a specific bill of fare. Mundell puts us on the direct route to a whole trail of suppers where we can graze and browse our savory way through Vermont.

There are Strawberry Suppers (mostly in June) to go to, Sugaring Suppers (first in early spring, but they can come again), Hunters' Suppers (venison and game), and Harvest Suppers (when the crops come in).

In addition there are Chicken or Turkey Suppers because it is a Saturday, and suppers that are given almost every Sunday. The suppers take place on town property, the commons, or in community (mostly Baptist or Congregational) churches. They are strictly nondenominational dinners; outsiders are welcome, and even encouraged to come to these meals. They are usually held to raise money to pay the minister's salary, fill up his cupboard, and buy clothes for his kids. The ladies' auxiliaries of the churches put the dinners on. They do most of the cooking and hope that the hall or lawn on which their dinners are held will be filled. You can be sure your greeting will be warm and genuine. Many people from out of state who go to these same dinners year after year have built up a community of Vermont friends, a community to which they feel they belong. There is no more authentic local food in all the country; it is a chance for a genuine taste of Vermont and its people. Most suppers are $6 ($3 for kids), and there are no taxes or tip.

You can make a fine career of keeping yourself fat on these suppers. Here are some addresses to feed your curiosity and your appetite admirably. The types of suppers follow, then their locations.

The Strawberry Supper can be held when the strawberries come in (so that they are fresh local Vermont strawberries, not California "walnuts"), and the dinner itself can be anything at all. Let's say it's a New England boiled dinner. This would be a nice piece of meat—a London broil or a shoulder cut—a nice piece of turnip (if you're lucky, Gil's feather), onions, carrots for color (because you've got to have color), and parsnips. It is in the dessert that the strawberries come—in the strawberry shortcake—and you can be sure the cream will be real whipped cream, not shot from the nozzle of a spray can.

The Hunter's Supper is the rare opportunity to eat like the pioneers and the Indians. Deer, bear, rabbit, and raccoon are often the vittles for these suppers. Also on the table are the fruits of the season: squash, the king of the big-game vegetables, and turnip. Chicken potpie is available for those who prefer it.

There is usually a surcharge for game, but we are talking about a top of only $15 a feast. Reserve early for this one. As hunting season starts in November, and game has to hang two to three weeks at least, Game Suppers, as they are also called, won't start before the third week of the month. Call or write ahead to the towns listed below to find out who's doing what and when.

The Harvest Supper: fresh fall vegetables—including carrots, beets, and turnips—scalloped potatoes, rolls, and pies surround sliced glazed ham, chicken pie, or turkey or corned beef and home-baked beans. Home-baked beans figure in a lot of these suppers; if a calamity happens to a Vermonter, the first thing another Vermonter says is, "I'll put on some beans."

The Sugaring Supper is for the months when the snow flies. Like many festivals held during the winter, it is the most convivial of all. Here's why: After a dinner of baked ham, baked beans, deviled eggs, cole slaw, potato salad, and rolls, your place at the table is filled with a pan of packed snow. A server then passes with a pitcher of hot maple syrup and pours it onto your snow. The snow almost melts, the syrup almost solidifies, and what you have left is maple brittle.

Pickles are served on the side to make you want to eat more, which you will. The process is repeated as long as pans, snow, and syrup hold out. Each serving looks like a crazed crepe or a maple pancake. Doughnuts may also accompany this festive dessert. Afterward, when songs are sung, if a neighbor offers a hand in friendship, chances are it will stick.

But there are more, so many more suppers; this list gives you only a hint of what's going on and what you've been missing if you've been keeping to the straight and narrow. There are Roast Beef Suppers (these are usually given by firehouses), Turkey Suppers, Chicken Potpie Suppers (but ask for a hornpout), Peach Shortcake Suppers (the one in Dummerston Center is famous; people come hundreds of miles each year for it). The list of communities that follows is, believe me, culled from many temptations. Each entry should not imply only one supper per entity, for many little towns do several events and some even many. The menu is annual and can change with each year. Inquire ahead of any community you wish to join, or of several, as it is a way to travel in Vermont and find the taste that suits you.

EAST DOVER CHURCH SUPPER
Mrs. Judy Keith
East Dover Baptist Church
East Dover, VT 05341
Tel. 802/348–7947

This is an especially good address for the Strawberry Supper; it's held in the picturesque Dover town hall. Not far from the town hall site and up the same road can be found a good place for lodging.

COOPER HILL INN
Cooper Hill Rd.
East Dover, VT 05341
Tel. 802/348–6333

Cooper Hill Inn is on the top of a hill from which you can see for miles and into three states. It may be the best view in Vermont. Not especially elegant, it's a very serviceable turn-of-the century white clapboard farmhouse. Breakfast is served in the rock-maple lined dining room from whenever you get up—a welcome convenience for skiers. The prices are easy, and Mount Snow is only 5 miles away.

Down in the valleys, other supper sites open more doors to easy exploration.

HALIFAX GRANGE SUPPERS
Joan Courser
Box 27
Halifax, VT 05358
Tel. 802/368–7733

Here they hold more than five public suppers a year, featuring strawberry, peach shortcake, game, meat loaf, and chicken potpie in various seasons.

DUMMERSTON CENTER SUPPERS
Marion Gassett
R.D. 6, Box 227
Brattleboro, VT 05301
Tel. 802/254–8182

These suppers at the Grange Hall are some of the most interesting and well-attended in Vermont. They have a tremendous following from everywhere, it seems, or at least from Connecticut and New York. The Peach Shortcake Supper takes the palm for the best.

WARDSBORO CENTER SUPPERS
Wardsboro Town Hall
Box 48
Wardsboro Center, VT 05355
Tel. 802/896–6055

Another perennial favorite of the supper circuit, Wardsboro (on Rte. 100, 10 mi north of Dover) has many— spring, summer, and turkey—and it always puts out a dinner with some surprises in it. Here you are likely to see a Gil's feather turnip or have a pie with a catfish in it.

NEWFANE SUPPERS
Newfane Congregational Church
Newfane Town Hall (Rte. 30)
Newfane, VT 05345
Church, tel. 802/365–4079; town clerk, tel. 802/365–7772

This town has two supper programs. Try to come to a supper that's situated on the village green; it's the most photographed spot in Vermont.

JACKSONVILLE SUPPER
Don Washburn
Box 241
Jacksonville, VT 05342
Tel. 802/368–2310

The Jacksonville Game Supper gets plenty of pressure. With rabbit, deer, and bear, why not? It's held every year, but contact them before the month of October to be sure to secure a place at one of three seatings.

Here, then, is your green trail to the goodness of Vermont; it goes through woods and over hills and into Granges and tree-shaded town halls. It is designed to get you into Vermont communities and country supper pleasures. Here you find something you cannot experience in a restaurant, ever. The price is right, the way is clear, the scenery is glorious, and the people congenial. So, come and get it in Vermont.

CHAPTER 6

THE SUMMER GARDEN

Waterbury, Vermont

There is a stretch of 20 miles or so along a state road in Vermont where you don't have to do much driving, for the town along it, Waterbury, is a concentration of tastes in itself. For many it is a winter place. During the season, skiers come plowing through it on the way to Stowe, praying for snow, yet it is an attractive spot all year long. In summer the leafy vegetation approaches green neon. The tumbling Mad River makes such a delightful series of refreshing leaps that people stop their cars to jump into it. The American elm still dwarfs the settlements of white houses beside the road. The second and third most popular of all Vermont attractions huddle here (7 miles apart), and both have something that you can put in your mouth. The churned, the squeezed, and the sugared all have their sources here, and it is a place bursting with flavor.

It is the summer garden of the middle of Vermont.

HIGHLIGHTS:
- Vermont sugaring: how to do it yourself—and the true and false of it
- A green mountain of coffee and the brew of the month
- Cool cider and videos in the hollow
- General stores of taste
- A spinning wheel of moose and bears

- The factory of famous flavors
- A green mountain of chocolate

LENGTH OF LOOP: 15 miles

LENGTH OF STAY: One night

Interstates 91 and 82 are to the east, but Route 100 is the road to take, for the Mad River is its companion.

Just 12 miles south of Stowe on Route 100, and 90 miles north of Wilmington, is nestled the little town that should be famous for its flavors. The small-town taste capital of America (or at least of Vermont), it deserves to be called. It is the village of Waterbury, our destination and headquarters for expeditions and forays—all of them extremely close by and logistically manageable (they don't stray from Route 100)—into the vast fastnesses of mountains of ice cream, chocolate, coffee, and taste.

Waterbury itself is hardly a headliner in the tourist industry or on the tongues of the tens of thousands who come up Route 100, nor is it a regular feature in picture travel magazines featuring stories on New England towns. Waterbury is too close to Stowe, and so it is neglected. It isn't fancy: On its streets there is no parade of sleek skiers. Waterbury is a worker's town; for color it has only the need of paint. Maybe that is why so many food companies are here, for there's a plentiful supply of workers. This little town boasts no covered bridges over the Winooski River. The town common looks common, but the library is well stocked. The train that will get you to Montreal in an hour still leaves from the station (and it's a good place to go from). The people founded the town in the middle of winter and come from tradition that sticks (and so does most of what they turn out).

Maple sugar is the great New England contentment, and it can be yours. No other sugar will give you quite the same taste. Certainly not cane. Not beet sugar or anything of only sucrose and dextrose. Maple sugar is different. It also contains fructose—fruit sugar. It sits so sweetly and lightly on the tongue that it never cloys the palate. It is delicate, and it has a body, in its pure early spring rendering, that is almost ethereal.

Now does that sound like the maple syrup you know?

The operative words are pure and early springtime. Many maple syrups are counterfeited. In fact, along with pictures of Ben Franklin on our currency, maple syrup may be one of the most counterfeited substances in America; the most common way a shipper will cut it (and his costs) is to blend it with corn syrup. Nothing wrong with corn syrup, you might say. But it is not maple, next to which it strikes a darker, more lugubrious note. Maple syrup is the undisputed sugar of pure crystal taste.

It comes from pure crystal sap. The colorless fluid runs like water, looks like water; in fact you cannot tell a bucket of it from water itself. It is odorless and tasteless, too. Not until you boil it down and start the evaporation process do its recognizable properties begin to show up in the residues.

You have to boil it a lot. About 40 parts of sap yields only one part of syrup. If you start out with 40 quarts or pints of sap in the kettle, at the end there will be only one quart or pint of syrup at the bottom. Tedious though it is, there is nothing particularly tricky or backbreaking about the process, and the results themselves are a justifiable reward. Never will you have tasted syrup or sugar like this, even if you bought it from the store. Especially if you have bought it as "genuine." There is far more mystery to maple syrup than that.

For anyone with a sugar maple on the premises, or access to one in the woods, the mystery is solvable, for he or she can make the finest syrup for pancakes and a multitudinous variety of breakfast and dinner things.

Here's how.

First get a leaf of the tree in question or take a picture of the one you are about to tap to a botanist (or your local nurseryman) to make sure it's really a sugar maple. The outline of the leaf isn't enough, as there are many trees in the forest. Only one maple is the sugar maple, and tapping a swamp maple will do no good.

Next, the tapping itself. First you'll have to go to a hardware store, a good one. Probably one in small-town Vermont, or anywhere in rural New England will do; there you need to buy something called spials. These are silvery little objects close in size to thimbles. They are funnel-shaped on one end, for driving into the side of the sugar maple tree, and tab ended on the other, for hanging a bucket on once the funnel end has been tapped in. They shouldn't cost quite a dollar each, and several should be bought, in case you mistap and bend one. The idea is to pick out a tree stout enough to stand for the extraction of its juices easily; you should not be able to get your arms around it. The spial should be placed where you can trace the main shoot of the tree up its bark from its roots, which climbs toward the mizzen of the main trunk and not out to a secondary limb.

The spial should be tapped in up to the end of its shank, about an inch and a half, and penetrate into the tree directly through its bark. It will make its own hole, but it can be helpful to get it started with a drill. Once the spial is in, the fit should be very snug; you will need pliers and muscle to get it out. The tab should be angled so the handle of a bucket can hang down from it.

Nobody uses buckets these days; these are only for picturing in snow scenes on maple sugar tins. Unless you watch a bucket like a hawk (an owl at night), lots of things can go wrong with it. Raccoons and bugs and rain can get in it, which can defile, pollute, and dilute the collected sap. The thing to do is to hang up your sap collector for a week and forget about it.

Plastic bag collectors with galvanized metal shields are what everyone uses now. They hang down where the old buckets used to hang from the tab of the spial. A sleeve of galvanized aluminum fits over the bag, snugly covering access to it from the outside and preventing stray twigs, bugs, curious raccoons, raindrops, dewdrops, and other droppings (hawks' and owls'?) from dropping in.

It is in the middle of February (about) when you want to tap a sugar maple, just as soon as there are a few sunny

days to drive the sap out of the roots and suck it up the tree: when the air temperature mounts to about 50°F in the day and then plunges dramatically at night. The sap in the tree goes up and down, too, with the rising and falling temperatures, like mercury in a thermometer, past limbs and spial holes, racing from the base to the branches by day and spending the night in the roots. Thus, the variation in temperature shoots the sap through the spial and into your bag.

This is the time when the taste of the sap reaches its peak as well. If you try to collect sap earlier, the temperature does not vary enough to make the tree behave like a water pump. If you collect it too late in spring, the sap spends too much time out in the branches, and the forming buds change the taste of the sap and of the syrup. It seems there are as many changes in grading maple syrup as there have been for German wine appellations. Let your taste tell; in this case it will do a far better job in grading than anything printed on a can. There is no better education on what maple syrup should taste like than simply making it yourself.

After about five days, there will be enough liquid in the bag to fill the largest kitchen pot.

Some people advise that the next step be accomplished outside in the air with wood fires to heat the sap in the pot and bring it to the boil. However, in February the air outside is still quite cold, and the pot, or pots, that you use must remain uncovered so that the steam can escape, leaving the syrup. This poses the risk that wood ash will wind up in the pot and the smoke from the fires will give the syrup a smoky taste. Therefore, the kitchen is the right place for your experiment.

The same people who tell you to do your cooking in the cold will tell you that you run the risk of peeling your wallpaper if you cook the sap in the kitchen. This is true. But for this reason, and also for the canning of vegetables, jams, and fruit preserves, kitchens should not be papered. Assuming yours isn't, or that you have the good sense to open all your kitchen windows and doors first, or perhaps, that you want to correct a previous error with wallpaper, put your largest pot filled with sap on your largest burner and turn on your heat to high.

At first it will seem like boiling water for pasta.

As the level of the liquid in the pot descends, however, it predictably thickens. A soft boiling roll comes to the surface; you can stir it occasionally and the droplets on the spoon will thicken.

It will begin to take on taste. After the boiling has gone on several hours (per few quarts), only a few inches of liquid will remain in the pot. It will begin to take on color, the taste will intensify, and you must be careful. When the yellow color is bright, the taste tantalizes, the viscosity of the liquid slows, and the critical mass of the syrup is achieved. If you heat it much further it will turn to sugar. Should this happen, as it does to everyone, pour some water into the pot, stir, and you will have syrup all over again. There will be 11 pounds of it to the gallon; this is the legal weight for maple syrup in Vermont and how the state judges whether it's pure. But no weight, only the tongue, will tell you if it comes from February.

Accomplish this (everybody with a tree should try it once), and you will wind up with a syrup that is unattainable at any price. The collection is passive and the work part consumes only putting the pot on the burner, turning on the heat, and watching it at the end of the boil. For plugging the holes left in the trees, wine corks do nicely. Like the best olive oil from Italy and from France, this is the kind of maple syrup that is not exported. Those who live here get it all.

GREEN MOUNTAIN COFFEE ROASTERS
33 Coffee La.
Waterbury, VT 05676
Tel. 800/223–6768

As you cross the little Winooski River coming into Waterbury, Route 100 turns into Main Street, and the **Green Mountain Coffee Roasters** appears on its aptly named Coffee Lane. You will have to nose down the alley to get there, as the coffee company is behind Perkins' kitchen supply store (look in here for hard-to-get hotel-size skillets and pans). The Green Mountain is a small store in size but a leading purveyor of coffees throughout the New England area. It is a good place to aim for on any morning. For 40¢, if you bring your own mug, they'll fill it and hand you a newspaper. Chances are there will be tongue-in-cheek ads touting "Factory Seconds Sales" at Ben and Jerry's ice cream factory just miles ahead on the road, and you will get a foretaste of the special kind of nutty place it is. You can take your mug of coffee into the fresh air out back and look at the alley or ensconce yourself at an old wooden table and chair and read your paper like a local (arriving customers will stare at you longingly). The Green Mountain is the best coffee deal you'll get in town. If you don't have a mug of your own, there are plenty on hand for sale, plus home-baked cakes, chiffon cream pies, and sticky buns. A wide variety of coffee gadgets—percolators and assorted paraphernalia, bean grinders, paper filters, and espresso makers—are tucked into every nook and chubby wooden cubby hole where the store displays its stock. There is a coffee-of-the-month-club program that delivers discounts with its beans and a rich range of Green Mountain Coffee. Mail order is the chief business at Green Mountain Coffee Company.

A warning, however; this is not only a coffee purist's kind of coffee outlet. Pure coffees are first on the list but not to the exclusion of all else. There is Celebes coffee, for example, and coffee from Sumatra (*see* Chapter 3, Berkshire Coffee Roasting Company) and other exotic places, but Green Mountain also offers flavored varieties. The weird and the bizarre are their cups of tea, too. More than 50 kinds of bean and flavored coffee are roasted and sold by mail or to take home. There are six fresh-roasted brews of the day at the Waterbury location. Try some of these at your own personal coffee tasting; they'll do more than open an eye: Viennese cinnamon, Swiss chocolate, mandarin orange with amaretto, rainforest nut, or Irish cream.

Green Mountain's most popular coffees are still the unflavored, however, with the perennial favorite Colombia Supremo topping the list, while hazelnut heads the choice in flavored beans. To keep the flavored and unflavored beans straight, two grinders are used; the grinder that grinds the flavored will never grind (and therefore contaminate) the unflavored bean. The coffee club can tailor your choices to its program. Discounts entice you to join, and you can taste your way through every kind of Green Mountain coffee in your own home.

About 5 miles north on Route 100, just after the red brick church, keep your eye skinned for the clapboard-sided group of cozy buildings called the **Cold Hollow Cider Mill.** One building is yellow, one is red, and one is baby-blue.

COLD HOLLOW CIDER MILL
Rte. 100N
Waterbury, VT 05676
Tel. 802/244–8771 or 800/327–7537

Shall we stop? you wonder. After all, it is just a cider mill. Consider, however, that this one is the third-largest attraction in the state of Vermont.

Here you can find more than just a drop of cider to wet your whistle and a bargain or two in the apple bazaar. Run first for the general store and its gallery of local food. Be warned, however; the general store comes with its own bakery inside. Through its plate-glass picture window can be seen the Cold Hollow team of apple bakers at work, deftly making little apple things to eat on the run.

To accompany the mulled cider are hot cider doughnuts at 25¢, and tart and tangy they are. Apple pies are fresh out of the oven each day, with noon the best time to strike while they're hot. There are apple strudels and cinnamon apple squares as well.

Also to graze on, as freebies, is an amazing variety of samplers. Should your budget be squeezed on the road, this is a very friendly place to know about. You'll find enough free snacks so that you can skip buying lunch. Paper cups on a tray are filled with hot or cold cider according to season. Jellies, including onion, come in smears for crackers, along with maple butter, Vermont (vegetable) salsas, and sometimes, if you are lucky, promotions from other food producers in the state—a range of Cabot's Cheddar, for instance.

The shelves, bins, and barrels of the general store are laden with Vermont favorites and specialties—fiddlehead ferns, a host of hot and sour sauces, Vermont common crackers, Blanchard and Blanchard salad dressings, and other things that go pop in the mouth.

The best treats of all are the specialty items that are standard stock and trade to the mill. Pure cider jelly is perhaps their hottest item, and an old, traditional product it is. Simply cider that is boiled and boiled until it reaches the jelly

state, it is firmed by its own natural pectin. Cider jelly is a clear, sweet amber product that generously holds and offers the essence and sweetness of apples and nothing more. Parents can watch their kids assuage their sugar cravings and have confidence in it.

Applesauce and apple butter come in one-pint jars. Another good bet is hot spiced cider concentrate (in liquid form). Serve it hot at Thanksgiving for a surefire hit. The apples come from the Lake Champlain region and are mostly McIntosh (certainly the big local favorite in apples), but Cortlands and Northern Spies are used, too. You shouldn't leave the store without a zesty maple-horseradish mustard, sold in 8-ounce jars for $3.95. Try that as a Vermont marinade for your roast beef and be content.

Now for a tour of the mill, one of the largest in New England. Begin with a charming little movie of the journey of an apple from the orchard (on the banks of Lake Champlain) to where you are. In the summer the theater is set up in the apple pressing room. In fall, when the apple press is operating, the film is shown in another building. Working an apple press is an operation equivalent to feeding time at the zoo. One hundred tons of pressure comes down on a fleshy mound of apples and squeezes the seeds out of it. A bright flood of amber juice cascades down a stainless-steel vat. It is then pumped into an adjoining room, to be bottled by machine and smiling cider workers.

You can buy a jug if you want (no sorbates are used; *see* Chapter 2, Ellsworth Farm), and one gallon costs $2.85. That and most other Cold Hollow products are also offered by mail.

If you stay on Route 100 North to almost the Stowe town line, you'll come upon a special, rare treat: the great red barn and impetuous wood menagerie of the **Spinning Wheel Sculpture Gardens.** It features an indigenous style of artwork that has grown up around Waterbury.

THE SPINNING WHEEL
Rte. 100N
Waterbury Center, VT 05677
Tel. 802/244–8883

A ballerina appears on the horizon. Looming 11 feet tall against the sky on the points of her toe shoes, she is shaped to exquisite dimensions. The black peelings of rubber on the road tell you her appeal is instantaneous and arresting; so are the giant moose and bear nearby. These are the wooden wonder sculptures of Max Osorio.

The Brobdingnagian figures are so unusual that you have to stop. A 12-foot-high American eagle holds a snake in his talons. The more-than-basic moose has a face of wood grain and skin of bark. A variety of menacing bears is topped by a 16-foot monster with bared fangs. Several cuter ones are only knee-high and cuddly. There are Indian chiefs and a jumping fish, squirrels, rabbits, and just plain woodsy critters. Prices range from $45 to $4,000 and are worth every bit.

If you want to watch the artist at work in his shop, Max welcomes you in. If you accept the invitation, surprise him. Bring a pair of earplugs. The rasp of the chainsaw precedes its biting into a hunk of pine; a 5-foot bear head emerges from the flying chips, and the price for this beast is about $300. In the barn a shop and souvenir stand offer upcountry products. The best buys are Vermont quilts and shearling slippers that are a treasure on cold mornings.

From here it is only about 8 miles back south to Waterbury's number-one tourist attraction (number two for the whole state of Vermont): **Ben & Jerry's Ice Cream Factory.**

Above the Vermont landscape, the second floor of the building lifts its head, painted a whimsical peppermint pink, blueberry, and ice mint; the bottom stands out in conventional black and white.

BEN & JERRY'S ICE CREAM FACTORY
Rte. 100N
Waterbury, VT 05676
Tel. 802/244–8687

This is an ice-cream company with a reputation for community service as well as for flavors, but the tour costs a dollar, and they have no 800 number. Nevertheless, upwards of 250,000 people gather inside the doors each year for the tour and a slide show, which is continually updated and changed.

The tour lobby is festooned with ice-cream memorabilia. There are old, handwritten ice-cream recipes (stained), a statement of operating principles (à la Charles Foster Kane), and a miniature model of the factory—including secret parts you won't get in to see—that children love. Tours begin whenever a large enough group (10–15) of visitors has gathered; the wait is never long.

All ice-cream and candy factories have some things in common: lots of pouring milk and workers who walk around in white hats. The milk is reduced in volume and blended through spinning machines and taste is added through flavor-feeding ducts; the Waterbury factory turns out 9 million gallons of ice cream and frozen yogurt products every year.

For the slide show visitors are cornered in a little theater where they are shown Kodachromes of Ben and Jerry, more Kodachromes of cows (Holsteins), and of the concoctions this team has brought forth. There is also a slide of Ben in Indian garb; the audience is plied with some of the corniest jokes and wordplay as ever made the pages of *Captain Billy and His Whiz-Bang.*

The tour culminates with a tasting of what is called the "scoop du jour." See what I mean? You emerge into a boutique full of cow socks, cow hats, cow sweatshirts, cow T-shirts, and so on.

For me there is one flaw in all of this: Ben & Jerry's is an ice cream that is strong on flavor but weak on cream. The taste of the cream itself does not stick in this brain; it is not voluptuous. This may be the fault of the cows the company pictures so proudly on its shirts: Holsteins.

Their black and white goes very nicely on a field of green, but how does their milk whip up in a cream? Not so beautifully; when it comes to cream (and cheese), you're in better company with Guernsey or Jersey cows (for a fuller discussion of this, *see* Chapter 4, High Lawn Farms and Cheesecake Charlie's. Also, *see* Chapter 5, Cabot Creamery).

However, if you think Chocolate Chip Cookie Dough is something to put in your mouth, or that New York Super Fudge Chunk goes more that just clunk, Ben & Jerry's may be your piece of heaven. The item that I appreciated most I found in the boutique: a real ice-cream scoop. It was the kind the ice-cream parlor men would use to dig out those great balls of flavor they dropped in a frosted: pure vanilla, plain chocolate, and real strawberry fruit in a luscious cream that ran down your chin and that you rolled into your mouth with your finger.

We are still looking for that.

Picking our way south through Waterbury and back across the Winooski River, we pass a few fast-sandwich places (as opposed to fast food) you should know about in town to help stave off hunger pangs.

In the center of town is **Chives** (corner of Park Row and South Main). It's a clean, well-lighted deli, a drop-in spot offering good sandwiches at good prices (under $5), lip-smacking soups by the cup or bowl for starters; a good dinner of both will cost less than $10. **The Crust 'n' Cauldron** is just around the corner, and it is here the ethnic specialties of the town—the Polish sausages, the pastas, the tidbit—show up, at prices that are a bargain.

For places to stay, there's one almost across the road from where we are going, and it is as good as any and better than most. **The Grunberg Haus** (Box 1595, Waterbury, VT 05676, tel. 802/244–7726), owned by Christopher Sellers and Mark Frohman from San Francisco, has 10 rooms. Mozart is a Grunberg feature—Sellers plays on a concert grand—and so are the pleasurable open spaces out back with hiking trails that are suitable for cross-country skiing in winter.

Across the road is the meritorious and serendipitous **Green Mountain Chocolate Company:** serendipitous as in you wouldn't normally expect to find excellence behind such a simple front, and meritorious in that the chocolates inside are simply the best.

THE GREEN MOUNTAIN CHOCOLATE COMPANY
Rte. 100S
Waterbury, VT 05676
Tel. 802/244–8256

The place is inconspicuous, a redwood log cabin; the sign is small on a blue awning, and inside there are only three counters. Albert Kumin, formerly executive chef of the Four Seasons in New York and White House pastry chef for President Carter, is the man behind the glass cases. The cases are filled with remarkable challenges for sweet teeth: number one are the chocolate truffles, little round soft chocolate nuggets for taking after dinner with coffee. Also spectacular is the butter crunch, toffee dipped in milk- or dark chocolate (as you like it). The fudge is like you have never tasted before. It is cut into sections, caramelized between the layers, and enrobed in dark chocolate. My personal favorite is bark—lightly toasted almonds (or other nuts) held in the dark grip of thick bittersweet chocolate. You keep it cold and break it apart with a hammer. There are other, traditional favorites, too—dainty chocolate cups with raspberry or mocha, and checkerboard praline. All are made in the basement below your feet and are fresh as today at the Green Mountain Chocolate Company. There is a new selling outlet 4 miles north (containing a little museum with chocolate memorabilia), but here's where the creation happens, and freshness counts for more than you might think in good chocolates because of emulsifiers. Emulsifiers are basically a type of preservative used in most commercial chocolates to give them a longer shelf life, but they take the edge off a fine chocolate taste. To use or not to use emulsifiers, that is the basic chocolate question.

The fine chocolates of Europe never, *never* use them. And the Green Mountain Chocolate Company of Waterbury, Vermont, is one of the few American companies that do not use emulsifiers either. That is why their chocolates win so many awards. Come up here to taste them. They have a catalogue of what they do send (by express), and you are guaranteed to eat it fast.

CHAPTER 7

INNS FOR ALL SEASONS

Cruising New Hampshire

When Robert Frost, himself a New Hampshire man, said good fences make good neighbors, he may have been thinking of the relationship between New Hampshirites and Vermonters. Although the two states adjoin each other, a stranger might think they have nothing in common. Vermont is the most liberal state in New England, New Hampshire the most conservative. Vermonters' most cutting humor is saved for citizens of the Granite State, and New Hampshirites reserve a special ire for Vermont.

New Hampshire has such a self-reliant tradition that it declared independence from Great Britain a full seven months before the rest of the colonies. During the revolutionary war, its men advanced into action under the blood-stirring cry, "Live Free or Die!" Anyone who has been to the state since can tell you that what was the command has become the state motto and is still a way of life. New Hampshire people have the lowest tax burden in the nation: They pay no state income tax and there is no sales tax. With this in mind, then, let us travel New Hampshire roads by New Hampshire inns. Most roads go along rivers; the clean, rapid power that once turned the wheels of machinery now provides a new bond between these once disparate states. Along their bright river flows are found the microbreweries producing the newly prized and highly celebrated micro-beers of New England.

HIGHLIGHTS:
- Catamount, the Amber Panther of White River Junction
- Hanover, the capital of beer: ale, lager, and Weisbier
- Duck and porter, and how the new food affinities work with beer
- The New London Inn: buffets and a home for the holidays
- The John Hancock Inn: Some things never change—and so much the better
- Harrisville and its millpond
- Monadnock and its mountain

LENGTH OF LOOP: 220 miles

LENGTH OF STAY: Three nights

Traversing the bottom of Vermont or coming up Interstate 91 from Massachusetts, you reach New Hampshire across the Connecticut River.

Taking the Interstate is the fast way, but crossing the Connecticut River on Route 10 above Northfield, Massachusetts, puts you in the right spot and frame of mind to realize how wide and glorious this river really is. It is perhaps the most underrated river in New England. The Indians called it "next to the great river with tides," which is what Connecticut means. The deep, opal waters twist upstream past islets and sweet-smelling border pines that frame verdant green patches; the river seems to go up to forever and its waters slide down from time.

You feel like an 18th-century trapper going up into the land of the Mohicans and Mohawks who once lived here. You have the feeling in your bones and the drumbeat is in your ears. New Hampshire does nothing to dispel the impression or persuade you that it is mistaken. No malls sprout in the green valleys, and no urban sprawls: just here and there a silo, a white steeple, a fence around a sprinkling of cows. Follow Route 10 to routes 12 and 12A northward along the river.

At Hanover, Dartmouth College rises up from the plain on a slight stooped hill, its white bell tower thrust into the sky and looking very little like the frontier outpost "for the education of the youth of the Indian tribes" it was erected to be. Now its students come from all over, but Dartmouth has stayed a small campus, with less than 5,000 students. A double row of brick buildings of the neatest and most orderly kind makes up a compact commercial district; Main Street ends abruptly at the college. The **Hanover Inn** is directly across

from the green (called a quadrangle at other schools). The inn is more than part of the college, which owns it. It is the capital of beer in New England.

HANOVER INN
Main and Wheelock Sts.
Hanover, NH 03755
Tel. 800/443–7024

The building, made of pointed-up brick, has an elegant 18th-century look, with fans and scrolls outlining the mullioned windows. The advantages of staying in rooms on the campus are many and considerable.

The **Hood Museum** (tel. 603/646–2808) is just outside the door of the inn. This is the largest art museum between Boston and Montreal, with an important Impressionist collection. Staying at the inn makes it an annex for your personal use. The **Hopkins Center for the Performing Arts** (tel. 603/646–2422) is on the same street, with three theaters offering dance, music, and drama. The setting blends what could be termed a petit urban sophistication with the gem of the ideal college town. You walk to performances. The crime rate is so low that people still leave their houses open and cars unlocked in the street. The Dartmouth Book Store, an excellent browsing place, is at hand, available between performances and between meals; everywhere you go, you encounter an industrious and cheerful breed of people known as students and faculty. A few days' stay at Dartmouth is like going home to the tonic of youth.

The cable TV in your room provides access to the sort of intellectual pursuits now required of every contemporary graduate and undergraduate, C-Span and American Movie Classics. Room service is rapid and cheerful, so there can be no lack of grazing entertainment even in a snowstorm.

A more delightful pursuit, however, and one we have come chiefly to take up, lies a short drive (5 miles) through the woods and across the river to the lair of the Amber Panther of White River Junction.

CATAMOUNT BREWING COMPANY
58 S. Main St.
White River Junction, VT 05001
Tel. 802/296–2248

One of the results of living free or dying is that there is not much state money to invest in start-up capital for small businesses. Because this is how **Catamount Brewing Company** was founded, it started on the Vermont side of the river, where small industries, especially with an artisanal flair, began to flourish in the '80s. But Hanover, in New Hampshire just across the confluence of the Connecticut and White rivers, considers White River Junction as its own backyard, and Catamount, which after all sells beer, is very happy to have this proprietary attitude shown by a college town.

The story of Catamount Brewery and its special success may be typical of many such stories with local food and bev-

erage products that are coming out of the north. The secret they share appears to be the delivery of a high-quality product through a manageable scale of production.

Catamount is a microbrewery producing what have become known in the business as micro-beers. What is a micro-beer? Simply, it is a beer from any company whose total production does not exceed 15,000 barrels per year. By contrast, for example, Budweiser produces 86 million barrels—which makes it a mega-beer.

Catamount Brewery started small, putting out 3,000 barrels in its first year, 1987. Since then its production has quadrupled to 12,000 barrels, which do a disappearing act in the states where they are sold, chiefly Vermont, New Hampshire, and Massachusetts. New Hampshire has the highest beer consumption rate per capita in New England and even outstrips Wisconsin. What Catamount's customers seek out is an interesting range of beer varieties, each with a highly individual taste.

Before you throw up your hands—especially if you are about to say, "I don't even like beer"—hold on. Wait until you have tasted a micro-beer. This brew may be for you.

Catamount offers regular tours of its brewery, a formerly abandoned 19th-century granary. The brick building is never closed from June to November and has tours seven days a week (Saturdays only, December to May). A shop inside sells Catamount gear—sweatshirts and such with big cat logos that reproduce the amber panther of the beer's label—as well as beer, so whenever you walk in until three in the afternoon of any day, someone will be there to greet you; the brewery is through a door at the rear of the shop.

The aroma of a brewery is very tart, but after a few moments you will fail to notice it, so natural is its attraction. Philip Gentile, the company's marketing director, comes out to lead the tour. He is a man still on the sunny side of his forties, like most of the 22 employees in the company. His blue shirtsleeves are a match for his eyes; he is the sort of fellow who a generation ago would have been extolling the virtues of his infant company's chardonnay.

Now such companies make beer. His fascination with it and his objectives seem ever the same: working with pure products of nature to make something people will love to drink (and it might also help if the product does well at the box office). The tour starts up a flight of steps to the malt room, where the malt is viewed with the hops.

Beer is a product of sugar in plants, as is wine, but in beer the sugar comes from grain and not fruit, and water is added. Malt is barley that has been sprouted; the growth of the sprouts produces the plant's sugar, from which the alcohol will come. Toasting the malt fixes the sprouting so the sugar can be extracted. This is not an operation that you can see on a sprouting or toasting floor the way it is done in Scotland (in some Scottish distilleries). At Catamount the grain (malt) is delivered (mostly from Wisconsin, but there is some English malt, too) already sprouted and toasted. It is sweet to the taste directly from the sack; someone in our party said it would make an interesting breakfast cereal.

The finished malt is fed into the milling machine, the first step in production. The ground malt flows through a

HOPS

chute downstairs to be brewed. The brewing machine is essentially a giant copper boiler installed in a brick cylinder with a fire (propane-generated) burning underneath. The malt is mixed with water and the two are cooked at a strong rolling boil at something slightly over 212° F. This solution of grain and sugar is called the wort. It percolates like coffee, leaving the dregs of the malt behind after the wort is extracted by siphon.

The wort is cooled to 64° and pumped into the fermentation room next door. With the help of added yeasts, fermentation takes place. Top-fermenting yeast (which ferments on top of the tank) is used to make ale, and bottom-fermenting yeast is used to produce lager; this is the main division in beers.

It is at the time of fermentation that the hops are added. These are most interesting plants; we examine them and pull them apart in our fingers, to smell and to taste them. They have heads that look like a ball of basil, with very green leaves surrounding sprigs of seeds that dip down from the center and have a smell and taste of amazing puckerishness. An herb that seems to do to beer what tarragon does to chicken, it gives it the zing of extra character. Hops are found throughout the northern latitudes of the world, in Germany, England, and Vermont; but Catamount especially likes those from the northwest Rockies. Beers with a puckerish or very dry quality to their taste are said to be well hopped; hops are responsible for the taste a beer finishes with, the lasting impression it leaves in the mouth.

Ale is a beer that finishes fast; more time is taken to make lager, which is the German word for "stored." Both styles of beers spend four days fermenting in their vats; after two weeks of conditioning and filtering, the ale is shipped; the lager is kept for three weeks more—up to six weeks for a pilsner, which is stored the longest of the lagers and so is the most expensive to make.

The beers at Catamount are made in batches of no more than 1,000 gallons, exactly what the term handcrafted means when applied to beers. No pasteurization or stabilizers are used for shelf life. Micro-beers depend on cold storage, as pasteurization decimates taste and food value. The ale is delivered to the Hanover Inn when it is two to three weeks old and kept fresh by means of a tight, consumption-oriented schedule.

The tour ends with a tasting and the opportunity to buy souvenirs and beer. The ales come in Gold and Amber. The Amber is in the style of Bass Ale; this is not surprising, as Catamount's founder spent a year in England studying its brewing. His beer, however, has no overseas voyage to make and is especially appreciated for its lusty bite and fresh zest.

Porter is a combination of ale and lager originally named for the porters of London, who especially favored it drawn from separate kegs in a pub. It is malty and thick like a stout (a shade darker porter), and it strikes a note in the mouth that also has hints of chocolate.

There was Christmas ale to finish with, a completely different kind of cat. It is made with Cascade hops from the Yakima Valley in Washington state, which produce a brew that is very aromatic and puckers the palate.

All of these are quite separate from beers that are drunk to quench a simple thirst. These beers provide a variety of backgrounds to stand up to even the most demanding menu, and this is the promise for the night. I am intrigued enough to gamble an evening's dining to see what micro-beers like these can do.

We dine at the Hanover Inn, in the impressive fireplace setting of its Daniel Webster (another New Hampshire man) Room. The dinner is accompanied not by the appropriate wines, but by beers. This is a new passion sweeping into the country from its northern edges, especially in places like the Northwest and New England, where forward-thinking beverage directors, hired from some of our best universities, have an open mind and knowledge about this new beer taste.

The Hanover Inn's beverage director, Richard Du Mez, provides the basic key for beer to wine conversions; on this basis the selections for dinner are made:

Pilsner	*Chardonnay*
Weisbier	*Champagne*
Porter	*Red Burgundy*
Octoberfest	*Cabernet Sauvignon or Brown Ale*

From among the 50 beer varieties available from the inn's bar we choose the following: Oldenberg (Kentucky)

Pilsner, perhaps the best of the micro-beer pilsners; Old Peculiar, a benchmark of legitimate English brown ale taste; Wicket Pete, a lusty micro from California; and Catamount's Octoberfest, the accompaniment for any spicy or deeply flavored meat.

At dinner the pilsner does behave like a good chardonnay. It goes with almost everything that we order for our first course. The cob-smoked ham comes from Gould's smokehouse in nearby Piermont, New Hampshire. Made from a leaner pig fed on milk bread, the meat defies any easy description. It is as mild and soft as veal. In their hard-cider butter the roasted Maine oysters are particularly pungent with pilsner, the smoked sea scallops deliciously subtle.

With the next course—native lamb with tandoori-oven pungencies, duck done in New Hampshire maple syrup, grilled tuna, and Jamaican seasoned swordfish—comes the heavier porter, Octoberfest, and brown ale. All of these entrées make strong cases for beer at the table.

It should be mentioned that there is a fine wine cellar at the inn (with more than 600 choices). A representative bottle opened to taste is a Corton, Clos du Roi, 1983. We try it along with the memories of the duck, which had been prepared in slices off the breast in the French manner, served with the leg and thigh sauced and cooked separately. The wine gives a cast of seriousness to the evening and sharpens up our critical faculties. Right away, the duck strikes a discord; still fat under the skin, it had been imperfectly rendered before serving.

After this, a sound sleep is a safe presumption in the four-poster acreage of the bed. The peace and quiet of the streets seeps up, and we are wrapped in dreams. The next day starts with breakfast of coffee and a good corn muffin (stone-ground cornmeal is used; the Hanover's muffins find favor among those who think muffins should not taste like cake). We lingered over a second cup beside the windows of the Daniel Webster Room overlooking the green.

Cruising the inns of New Hampshire to sample its foods, one should observe certain criteria: The inns must all be in very small towns; they should be set on a quiet green or its equivalent; they must have kitchens of repute; and all must date from the 18th century.

Follow Route 120 south out of Hanover to the signs to Interstate 89 south toward New London, New Hampshire, only about 25 miles away in the lap of Mt. Sunapee (skiers take note). The **New London Inn** adjoins the campus of Colby-Sawyer College.

NEW LONDON INN
Rte. 114 (S. Main St.)
New London, NH 03257
Tel. 603/526-2791

This is quite a different sort of inn from the one we have left. The sign over the door says 1792. The building stands on the main street as it starts to wend its way out of town. Painted white, it has a lovely old double veranda and is diagonally across from the campus of the small New England college. The inn's maintenance, however, seems far less than corporate, and the college remains aloof and stand-offish. If the Hanover Inn is a place for keeping appointments and dressing and going down to dinner and theater, the New London Inn is more like a temporary home, a place for kicking your shoes off and relaxing in deep cushions and wicker. There is the smell of mustiness, and an overlay of antiques placed without a nod to designers (pay special notice to the grandfather clock); a feeling of time past pervades it. You learn that the stump of belfry of the onetime college chapel is haunted. The trails of Mt. Sunapee State Park and its mile-long beach on the lake are only 12 miles away. Admission to the park is $1.50. Prices of the rooms at the inn are a bargain, too.

A dining room in upholstered green looks out on the green of the college. Meals became a respected commodity at the New London Inn after a young chef took it over some years ago. She has since departed for Washington, but her generous style still lingers.

Outstanding on Friday nights from June through October is the inn's "All You Can Eat Seafood Buffet." One price covers everything except what you drink. There are always four main seafood entrées. Selections typically include catfish, deep-fried or sautéed; grilled marlin from the nearby shores of Rhode Island; mako shark, from the same address; and fillet of flounder (some call it sole but *see* Chapter 1, The White Hart Inn). You can have as much as you like of each or just keep coming back for one.

Included also as part of the feast are 8 to 10 cold salads, potatoes (garlic whipped are often served), and seasonal vegetables; jumbo peel-and-eat shrimp and oysters on the half shell round out the choices from the deep. There are also prime ribs of beef if you prefer or if you don't like what swims. The price for all this is $15.95 per person, which makes it one of the great inn food bargains in New England (it is rumored that the price is about to jump, perhaps all the way to $19.50).

Not to be outdone in the arena of thespian arts, the New London Inn offers a dinner and theater package with the lovely New London Barn Playhouse only a few miles back up the road. For $25 you get dinner at the inn and a ticket into the barn (yes, it is) for a play, often from the Broadway musical repertoire.

Among other inducements for coming to this inn is Thanksgiving, the event of the year. November holds the seasons in suspension in New Hampshire. Although far from the riot of color that marks autumn, a few leaves still cling to the trees, and the air has yet to attain its wounding razor's edge. The season is celebrated by setting out the bounty of the harvest in a traditional New England Thanksgiving buffet. This is begun lightly with a grazing salad of greens, tomatoes, and mint vinaigrette; a few leaves of endive add snap. Then come candied ginger French fries (fries with a difference); there are also three different pastas to toy with before the hot pumpkin soup. Turkey appears with sausage and corn stuffing that is a surprise for the textures in the mouth as well as the taste, and it is accompanied by a cranberry conserve. The native squashes are excellent choices, for one is an old favorite (acorn) and one is stringy (spaghetti). There are also turnip gratin, a celery root purée, and sweetly sautéed snow peas. Desserts include pumpkin pie, of course, maple-walnut tart, and other goodies.

The everyday menu is also enticing: salmon prepared medium rare and served with a chive and salmon caviar butter; fresh duck breast smoked over applewood, with a rhubarb sauce. And yes, they do have a muffin for New London. Let me speak for the chocolate-chip: a different way to start the day with coffee. It is crunchy on the edges and smelling of chocolate inside. Decidedly for those who want to have their muffin and eat cake, too.

There is always a fire in the sitting room. For Christmas the tree is set up on the first of December, and snow is a foregone conclusion this far north.

Leaving the inn and New London and driving southward on Route 114 we drop down through tiny towns like Vernondale, no more than a twist in the road, and enter a pine and hemlock forest. There are more moose-crossing signs than houses. Turn west on U.S. 202 and Route 9.

At Hillsboro, home of Franklin Pierce, 14th president of the United States and another New Hampshire man, there are Yankee fast-food places in shacks along the road, but hold out for Hancock. To get there, follow U.S. 202 south just past Hillsboro and turn right when Route 123 joins 202.

Hancock is the prettiest town in New England. The first building you run into after miles of forest is the post office; the Hancock School is just across the way; the Congregational meeting house is to the left of the post office, and the three stand out in the bright triangle of clapboard buildings with green trim in the center of town.

About three doors down the street is the **John Hancock Inn**. Started and owned by the famous founding father in 1798, it has been in continuous operation ever since, making it a contender for the title of the oldest operating inn in the state, a title also claimed by the Hanover Inn, which asserts continuous operation since 1780.

JOHN HANCOCK INN
Main St.
Hancock, NH 03449
Tel. 603/525-3318

Hancock, the village and inn, is much smaller than Hanover. There are no boutiques. Across the way is the Hancock Market. After that, and the little library, you run out of town, but it is the most perfect living picture of an 18th-century community and inn you could want. Automobiles are the only anachronisms to keep us from believing that somewhere in the 6-mile crossover of deep woods from Route 9 a barrier was penetrated through which we went back in time two hundred years.

The John Hancock Inn and its haunts form an almost perfect record of the end of the 18th century. Arrive just after noon when the full sun is upon it. Is it green or gray? The nuances of its putty-color siding do not show up in pictures.

The little Hancock Market across the street looks very shoppable and friendly. The neat brick building housing the Hancock library seems inviting and conducive to study. Nevertheless, the smells coming across the inn's parking lot are more compelling. The aroma of cooking bacon wafting from the kitchen vent makes us wonder if there can be a chowder simmering.

There are candles (electric) in all the windows and in the two dining rooms. The inn has been restored to reflect

the age and time when John Hancock owned it.

The inside dining room hugging a fireplace is an 18th-century gem of Colonial Americana. Its walls are sponge-painted red above traditional blue wood paneling. The rug is red, the tables are rock maple polished to a New England innkeeper's pride. The back tearoom looks out on a green woods, a view shared with the outside dining room, which has comb-back chairs.

The experienced innkeepers are Linda and Joe Johnston, who have installed most of the building's architectural changes in the kitchen. Enormous, about the size of four bedrooms, it has plenty of space to move about, for a locker to hang and age meat, and for sous-chefs and sauciers to carry on their work.

Chef Jerry Willis, a former restaurant owner himself, now concentrates on cooking exclusively and lets others pay the bills while getting paid himself. The mammoth South Bend stove at the heart of his labors pours out waves and waves of heat. On it he brown-braises chuck roast (for juiciness) of beef, the first step in his Shaker Cranberry Pot Roast (*see* Chapter 4, Hancock Shaker Village), from a traditional Shaker recipe. The Shakers had a sweet tooth that went with their meats; their pot roast continues as a great local favorite.

The chef will also be preparing whole beef tenderloins, pork tenderloins, game, and rabbits. The smell of bacon did come from a chowder; we go into the dining room to taste what had tempted us inside in the first place.

A plate of seafood chowder in a white china bowl is set down on the rock-maple table. Wholesome and elegant, the chowder contains heaps of bite-size pink shrimp cast adrift with bay scallops; tender, almost old-fashioned potatoes; and bits of cod for another color and pungent taste note. A glass of house chardonnay—aside from Champagne (Möet & Chandon) the wine list is all American—hits the spot. The sticky bun, for dessert, is deep fried in maple syrup.

For dinner the chalkboard menu has further enticements. Immediately appealing seem the hunter-style venison, the cranberry pot roast, and the braised rabbit. Rabbit is seen plenty on the road but rarely on menus, and when we learn that the venison is Australian (*see* Chapter 1, Nodine's Smokehouse), we set our cap for the rabbit. It is a wild taste of native game after all, and braised is one of the best ways to do a young animal.

To say rabbit tastes like chicken is to be imprecise and do neither animal justice. Rabbit (high in protein, low in fat) is rarely taken advantage of in America. Just as there are many chicken tastes, so are there many rabbit tastes. A rabbit over 10 pounds is good for a stew, and one so good as rabbit can hardly be made from chicken. The taste is spicy, will hold wine and a few bay leaves, and the rabbit will be cooked till it falls from the bone and tastes just like what it is, game. When the younger and lighter animal is braised, the best part of all to eat is the neck. Some call it the necklace, for it extends in its vertebral column down its back. The local rabbit served here normally comes in quarters, like chicken or duck, but Willis, at your prompting, will prepare it the way he does for us: The forelegs and shoulders are cut away; the meat between the bones is the sweetest to be found at almost any table.

Between lunch and dinner you can take little Route 137 out of town to the village of Harrisville. You turn right at the sign that says East View and drive into the forest for about 5 miles. Go around the lake, turn right at the stop sign, and go to the top of the hill. There you will find a mill and a pond.

HARRISVILLE DESIGNS
Harrisville Weaving Center
Harrisville, NH 03450
Tel. 603/827–3996

The design center is in the loveliest old mill on a millpond you ever will see. People who search out the rare, the exquisite, and the old in the world should make tracks here. You can see it's off the beaten path, and that is perhaps why it remains the pristine marvel that it is.

The center's tradition in textiles goes back more than two centuries, and unlikely as it may seem, the brick building was a focal point of the Industrial Revolution as well as a major hub of world traffic in weaving and weavers. A weaving festival goes on here all summer, and woolens are sold all year long. Since 1972 the center has sponsored a series of weaving workshops that give students the opportunity to study with gifted instructors in the unique atmosphere of this special village.

Built originally as a storehouse for wool from locally raised sheep (a principal New Hampshire farm occupation through the 1700s), the renovated Harris warehouse now serves as the design center's studio. It occupies the precise center of the village on the edge of the millpond, bathing in the quiet reflections of summer and fall. For visitors there are things to see and feel and smell inside, especially the spun wool. Woolen yarn has been spun in Harrisville since 1790. Farmers originally sold the wool from sheep they had raised for meat to weavers, who spun it into yarn and turned it into products such as shirts and blankets. Eventually a factory was built to do all this, and so the Industrial Revolution came to small towns in New England, far from the industrial centers like Lowell, Massachusetts.

Next, wool-buying went west in the 1860s along with the farmers opening up the frontier under the Homestead Act. In the late 20th century things have turned around again: Sheep are back in New Hampshire and so is their wool. At the design center local artisans offer goods woven and knitted from local wool for sale among the looms and spinning wheels. Harrisville Design woolens sold in selected locations around the country serve notice that the little town is back as a major artistic force in weaving; its products are listed in the Smithsonian Institution's gift catalogue. What this shows is that the little hamlet is re-establishing its rightful place in its specialized and traditional field and that the terrain around it is filled not only with woods and sheep but with talented designers. The indications are that the creative surprises and explosions that are about to occur in New Hampshire will make it the Vermont of the 1990s.

Outside, the rest of the little town extends along its water courses. From here there is very little to stop for as the road tumbles toward Massachusetts besides odd old Mt. Monadnock.

Odd old Mt. Monadnock, completely burned on top at the beginning of the century and bald on its summit, is said to be the most-climbed mountain in the world after Fujiyama. It is the kind of mountain that at an elevation of 3,166 feet will make you sweat in the heat or warm you up in the cold. But if your children grow tired on the climb and they cry and complain, it is the sort of mountain where dads lift their kids up on their shoulders and continue to the top. It is exactly the sort of mountain and exercise to head for after a weekend of dining in the Live Free or Die state.

CHAPTER 8

OVENS AND WATER WINGS

New Haven, Providence, and the Islands

There are two things of unrivaled repute in New Haven: Yale and pizza. Of New Haven's pizza it can be truly said its reputation in America is deserved and unimpeachable. The Italian fifth of the city's population has given the pizza an especially long, unbroken recorded history here. Pizza has also worked itself up the taste chain of the nation to challenge the hamburger for the position of number-one American dish. New Haven has the pizza of record. "As good as New Haven pizza," is the saying all over New England as they hand out slices of anything from pastrami to bologna. Making not even a concession to Naples, New Havenites argue that their pizza is the best in the world. Until you have tasted the Great White Pizzas of New Haven, they say, you are no fit judge of pizza at all. So this is the interesting challenge posed for us in New Haven: to find its very best pizza (including the rare, and much-discussed, Great White), to chew it over, to analyze it, digest the results, and declare a New World winner.

After that, we'll go on for a dip on the beaches of Rhode Island, stop in at an unusual new oven, and maybe cast a line for some (blue) fish and chips on the islands off the coast.

HIGHLIGHTS:
- Pizza and man in New Haven
- Wooster Street — The Great Mozzarella White Way
- Highlights of Pepe's and Sally's
- Hamburgers: the place where Louis dwells
- The Mediterranean trail
- The white sands of Rhode Island
- High watch from an ocean palace
- An oven in Providence
- Martha's Vineyard — the sea surrounds us
- Nantucket sleigh rides and the warmth of winter
- Block Island — where the shores of Europe and America meet

LENGTH OF LOOP: 58 miles
LENGTH OF STAY: Two days

From the south, if you are not driving, take the train to New Haven. All the rental agencies are at the station. You've ducked out on 105 miles of not-so-easy driving, and you're on your way.

The center for pizza in New Haven is Wooster Street, the core of an old Italian neighborhood. It could be a village street in any small town, made up of a procession of blocks of neat two-family Victorian and frame houses, a children's playground, a sweetheart of a sweetshop (at No. 235), and several eating places. The most important of these are two pizzerias (restaurants where only pizza is served). They make pizza the old-fashioned, Neapolitan way. Pizza and the word for it came to America from Naples and the Neapolitan word *picea*.

Because of this heritage, all pizzas on Wooster Street are made in hand-built brick ovens that shoot temperatures up to 800° F and beyond. The hand-pounded dough bakes on the porous brick surface so fast it does not dry out. Heat blisters puff very thinly from the edges, which are not pounded so flat, and these are so delicious, blackened and smoked by the wood from the fires, that they are never left on the plate. The dough itself is fermented and deflated for as long as three days; the mozzarella is not thrown from plastic scraps but from whole curds prepared by the best Italian delis. The fillings are freshly and individually made, and the pies are baked under a golden drizzle of the most virgin of olive oils.

These pizzas are so good that people stand in line in the streets for them even though one of these restaurants can hold a hundred patrons at a time. They take no reservations, which is traditional with pizzerias, and it's first come, first served. On the weekends the wait can be up to an hour in the street; pizza aficionados who come up from New York City regularly consider the two-hour drive and the wait in the street easily worth the effort for such a bargain in taste.

Another thing you should know when ordering pie in New Haven: Ask. Do you want mushrooms or smoked bacon, for example? These, and some other ingredients, can produce a bath of their own fat or liquid if left to themselves, so they are cooked separately and then singed on top, so that you don't get their whole dose in excess, just their taste on a toasted, thin crust, cooked like a delicate wafer and smoky in flavor. You should tell your waiter how you want each detail done. Do you like bacon fatty or lean? Know what you want and say so, and it will be done to your order.

Drive past the Yale Bowl and down George's Street into New Haven; pass Coliseum, turn right on Chapel, left on Olive to Wooster, and then left again. Here is the Street That Pizza Built, and all the pizzerias are on the left as you drive in.

There are two equal and undisputed champions of pizza on Wooster Street, and what is said for one, except as noted, is generally good for the other.

PEPE'S PIZZA

157 Wooster St.
New Haven, CT 06511
Tel. 203/865–5762

Pepe's, the very first, has its origins in 1925; the original Wooster Street pizza house, it is the one from which the rest of them spring, including the new (1938), and very hot current number, **Sally's.**

SALLY'S PIZZA

237 Wooster St.
New Haven, CT 06511
Tel. 203/624–5271

Next door to Pepe's, add the **Spot,** which is owned by Pepe's restaurant and considered its "annex." The three have more or less the same ovens, and it was the same Italian immigrant who originated them all. Frank Pepe arrived in New Haven from Salerno in 1925. A baker by trade, he went to work for another baker. On his own time he made "tomato pies." Loading them on a horse-drawn wagon, he drove through the streets, selling the pies at 20¢ each. The pies were crushed tomatoes and grated Romano cheese on bread and nothing more, but they were good. Pepe saved his profits and bought a shop next to the bakery where he worked. He was a mason, too, and built his own brick oven: 9 feet by 18 feet, it stood over 6 feet tall. It was wood-and- coal-fired, and it sizzled pies at 800° F. The floor of a pizza oven must be brick (a porous material) to get the heat into the dough fast enough to cook it without drying it out.

Today as you walk down the four blocks of Wooster Street, Pepe's name is on two of the buildings, and his ovens are in three. His nephew Sal started Sally's; that place is still run by Sal's wife. The bakery next door to Pepe's, where

Pepe first worked, replicated his oven exactly and is now called the Spot. As if drawn by a magnet, other Italian food shops moved onto the street—big calzone and pastry operations clustered around Frank Pepe's. There is plenty of parking in Frank Pepe's big lot; license plates come from as far off as California, and parents and children all darkly resembling one another get out of cars and walk up to the restaurant as if they had appointments at a shrine.

Inside Pepe's the space is well organized. Booths line each side of a center aisle that wraps around a wall to a double file of more booths on the other side. On the left is a priceless and princely old oak bar with a long brass rail. The superb brick tile oven runs the entire width of the end of the room. Its cast iron shutters resemble black grates in a boiler in the belly of a great ocean liner. Pictures of Frank Pepe and his pizzas decorate the wall. The booths are numbered up through 30 or so; as soon as you sit down, a waitress appears to take your order.

Each day pies are usually available in two categories—red and white. If this is your first time on Wooster Street, and unless you are a glutton for tomatoes, you must order a white. Of these there probably will be several choices, including the original fresh clams or broccoli. Come in a party of four and order them both. The fresh clams are cherrystones from Rhode Island, opened fresh each morning. Baking softens them up. The cherrystone pie is the most brilliant pie on the street. It is like eating clams casino on toast.

The place is clean and brightly lit; all the workers wear white; the men who stand by the hot ovens ply the pie dough in white baseball caps. In the kitchen the tin ceiling is painted white; in the dining room it is painted mahogany. The long pizza paddles that deliver pie to and from the heat seem ancient enough to have rowed a slave galley. Romano cheese is still what they put on pizzas, 70 years after Frank did, unless you are stubborn enough to ask for Parmesan.

One way people get around the wait for a pizza is to call ahead and order a take-out. When the weather is right, people from the neighborhood stream through the line all night long, going to eat their pie in the park a block farther back along the street, where the kids play. You could do the same if you don't want to wait.

The pizza comes to the white-paper-covered table on a tin tray. Each person is given a knife and fork and a napkin but no plate. The first thing to do is take a slice of pizza in your hands. The cherrystones are under a thin yellow film of olive oil and the broccoli is like a relief map of Ireland oozing out of a field of velvet cheese. You never see broccoli come out as bright green as this unless you blanch it first.

The taste comes on totally unexpected and original. It is the subtlety and perfume that is such a surprise. First, there is the delicious scent of garlic floating on a flavor of the oil, but nothing is overpowering. You taste one, and then the other. There is a blend of broccoli with Romano and Parmesan cheeses, and the taste of the cherrystones is sweet. The platters turn 'round and the hands dip in. We have never tasted onions (we asked for them) cooked so well before. They are tender and pearly, tasting so subtly; nothing is wet or burned.

We ask ourselves, as you will, where we have tasted pizza as good as this before. For the crust it takes some deep digging into the memory: once, on the bus from Naples to Pompeii, for the crackle of the buttery fat bubbles on the edges; other times, in Paris, for the toasty crunch of its thinness, at the Casa Nostra on the rue des Belles Feuilles where they do a *feu de bois* (wood-burning fire). For the equal of New Haven pizza in America there seems to be no comparison. As for the clams, the broccoli, and the finesse of the rest, I cannot vouch for Naples. But when it comes to authentic pizza, here is the best in America, here is where a visiting Italian, brought to taste pizza, would be happy with the results.

Something else in New Haven to come for, as fresh and original as pizza in its own time, is the hamburger. The same city that gives us excellence and superior quality in what may be America's number one dish, was originally the site for the national dish that pizza now rivals. Hamburgers figure prominently in New Haven history and tradition: It is the place where hamburgers were invented. The very same grills at the very same site are still turning out examples of what became an American trademark and passion. Is it any wonder, then, that food lovers and the curious, historians as well as the hungry, still beat the same trail to the same door at **Louis Lunch**?

Louis Lunch
263 Crown St.
New Haven, CT 06510
Tel. 203/562–5507

It will do no good to reserve; it isn't done. Just call ahead to find out if they're open. Louis closes in the afternoon, and lunch is all they do; that's it. The city's historical society moved quickly to save the hamburger's birthplace when Louis' original location was menaced by urban renewal around 1970. The little building was picked up on wheels—cast-iron grills, walls, utensils, and all—and plunked down where it deserves to be, right in the center of the architecturally rich downtown. It's just around the corner from the revivified and beautified Shubert Theatre. The pre-Broadway-tryout landmark is yet another legitimate slice of American history; it rightfully bills itself as Birthplace of America's Greatest Hits. In this theater the scores of *Oklahoma!* and *South Pacific* were first played before paying audiences.

Louis itself is the cutest eatery you've ever seen, with its original leaded windows, wooden booths, and benches still intact. Crowds line up for their one offering: the original hamburger. Perhaps because Louis invented hamburgers, they still make them the same way; there is not a drop of catsup in the house. The burger itself, thick and charred, comes on crusty bread, not buns. Onion or cheese is the only garnish they will allow you at Louis. It is a true slice of history: New Haven at the turn of the century.

At the end of Wooster Street, stop in at **Frank and Mary's** (No. 102) if the car's got room for super subs; meatball

is recommended. The entrance for Interstate 95 looms before your eyes at the end of the block. Go right up the ramp in the direction of New London, and you're off to the bright, sandy beaches of Rhode Island.

I–95 is both a blight and a blessing: a blight because it obliterated the landscape along its right of way clear up to Boston, and a blessing because it shot the traffic forward and left a lovely shore in a vacuum. Here a necklace of white sandy beaches nestles like pearls in aqua waters. They remain secluded along Route 1A, seldom seen by strangers, staying remote and providing a rare respite on the coast.

Of these idyllic spots the best to visit are two: **Watch Hill** and **Misquamicut Beach,** Rhode Island. The latter is in

Misquamicut State Park (entrance on Route 1A in Westerly). Watch Hill is a Victorian seaside spa with uncommon views from its hill and a long sandy beach—a place to head for in summer. (Although Stonington is worth a look for its fishing port, Connecticut beaches are not outstanding. Trapped by the sandbar of Long Island, Connecticut beaches have murky waters and are frequently polluted.) In Rhode Island the ocean returns to its coast, and with it, thundering waves and cleansing surf.

It's not the ocean that brings most people to Watch Hill, though. The main attraction is higher up. On the promontory known as Watch Hill, commanding a view over tides, peninsula, sand, and dunes, is the old and delicious hotel known as **The Ocean House.**

THE OCEAN HOUSE
2 Bluff Ave.
Watch Hill, RI 02891
Tel. 401/348–8161

Opened just after the Civil War, The Ocean House is the last of a kind. It is a faded lady from a time when the brightest gems of America's elegance stood on the shore of Rhode Island. It was the kind of clapboard castle, much repeated in Victorian hotels and spas, that sprang up in forests and on lakefront sites where there had once been timbered forts. These hotels made a circuit for only the very rich to travel. Vacationers arrived on trains pulled by steam engines and were driven the final miles by horse and carriage. Now The Ocean House is more accessible to everyone; its clientele is no longer of the millionaire class. It is the romantics, writers, teachers, and others who will pay any fee—not to recapture perfection but to be close to its residue. The price paid is that where there was once elegance, there is now mildew, but The Ocean House is still a memorable place, cluttered with American ghosts and dreams.

There are cobwebs on the ceiling, the paint is peeling, the rugs are threadbare, and exposed pipes (fire sprinklers) run the length of the bedrooms. Returning guests find old fixtures in the bathrooms romantic. The beds creak; on a summer's night this can be romance, too.

Outside, the expansive decks bask in the sun. Inside, the dining is good in the restaurant. Roast leg of lamb, roast beef, roast fowl, and catch of the day from the sea are the generous choices. Potatoes and fresh vegetables are served on the side, and everything is under gravy, hearty and honest.

The Ocean House has gas stoves that stay lit during power failures; this is a place where hurricanes come. In case of storms, gas generators take over; the telephones always work. In times like these the villagers from the shore come up the hill to where the waters cannot reach; Tiffany globe lights are set out for dinner (there is never an open flame), and every guest gets a flashlight for the walk back to the rooms.

At night the wind blows through the cupola on the roof. The awful thought comes as you listen that places like this are anachronisms. One by one they are disappearing and cannot be replaced. The opportunity to know The Ocean House while it lasts is a privilege for which lovers of poetry in places, and certainly wood, should still apply.

For recreation it is just a little walk down the hill to the oldest carousel in America (The Flying Horses) and the gingerbread section of boutiques in the town of Watch Hill. Down a narrow spit of land with a bird sanctuary to one side is Watch Hill Beach, a real, foamy ocean beach with ribbons of aqua breakers and hissing surf. Try it, for it is as good as anything on Cape Cod.

As the license plates indicate farther east along Route 1A, which follows the spit of sand and pine barrens,

Misquamicut Beach is relatively free of vacationers but busy with locals. It runs on for miles, interconnected with others, enormously wide, seeming to offer room for everyone.

Beyond Misquamicut, no part of the small state of Rhode Island is very far from another. Nevertheless, should we aim for the bright seas, mausoleum glories, and onetime America's Cup site of Newport, a name that still conjures up images of its rich past, or strike out for other, more contemporary parts?

You can go to Newport if you want. It does take time, but it is not far. The millionaires' mansions, such as the Vanderbilts', abound by the sea, and there are still yachts worth millions in the marinas. Nearby are endless tracts of trendy restaurants, all with porches and patios, indifferent pastas, and nice salads of arugula (but by the time you read this the switch could be on to mesclun).

The food capital of Rhode Island, however, is Providence. George Germon and Johanne Killeen have made it so. Their restaurant is **Al Forno.** After six years it has become as hot as its name.

AL FORNO
577 S. Main St.
Providence, RI 02903
Tel. 401/273–9760

From the coast, take Route 195 to Exit 2. Bear right as you go through the lights at the foot of the ramp, and the way will lead to South Main Street. The restaurant stands alongside the shops of a reconfigured tire factory, which also played a role in the renaissance of the city. There is parking around the corner and in the rear for Al Forno.

You never know what is going to happen when you walk into a restaurant you've never been in before on a food adventure. At Al Forno they don't take reservations; it's first come, first served, and come as you are. Al Forno started out a Provençal and Italian restaurant. After taking just the first few steps in its development, however, it decided to drop the Italian part of the menu and go with the Provençal, ending up as a Provençal restaurant with an Italian name.

There is a philosophy in Provence for cooking meats. Many things—feed, grasses, breed of animal—put flavor in the flesh. One of them, however, is often neglected in this country and rarely even mentioned: Fire carries flavor. The source of the flame also puts taste in food. If you start with hardwood charcoal (as they often do in countless little bistros with brick ovens that glow in the night on the hillsides of Provence), you are putting the taste of the tree into food.

Meats—game, fowl, and fish too—cooked this way come from the *forno* (*four* in French: "oven" in English) frequently sauceless. There is a crackling of skin or charcoal or both that makes for a delightful seasoning, and then all the herbs in the world are mounded on top. Wild thyme, tarragon, rosemary, and oregano are the staples. This makes for a very healthy and delicious diet. Some of the oldest people in the world live in Provence, and this is why.

Cooking over hardwood fires would be an original food formula, a diet, so to speak, and nothing more, had it not developed in an especially fragrant and unique part of the world where diet is only considered after it has satisfied the condition of flavor and then is easy to stick to and live by. This formula and spirit have been captured at Al Forno. (For styles of Provence, *see also* Chapter 10, Olives, as well as Chapter 2, The West Street Grill.)

Here chicken is split down the middle, grilled over the coals, and buried in herbs. Lamb and beef are done in much the same way. Naturally most of the fat drips off onto the coals; what you are left with is the taste of the meat, the wood, and the greens. There are three ovens at Al Forno, all the personal creation of George Germon. They conform with the demands made by Provençal cooking for heat; a fireplace provides for warmth of atmosphere in a room made of stone. The bricks are both firebrick (smooth) and non-firebrick (porous) to handle different kinds of cooking and baking. Diners usually start with a pizza for the table. It is thrown free-form directly on porous bricks and crisped at 800° F. Veal tenderloin, about 5 inches long and 1½ inches thick, is grilled over the coals and then sliced into pieces and served

OLIVES

with a rosemary apple sauce over grilled polenta. It is infused with the taste of rosemary. There is also what is listed as Dirty Steak, so called because it is simply dropped on the coals. Duck is first grilled, then glazed to a light mahogany shine with caramel. The crackle of its skin is of unexcelled sweetness. Grilled radicchio arrives with mozzarella from an Italian supplier across town (you will hear more about him later). Johanne Killeen pays special attention to details like her cheese and the olive oil that is drizzled on the cheese, to be sure that no part of it is grapeseed oil (*see* Chapter 10, the Ritz-Carlton cooking school).

Potatoes roasted in the oven go mostly with fish: floun-der, fluke, blackfish (*see* Chapter 9) hand-picked live by Johanne and George from their seafood supplier. As in

Provence, seafood is no stranger to the larder. The littleneck clams Al Forno must be tried without fail; they are fresh, baked in the oven with tomatoes and white wine and garlic.

The ice cream is homemade and hand-cranked. The chocolate truffles are also made in-house, as are individual chocolate and hazelnut cakes, called baby cakes; but you must leave room for the Grande Cookie Finale. This is six kinds of cookies, all hot from the oven and baked to instant order. They are warm and exquisite in the mouth.

Ricotta fritters follow.

Provence is only part of what figures in the Mediterranean scheme of the city: A slice of the Italian hill towns is only a drive away across the hills of Providence. You approach along Atwells Avenue. Your arrival in the Federal Hill neighborhood (Providence's Little Italy) is signaled by a great metal arch that vaults over your head and the road. Cars are never any good in hill towns unless they're Fiat 500s, so it is wise to park what you drive. No matter where you turn, you won't have far to go.

In this Little Italy the streets are paved in brick; old-world lanterns light squares where the cool of fountains soaks the air in summer. People pass in and out of cafés and shops, occupied almost exclusively with the business of buying food. Inside the arch, at 134 Atwells, is the restaurant known as the **Arch** (tel. 401/357–8822). Most of Providence's Italians, who came to this country in the early part of this century (like most Italians in America), came from southern Italy. Although the streets of Federal Hill could be from a sketchbook of Umbria (northern Italy), the menu is strictly southern. Featured here, and throughout Federal Hill, is traditional southern fare such as veal parmigiana, eggplant in the same style, a variety of antipasti, and so on. Many of the cafés set their tables outside by the fountains in summer; the street is a shopping and dropping-in place offering food items almost exclusively for immediate consumption and to take home.

Shops spin out fresh pastas, Italian butchers offer pounded Italian cuts, and Italian groceries scent the air with cheeses and hanging spiced meats (Al Forno's mozzarella supplier, **Tony's Colonial Food Store,** is at 311 Atwells) and tempt you with glorious creams and custard creations to eat as you walk. **Caserta's Pizzeria** (tel. 401/272–3618) is around the corner at 121 Spruce Street; it's a place everyone born in Rhode Island has heard about and comes to. Heat from the oven and fragrances of oregano and leavening dough waft from its open doors. Caserta's has the reputation of making the best pizza in Rhode Island. Should you choose to compare it with Pepe's of New Haven, always remember that the slice in hand will compare favorably with the one you can only remember.

In every city with an Italian section there is a **Blue Grotto** restaurant. Federal Hill is no exception, and theirs is at 210 Atwells (tel. 401/272–9030). This is a delightful, formal place with little round tables in dim, romantic lighting; the waiters are in black tie, the use of marble is lavish, and the veal, scampi, calamari, and salads are a celebration of Capri—light and summery. In case you are in shorts and a T-shirt or have simpler cravings, there are all sorts of simpler restaurants. The best of these is **Angelo's Civita Farnese Restaurant** (tel. 401/621–8171) at 141 Atwells. Here is the place for homemade pastas, instantly served, and real Italian home cooking, where the waiters all wear smiles and soiled aprons and the wine flows like the water from fountains. Then, for dessert, you must stop in at **Pastiche** (tel. 401/861–5190), at 92 Spruce Street, especially if you are partial to chocolate and a good coffee to match.

Now there are only a few miles (35) to go down Route 95 to Route 4, then to U.S. 1 to get to the coast. From here you reach the islands: Nantucket, Martha's Vineyard, and Block Island, similar in topography, if not in size, have been given over almost entirely to the benefits of the sea and its produce by people who have come out to visit or live on them since their discovery by the first Europeans. The produce of their fisheries, which are contiguous to and resemble those of Cape Cod Bay and the Atlantic, is covered in the chapter on Cape Cod (*see* Chapter 9, *below*).

Ferries link the cape with all three islands, but Block Island is also accessible from Point Judith, Rhode Island. Before getting on a boat to go, however, you might reflect on what you are seeking. The three islands are wonderfully diverse in mood and style.

Nantucket Island is small, with two towns, Nantucket and Siasconset; in summer it is a noisy, honking place, and if you come by car you must have a reservation to get your car on the ferry. Beaches are crowded, guest houses overflow, and the native population often barricades itself from a tourist population that in some summers outnumbers them by 100 to 1. People with porches plant themselves in their rockers and read their papers, ignoring the crowds as they go by from the ferry gawking as if the readers were exhibits in a theme park.

Still, there is good reason why so many come. The streets of Nantucket are picture-perfect and quaint. The island is blessed with a balmy climate bright with warming sun and bathed by delicious breezes from the sea. The beaches lie like golden wreaths around a dramatic shoreline.

For quite some time a century or so back, Nantucket was the absolute hub of the world whaling industry. Although the planet and its attitudes toward whaling have changed a great deal since then, the island has not, and the battering sensation of being in a little boat propelled by the fury of a harpooned whale is still called a "Nantucket Sleigh

Ride." (Not that its people these days would do anything so unfriendly to a whale.) Many of the homes of Nantucket are in the Greek Revival style favored by the whaling captains who went across the sea and brought back chests of innumerable odds and ends, such as a door or a copper mantel for the fireplace. Finally, in old age, the captains pulled their families up around their ears and went to sleep.

Nantucket has become, all over again, a place of retirement. Noisy in summer, it is one of the best places on the East Coast in winter, and here increasing numbers of senior New Englanders come to buy year-round homes. The December air is comparatively mild (because of the Gulf Stream), but the streets are lightly covered with snow, the community is close-knit, and it is in winter especially that the visions of old Nantucket come back from the past intact. Winter is the right time to see it. Residents scurry about to activities in the local churches and clubs, lectures in the libraries, or concerts in the schools. Art gallery cocktail parties draw residents and visitors, new arrivals are warmly received, and inhabitants like to say they are glad they didn't move south.

The **William Hadwen House** (96 Main St., tel. 508/228–1894) is a good place to start sampling this true Nantucket atmosphere and style. Straightforward examples of the hodgepodge that Greek Revival architecture had become by the mid-19th century, Hadwen House and its next-door neighbor are collectively called the two Greeks. The Hadwen House is a virtual museum in itself of Revival appointments such as the white columned portico, the circular staircase, marble fireplace mantels, and the cushioned opulence of Victorian furnishings.

Directly across the street, the Starbuck houses represent the wealth that came from whaling. Joseph Starbuck (notice the similarity with the name of Ahab's first mate in *Moby Dick*) built the three brick homes for his sons from the profits

he acquired through whaling; these mansions are known as
the **Three Bricks.**

For a look at what villagers and visitors enjoy together,
the months of November and December crackle with a cav-
alcade of warm, spirited events that crescendo at Christmas.
There are lists five pages long of weekend receptions. Several
are hosted by the Artists Association of Nantucket. The
Little Gallery at the foot of Straight Wharf, where the sea
comes in to touch the town, bustles with cocktails and

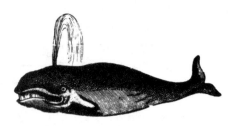

cheeses, and no more charming a place to view paintings
could exist. Evening openings are accompanied by refresh-
ments, and this is where you can take your first course before
dinner. *A Christmas Carol* is presented by the Theatre
Workshop of Nantucket at Bennett Hall on Centre Street.
Franklin Alive!, is a one-man tour de force put on at the
Unitarian Church on Orange Street that always draws an
audience, and there is a re-created Victorian magic lantern
show at the Harbor House on South Beach Street. More
moving still for Christmas spirit is Dylan Thomas's *A Child's
Christmas in Wales,* given in dramatic reading at the
Nantucket Athenaeum (the library) on India Street.

The **Whaling Museum** (tel. 508/228–1736) on Broad
Street is set in an actual spermaceti oil refinery. It includes

whale skeletons and scrimshaw, and its guided tour is salted with real live seafaring talk. It stays open until 4 PM in the Christmas season seven days a week. One-hour seal cruises (on board *The Anna W. II,* Slip No. 12, Straight Wharf) in the waters around Nantucket Harbor, with a Nantucket captain/naturalist, from November to April, offer the chance to get a moving deck under your feet for about as long as you will want.

On the first Saturday in December a Food Bazaar (11 AM to the dinner hour or whenever they finish up), with hot and cold selections, features the proverbial soup to nuts and more under a tent at the bottom of Main Street in a supermarket parking lot. You walk into the tent, take what you want, and pay what they ask, for Italian sausage, peppers and onions, clam and quahog fritters, Portuguese sausages, a host of chowders, hot soups and stews, bay scallop rolls (get several of those), chicken and steak, lobster bisque, steamship rounds (you point, they cut) of hot roast turkey and baked ham. For dessert there are cookies, brownies, and hot tarte chèvre. Just like that, you have tasted the best home cooking on the island.

On the second weekend in December the residential door decorating contest, with a grand prize, is a good excuse for residents to go around visiting one another.

But there is more; the artists and painters of Nantucket are no slouches either. Try the pot luck dinner and lecture at their **Studio Barn** (23 Wauwinet Rd.). Still another potluck is served by one of the island's brightest caterers at the **Unitarian Church** (Orange St.).

There are tree-lighting ceremonies, community sings, vocal quintets, and chamber music concerts, but the most festive and musical event of all is the great Christmas Stroll, on the first Saturday in December. This is just what it sounds like and is reason in itself to come to Nantucket in winter. The Nantucket Chamber Music Carolers parade through the town singing. They appear at prearranged and scheduled spots where crowds gather to hear them; sometimes they parade to their next stop, trailing their audience behind them through the streets in a tableau of an old English Christmas. The Community Bell Choir performs on a snowy Main Street stage. The Brass Ensemble also pops up on corners. They, too, are scheduled, but sometimes it's quite startling. They pump up a chorus or two, then move on to pop up and pump away elsewhere.

This is only a partial listing of the events you will find going on in Nantucket from Thanksgiving to Christmas day and beyond. For a more complete list, as well as for the aftermath, contact the **Nantucket Chamber of Commerce** (Main St., Nantucket, MA 02554, tel. 508/228–1700). For accommodations, the **Jared Coffin House** (29 Broad St., tel. 508/228–2405) is a Greek Revival home you can be very comfortable in yourself. It has slices of history throughout as well as apple pie.

There is no more whaling trade on Nantucket, but fishermen now come in all winter long at Children's Beach laden with what the island has become known for: scallops. These shellfish are some of the most sought after in the world; try to get scallops from the sea, with the roe on, if you can. The sticks of roe that look like little Havana cigars and are treated like gold in most of the world come right from here. Often they are discarded by chefs and fishermen because Americans throw them away, but try them, if you find them, under a light cream sauce served next to the scallops.

Get bay scallops also at the Nantucket restaurants that are open when these smaller and sweeter scallops run. They are proof that what you eat is from local waters, because most of the fresh fish and bay scallop catch taken starting in late fall is known and appreciated by local Nantucketers. It keeps them coming through the doors of their restaurants in hard times and even in winter.

The Sea Grill (Sparks Ave., tel. 508/325–5700) is a big, white family-style restaurant that features catch of the day. Bluefish start their runs in September/October; tourists won't touch them, but you should. They're a favorite with locals and visiting Europeans who savor the oily freshness that evokes the oysters of Brittany. Of shellfish there are the aforementioned scallops from the bay, fresh and brimming with brine all winter long.

The Beach Plum (9 West Creek Rd., tel. 508/228–8893) started out as a simple bakery and grew to fill a need for a small but pleasant place with food that is simple to order and eat and yet full of surprises. The small café has wood tables, towels for napkins, and moderate prices, too. The pasta (ravioli with chutney, for example) is typical of the surprises, but it is for what swims in the bay and the sea that we come. Nantucket bay scallops, smaller, sweeter, and roeless, are the order of the day and night in winter. They are served in numerous ways, but the Jamaican, and the fresh lime and butter sauces are stunning. Flounder in many of its fresh winter faces and fleshes also greets the diner, as do Atlantic salmon, tuna and swordfish, halibut and yellowtail—this last is sautéed and served with pasta. The big sea scallops and their cigar roe are a treat that comes only in summer.

Five miles off Cape Cod's southern coast, and a little less accessible to its summer weekend crowds, is **Martha's Vineyard.** This is a place where the laid-back come to lie back. There is a list of retiring celebrities who shed their performers' personas while here. They don't want to run into the neighbors, and on Martha's Vineyard, much larger than Nantucket, they don't. The Vineyard is a place of prodigious private parties (you've heard of the Kennedys?), narrow bridges, watery impoundments, varied terrain of scrub oak, pitch pine, pastures, old fashioned roses, ponds, and woods.

This was the part of the coastline that, seeing the wild American grape growing, Leif Erikson named Vineland. At the beginning of the 17th century, a passing European voyager saw the same thing and named it for his daughter.

Martha's Vineyard is a place of house parties; there are few cheap restaurants on an island where very little is cheap and no lobster pounds as these are known in Maine (*see* Chapter 12). From a food point of view, easily the most interesting place on the island is the tiny town of Menemsha. Sitting three miles from the western end of the island, the little lobster fishing village and port is among New England's most picturesque and unspoiled. When its fishing fleet comes home with the evening tide, the decks of the boats are laden with lobsters and traps. There are fish markets on the pier (try **Larson's,** tel. 508/645–2680; or **Poole's,** tel. 508/645–2282) that sell the crustaceans live or steamed to take home or on a picnic. Lobster rolls (*see* Chapter 12)—and these must be tried—are available at a shack down by the pier, but the restaurant for lobster is **Home Port** (at the foot of the pier, tel. 508/645–2679). Big and immensely popular, it also offers catch of the day in fish and other seafood. With its clear view to the west over the water, it is a great place to watch the sunset.

In Vineyard Haven the **Black Dog** (Beach St., tel. 508/693–9223) is a restaurant chosen by islanders themselves. It perches overlooking the water, and the favored tables are on the porch. Everything is island fresh, caught by islanders and bought on the island. Eating here is like eating in a private house. West Tisbury oysters and swordfish are offered, bugs (what lobsters are called here) are usually handy, and there is tuna and cod (either baked or poached and seasoned in a mustard sauce). Salmon is said to be wild; now and then there is bouillabaisse, as well as steamers and littleneck clams. You are free to bring your own bottle of wine, which does cut down on the cost.

Then there is **Block Island**—a place of which everyone
has heard but whose location hardly anyone knows. Block
Island is the island for people who used to go to Nantucket
before the crowds came. In summer Block Island is like
Nantucket in winter. Calm. You can walk up a meadow road
from the Surf Hotel to a fishing bait shack on the other side
of the hill, buy a few lures and a bucket of squid for bait,
haul it all back down the hill, and never see a car. Except in
the port, hardly anyone wears shoes.

At the harbor a few grand old wooden hotels face the
strand and dinghies are parked on the sand—it is like a
scene from an old flickering Robert Flaherty documentary of
Ireland.

The best-situated hotel is the **National,** which has a
long porch facing the shore where the fishermen beach their
boats and stroll up for drinks. It is a fine place for drinks, but
not so fine for food. The staff makes you wait too long and
then acts like you're disturbing them if you nudge them.
Everything worked fine here just a few years ago, but then
one of the partners left, and he was the one who made the
place go. Just around the corner to the left is the **Surf Hotel**
(Block Island, RI 02870, tel. 401/466–2241; closed mid-
Oct.–late May), a bed-and-breakfast where most of the Block
Island fishermen who park their boats down on the tide now
go. They beach their boats for the night and then are out on
the first tide looking for blues. The rooms are cozy and
upholstered in look; beds are a deep comfort in themselves.
The bathrooms are shared but clean and well cared for.

For lunch or dinner you will enjoy eating at **The
Ballards** (tel. 401/466–2231; closed Oct.–mid-May). The little
restaurant straddles a small spit of sand that is mostly swad-
dled by rippling tides. Out back is a little family beach, where
there's usually someone to watch the kids romp while you
eat. The tables are covered with atmosphere and oilcloth. A
few rooms can be rented upstairs. An array of flags flutters in

bright colors against the blue sky. At night there is music and dancing; many who know the place come here to get married. The tuna is yellowfin, grilled to the right turn and delicious. It comes with potato salad on the side. The lobster is trapped out here and served for two or four in portions that come in huge stainless-steel bowls. There is good chowder too; if every place on this earth were as good as The Ballards, everyone would go home from a few days of vacation filled with sweet dreams and contentment.

Block Island is a great place to explore on foot or bike; there is a beach with character for everyone, including some at the foot of great cliffs that loom up from the sea. On the tops of these are flat moors thick with hunting birds and fields of wildflowers. The restaurant with the greatest view over all of this, if you need a deck to sit on and a drink in your hand, is the **Spring House Hotel,** an ideal place to stay for comfort and service.

SPRING HOUSE HOTEL

Box 902
Block Island, RI 02807
Tel. 800/234–9263
Closed mid-Oct.–May

The Spring House is elegant and makes you feel like a movie star. The porches that surround the rectangular Victorian wood building make it an ideal spot for dining on the veranda and watching the sun go down. Food is presented with the sweep and panache of the best Continental hotels. The waiters and waitresses are 30 young students from Ireland with Metro-Goldwyn-Mayer brogues, and it's all that John Ford could ask. They start you off with pâté or a terrine that is green and spicy, either of which goes well with the Napa Ridge chardonnay. Scallops are served under a light herb sauce, and there are delightful pastas with pestos that tickle your nose and tempt the palate. The swordfish at the Spring House is always locally caught. It is often baked in milk to hold the flavor and keep it from drying out; it is usually finished with horseradish mustard, a great English and New England favorite. In the Victorian lounge you can retire to marble cream cheesecake or Irish cream cheesecake. If you come to Block Island, it would be a shame to miss either. Like the service, they are elegant.

CHAPTER 9

BLUEFISH, BERRIES, BEACHES, AND WHALES

Cape Cod

Of all the places along the East Coast where you can go down to the sea, test the waters, and eat the things that swim and bump along the bottom, there is no match for the kingdom of the sea on Cape Cod.

There are three kinds of water to swim in—the sea, the bay, and the sound. Four major kinds of fish are brought to its wharfs: striped bass, blackfish, fluke, and cod. All sorts of restaurants—better call them eating places—are on hand to serve them up, from six-stool raw bars (for oysters and clams) to silver-sided epiphanies of gables and clapboard resting on sand in their boxwood shade. Along 300 miles of carefully preserved shoreline the sand is so fine it blows from dunes that look like sugar hills. There are town streets where you can feast an antiquarian's eye. In old captain's cottages you can sleep in a dormer with a curtain over the sea beside you while the cry of the gull serenades your ear; you creak downstairs on an oak stairway into a breakfast room where the blueberry muffins and creamery butter are the same as those served on the Cape since the 18th century. In some places the fleet still comes in at 4 PM; you can walk down the planks of the dock and buy what pleases you— most particularly those great big, oily, oceangoing fish: striped bass, blackfish, fluke, and cod. Oh my.

HIGHLIGHTS:

- Dining in the 17th century: Thanksgiving at Plimoth Plantation
- Fruit on the vine and a cranberry tale
- The wise policy of honey and bees
- A walk in the wild bog
- Blueberries and roses
- Three kinds of water to swim in
- Blackfish and cod
- Fishing and the settling of America
- Quahogs and sundowns
- The pools of life
- The tables of Cape Cod
- Ship-to-shore swordfish
- The least and the most of the sea

LENGTH OF LOOP: 75 miles

LENGTH OF STAY: Three days

If at all possible, a good way to go is with a car that you can leave off at Provincetown, where there are rental agencies, thereby opening up the pleasures of an oceangoing return to Boston.

Before you zip across the Sagamore Bridge onto the Cape, you can experience how and what the Pilgrims ate at **Plimoth** (Governor Bradford's own spelling) **Plantation.** Two and a half miles south of Plymouth Rock itself is a reconstruction of the original Pilgrim settlement.

A stout timber palisade surrounds a huddle of wood-frame dwellings, each housing a pilgrim family. Behind the houses are kitchen gardens. Outside the stockade common fields are tilled to produce crops like those the colonists grew for export to Great Britain.

Anytime you visit, it is that day in the year 1627. Ringed within its half-mile of timber stockade, the plantation is a monument to Yankee ingenuity and craft. Here were a

people who stepped fresh off a boat from England, found a land they didn't own, and took it, found a plant they had never seen before (the cranberry), named it for a bird that didn't fly there (the crane), and made a juice that was too sour to drink. From this they made a fortune. They also invented Thanksgiving, for which they supplied the sauce that became indispensable for the feast. No matter what you think of the Pilgrims, and no matter how you spell their settlement, Plymouth is a starting point of both European history and European food in America.

The Plantation employs not one, but two food historians. Traditional Colonial recipes for bread, sauces, entrées, puddings, and desserts are researched, tested, and served. In the quaint wooden houses and other structures behind the timbered stockade, the serious work of the reconstruction of meals of Colonial America goes on. Meals were one of the few pleasures of this world permitted to the Puritans. We know how they were starved for the others, which might not have been possible to endure had they not had the pleasures of the palate to fall back on.

After you've entered the compound inside the wooden stockade, with working carpenters, baking kitchens, running chickens, and Puritan kids at play; and have been aboard the *Mayflower* replica in the bay, talked with actors playing at colonists, and been peppered with 17th-century speech, get set to take a real bite out of history.

Remember, however, the Puritans dine at noon.

Several kinds of meals are served in the atmosphere of American discovery: Most of the produce used for daily household cooking demonstrations, which go on under each roof, is raised on the settlement, with crops such as corn, barley for bread, and ripe pumpkins in season.

In spring, Easter feasts are presented; Mother's Day is marked with lunches and dinners. There are escorted herb walks, kitchen demonstrations on Colonial methods of making sweetmeats and of using flowers, leaves, peels, and roots. Jam and jelly workshops are good in summer; bring your own apron and come away with jars of strawberry and rhubarb jam. In the English hearth cooking class you can learn how to prepare a roast or a soup on the fires you'd keep going all winter. You also learn what woods should be used for what flavorings. In New England, definitely try sugar maple.

The high enjoyment season for dining arrives today just as it did for the Puritans, during the harvest. In the months of October and November, when food is most plentiful on the plantation, the Harvest Feasts are on. Separate dinners mark the harvest and Thanksgiving. They are 17th-century or Victorian (Thanksgiving) in style, and are

served in a festive banquet hall spruced up for the events
with wreaths, antique tapestries, flowers, and a fire roaring
in the hearth. For the Victorian feasts there is a chef in a high
toque blanche (white chef's hat) standing at a groaning board
under pineapple chandeliers.

As the preparation of meals for the village is a part of
its daily routine, you can get close to a particular Pilgrim and
ask all the questions you want. The day begins with each
housewife coming out of her one-room frame house and

walking up the grassy mall to get a food basket (prepared
under the supervision of a food historian) from the storehouse at the end of the block. Tucking it decoratively under
her arm, Mrs. Puritan then proceeds back down the green to
her home. As the Puritans' main meal came at noon, she usually begins directly to prepare the food, and you are invited to
join her as she enters her home and puts on an apron. You
can ask her questions or just watch, as you wish.

In the basket could be a choice variety of historical
foods. To start with, there's a nice cod; after all, they don't
call it Cape Cod for nothing. The waters of Cape Cod were
so rich and teeming with life in 1627 that it is today estimated
that two men fishing a single morning could bring in enough
fish to feed the whole town.

Aside from cod (the codfish took to salting very well, and this is why they were favored in 17th-century Europe) there are bluefish, blackfish, clams, and mussels to fill out the daily larder from the sea. These last were frequently served in this interesting and now forgotten way: They were "seethed," as one recipe at the Plantation puts it—that is, very slowly simmered in beer. The mussels were often served with boiled salad. Vegetables, on the whole, were frequently served as broths and soups; here the lettuce is boiled, like cabbage, and it goes so well with "seethed mussels" that both make a contact with our past worth reviving.

Curd cheese fritters are tasty in a modern fast-food way. The curd of the cheese (ricotta could be used) is fried, like a pancake, in oil. What kind of oil did Mother Pilgrim use? Why, it was olive oil, imported in barrels from Italy by way of England. (There were only three milking cows in the colony, so no butter was available for frying.) These early colonists were more Italian or Provençal in their cooking techniques than later Americans became. Herbs and spices were in much greater use then than now. Meats were stewed with marjoram and thyme or roasted with mustard seed (as is still done in France). Grains were prepared as breads or pancakes, and sweet and savory puddings were popular.

The **J. Barnes Plantation Bake Shop** on the grounds makes it evident that there was far more to Colonial baking than mere cornbread and pumpkin pie. The almond cakes, which have a light and airy finesse, are made the 17th-century way, with a grind of nuts, sugar, egg whites, a touch of rose water, and nothing more. Our beloved cheesecake, considered so modern and tracing its roots to New York, actually is from an English recipe that was finally published in 1671. Most of the sources of these recipes are books such as *The English Housewife* by Gervase Markham (1615, London), and Thomas Dawson's *The Good Housewife's Jewel* (1597, London).

The individual gardens that back up each house were supposed to suffice for the colony's needs. The greater outer fields full of corn and tobacco (an instant export commodity), provided the barter that was essential for overseas shipment to England to pay for imports like hoes, hatchets, and Italian olive oil. Turkeys were sent back live on boats (or else how could Gervase Markham have provided us with a turkey recipe as early as 1623?).

Of agriculture as a just and efficacious pathway to riches, the opinion of America was fixed in the voice of Charles Pinckney of South Carolina during the Constitutional debates at the close of the 18th century: There were three pathways a nation could choose to acquire wealth, he said. One was the Roman way of conquest, which was obviously "robbery." The second way was that of commerce, which was "generally cheating." Lastly there was the way of agriculture, "the only honest way, wherein a man receives a real increase of the seed thrown into the ground, in a kind of a continual miracle wrought by the hand of God." Then as today, to those who till the soil the increase is no accident; it is a miracle.

Before venturing out into the 300 miles of Cape Cod's sandy beaches, you first need to plant a foot in the bogs. The cranberry bogs of southern Massachusetts are responsible for half of the national crop of that berry and the establishment of a food company that is intimately linked to the local environment and its history. This small red fruit, so well known on American tables come the end of every November, is, in the picturesque setting of the tidal bogs where it is found, a highly profitable cash crop. Were you a berry rancher, you would forget all about blueberries, strawberries, and even grapes. You would lick your lips over the profits accrued from cranberries. These are the most lucrative berries in America. (Prices in 1992 averaged $1,200 per ton. This compares to $1,100 for North Coast, California, chardonnay grapes.) The Ocean Spray Company, founded on this single fruit and located in the heart of the cranberry bogs, has created a visitors center to inform the public on cranberry use. Last year its **Cranberry World** played to 350,000 guests, who were also plied with juices and cranberry cake.

CRANBERRY WORLD

Ocean Spray
225 Water St.
Plymouth, MA 02360
Tel. 508/946–1000

The first thing to know about Ocean Spray is that it is not a food company like all the others. In 1930 America was in the teeth of the Great Depression. People were selling apples on the street, and the bottom had fallen out of cranberries. Farmers couldn't get a fair return on their labor-intensive (as you will see) crop and, as farmers were doing all over the world, they looked for a financial solution that would leave them in control of their lands. Like many other farmers in the fourth decade of the 20th century, they formed a cooperative. The worldwide depression had inspired farmers in Champagne, in France, to do the same. Cranberries are a fruit that grows on the vine, and a marketing solution similar to that used for grapes worked for them as well: to sell the juice from the fruit.

From a shaky sauce company a new and more viable business opened up for the three cranberry farmers who had created the co-op. As the co-op took off, in the 1930s other farmers hurried to join, and the small concern became the Ocean Spray Company.

There were other, subtle parallels to the old-world marketing of juices from the vine. On its own, the juice of cranberries was more than just tart to the taste; some people found it bitter. So from the production of other vine juices (grapes) it was learned that in other places (Champagne) the juice of several varieties of grape could be blended together to ameliorate a deficient taste and make the final one more pleasing than any of its individual parts (this is the story in Bordeaux, too). In this way the juice of other fruits was blended with that of cranberries to make a juice that had a sweet yet puckerish taste. Cranberry with apple juice was hit upon, then cranberry with raspberry. Finally the farmer's co-op grew to its current 900 owners on the commercial viability

of a juice that is seldom tasted on its own. "Stretching" the cranberry with apple juice (or sugar and water) can also leave many more cranberries to expand into new markets as Ocean Spray reaches into Europe.

What this berry is and how it has grown and made its fortune is the subject of a self-propelled tour at Cranberry World. You wander through the displays, pushing buttons, activating video screens, unleashing color slides, or looking at early TV commercials. Almost anything that has anything to do with cranberries is part of the focus of the 45-minute show.

There are many more varieties of cranberries in the world outside the doors of Cranberry World. Each variety has its own clock in its genes, and it ripens differently. This separation of flowering and harvesting cycles is a device to protect the total crop against early and late frosts. What this means is that all over the bogs, throughout the months of late May through July, and then again from mid-September and into early November, somewhere on the Cape, cranberries are coming into flower or full berry ripeness. With their bright blazes of color, either in the flowering or in the ripening, this is an event of nature that no traveler to the Cape should miss.

The best places to see it are little inland towns such as Harwich, where the cranberry was first cultivated commercially by sea captains who wanted to keep their crews occupied while ashore. The cranberry is still the sole industry here. Harwich offers some of the most visible and accessible bogs to visit, as well as the most ambitious and salubrious of summer celebrations, the mighty **Harwich Cranberry Festival.**

HARWICH CRANBERRY FESTIVAL
(2nd to 3rd week of Sept.)
Vineline for yearly schedule and information:
Tel. 508/430–2811

The best thing about this festival is that it is a true community event. The festival marks the last days of summer and the moment after which everybody gets down to the serious work of the cranberry harvest—a sort of end-of-summer Mardi Gras. As the bogs begin to show a metallic glint, there are country-and-western Jamboree Nights at the high school, a 6-kilometer road run, Sunfish racing, a grand sailing regatta in Harwich Port, an antique car salon, an arts and crafts spectacular in three huge circus tents (yes, a bazaar of things to buy), and a closing fireworks gala done by a famous fireworks family that sets the fuses for much fancier towns.

Two things to remember in any season, however, are the **Brooks Academy Museum** (80 Parallel St., Harwich

02645, tel. 508/432–8089), which has a comprehensive permanent cranberry exhibit covering the history and culture of the fruit (fine old pictures and prints), and the bogs themselves. As in the best wine villages, the vines come right into the town. Possibly the handiest bogs to view on the Cape are right on Route 124 (Exit 10 off Route 6). Directly across from the Cape Cod Regional Technical High School are, as they say, "four or five lovely bogs." If you are confused, or for any cogent cranberry question, ask David Tobey at his liquor

shop, **J.F. Tobey & Son Liquors** (703 Main St., Harwich, MA 02646, tel. 508/432–0100), where he carries cranberry liqueur; light in alcohol, it is a true artisanal product.

Most of the Harwich bogs (for others, look by the firehouse on Bank Street) can be seen from the roadside. There is a six-room inn nearby, too, the **Inn on Bank Street** (Bank St., Harwich 02646, tel. 508/432–3206), where both people and rates are friendly.

To view the bog you can park your car on the shoulder of Route 124 and take a walk around by yourself. Depending on the season, it is wise to bring good walking shoes or calf-height boots. At some times of year the bog may be flooded, but if it is, the water will only be 1½ feet deep. The shrubs of vines are only chest high, and they resemble little trees when trained. It was a retired sea captain who, early in the 19th century, observed that cranberries produced most when exposed to blowing beach sand that covered up the runners, causing the vine to send down roots that sent up more plants, which then gave more berries. With the aid of a shovel, he produced the same effect on vines inside his own property, and cranberry cultivation was born. Now the bogs are covered with sand whenever they are resting.

From mid-June through July (depending on the variety of cranberry planted) the flower appears on the vine. As the sun dries out the waters, heads of flowers come out to float above the bogs on tens of thousands of reedlike stems, and for every flower to see there will be a berry to pick in the fall. The bogs are then flooded and the berries knocked off with poles, rakes, or jets of water. They float in the water and are scooped up, raked, or sucked up by machine.

With fruit, everything starts with the flower. Pollination takes about five days; when the fruit begins to form in the stigma, the petals, having done their work orienting the head and attracting the bees, begin to fall away. It is from the flower that the cranberry gets its name: It looks like the head of a crane. The anther is orange and long like a crane's beak, the head is a caplet of preened pink petals, round like a pod with an exquisite partridge eye inside that will develop into the berry itself; the whole flower floats on a reedlike neck and is one of the most beautiful blossoms in the wetlands forest. It is also the object of one of the most symbiotic assists that take place naturally on the Cape, producing results you can taste in two ways.

The total number of acres under cranberry cultivation in southern Massachusetts is only 13,000—truly a microclimate. A driving shore wind at an inopportune time could leave the area bereft of bees. If this happened during the critical flowering, there would be no fruit in the fall. So no chances are taken on nature and its whims; the cranberry farmer collaborates with the beekeeper during the flowering. During the time of pollination trucks stacked with wooden hives, from as far away as New Hampshire, pour over the Sagamore Bridge onto Route 6 and disperse themselves in the vinelands.

The beekeeper gets $38 per day per hive. Not quite two hives are needed for each acre of bog; the average farm of 16 acres uses 25 hives.

After the job is done, the beekeeper drives off with his hives and his money, the farmer has his pollinated fields, the little workers have their pollen, and you are about to get their honey. Cranberry honey is light red in color, with a semi-sweet aroma backed by a luscious, lip-smacking flavor typical of berry honey. It is available in shops around the Cape, or it can be ordered from **McLure's Honey and Maple Products** (Littleton, NH 03561, tel. 603/444–6246), one of the largest producers of honey in the Northeast. (As well as cranberry honey, they sell raspberry, blueberry, and buckwheat honey at $2 per 1-pound jar by mail.)

To see cranberries growing the way they looked to the Pilgrims, whose first landing was on Cape Cod, you can pick up the very beginning of the cranberry story 25 miles farther out on the Cape on the edge of the huge National Seashore Park, which encompasses 27,000 acres of protected, pristine sands, dunes, and woodlands.

PARMET CRANBERRY BOG TRAIL
Off N. Parmet Rd.
Truro, MA 02652
Province Lands Visitor Center
Tel. 508/487–1256

A wooden boardwalk leads out into a gentle sand-and-green glade where you can feel the air of a tidal bog, hear the shorebirds, and, in spring, view the pink and waving fields of flowering cranberries. The maroon and crimson harvest of berries that comes in the fall provides a banquet destined only for the birds and raccoons.

Red maple and button bushes sprout among the shrubs growing wild, as the bog, cultivated until the early part of the century, returns to a natural state. The trail is a half-mile walk that passes a freshwater pond. The many songbirds sing best when the sun is lowest. As you listen you will smell salt in the air. Beyond the pond the wild cranberry vines grow down to the sea where they are covered up by shifting sand, much as the captain saw them originally.

Another berry out here fed the Pilgrims and the wild turkeys: The wild blueberry is a succulent treat that, like the cranberry, had never before been tasted by Europeans. It eventually found its way into jams. Only one-third the size of the blueberry cultivated from it, the wild original still grows on the Cape. The third new fruit the Pilgrims found on the Cape was the Concord grape. The wild roses out in the dunes of soft blowing sand are as they were when they welcomed the Pilgrims. The aquifer is only a few feet below the surface, so the flowers get all the sun they need and drink all they want. When they lose their petals, the fruit appears and the pharmaceutical companies come out to the Cape to collect it (for it is very rich in vitamin C); you can use it, too, in rose-hip tea. For that is what rose hips are: the fruit of the wild rose.

Besides its roles as the site of the first Pilgrim landing and the home of the cranberry industry, the Cape merits examination for itself. This massive extension of land thrust like a bent arm into the sea was formed by the glacial push of the last Ice Age, shoveling out in front of it ground granite debris and sand. When the glacier retreated, what was left behind above the waters were Long Island, the islands in the waters between it and the Cape, and Cape Cod, a roughly 65-mile-long appendage of sand and dune edged with 300 miles of beaches. The curious shape of the Cape, like an arm flexing its bicep, is a water trap that separates the tides around it into three diverse kingdoms of seas.

Outside the elbow turn in the arm (the outer Cape) there is the Atlantic. Here great green swells surfed with white foam boom and sleigh ride on a smooth carpet of sand. Unfortunately the Atlantic's ambient temperature this far north is daunting, and the undertow is very strong.

The waters of Massachusetts Bay at first appear more friendly. Trapped by the arm of the upper Cape they laze all day in the sun, absorbing its warmth. The bay's shallow waters are tranquil enough for everybody. When the tide is out, pools of water filled with interesting marine life stay behind: periwinkles, small crabs, and occasional fish that children stoop to collect. The clammers come splashing out with their plastic tubs for the daily dig of long-necks (you need a license).

You can walk for miles out into the vacant flats with sand squishing between your toes, the sun coming down on your back, and the salt air tickling your nose. But do not forget where you are. Although you may have driven over land, you are 30 miles out to sea at the point where the bend of the arm tips toward the upper Cape. You must be careful not to let the fog come in at your back. It comes in wispy banks when the air of the sea side (3 to 5 miles away) rolls over the warmer bay water. Should you lose sight of land, the fog can engulf you, leaving you wandering around in circles, with the tide coming in.

Along its southern edge is the Cape's third kind of water, Nantucket Sound. Neither sea nor bay, open at both ends (but sandwiched by the Vineyard and Nantucket Island), it is palpably warmer than the sea, but not so warm as the bay.

Whichever seashore you choose, you'll find the warmest water temperatures, as any Cape resident will tell you, not in the obvious months of June or July, but in September or early October. Then the waters of the sea, warmed all summer long, lose the smallest amount of heat as they move up from the south in the Gulf Stream, bathing the Cape in its balmiest wreath of tides.

Along with the waters, the Cape has three kinds of village to visit. The south coast is fine if you have a house or friends there, or want to get fast to the fun, but it is the most cluttered coastline with the least access to the sea. Next are three towns where you can base your stay.

Chatham is on the Atlantic, and some say it is to Cape Cod what Beverly Hills is to L.A. **The Moses Nickerson House,** a picturesque, traditional Cape bed-and-breakfast, which once belonged to a sea captain, is the place to stay in this picture-perfect town where boxwood hedges are grown above head height to protect the little silvered houses.

MOSES NICKERSON HOUSE INN
364 Old Harbor Rd.
Chatham, MA 02633
Tel. 508/945–5859 or 800/628–6972

There are white-painted houses on the Cape, but silvered wood is the preferred style, the desired and highly paid-for finish for a house. The persistent wind blows sand that can take all the paint off a house in a winter gale. Originally, most houses, made of pitch pine (a local wood used for ships), which dried free of rot, turned a gorgeous silver in the sun. As local woods have been used up, newer houses are made of cedar (frightfully expensive); the complaint is, after considered discussion, that with cedar there's too much gray in the silver.

The main street of Chatham has nothing of the bare-chest and hodgepodge uproar common in other Cape towns. Going straight to the sea it is lined with restaurants that have the faint odor of tearoom about them. There are antiques stores with values from the reasonable to the uncertain behind blank wooden facades. On the other hand, the fish pier out on Shore Road is a continual delight to townspeople and visitors. From an upper deck gallery you can watch the boats come in with the afternoon tide. Usually by 4 PM the bustle reaches crescendo. People come down to buy their dinner to take home or at least to see what the pick at the restaurants will be. Even with its pier, though, Chatham seems more of a place where people go to get away from it all rather than to get in the swim.

North from Chatham along the road to the tip of the Cape is **Wellfleet.** Here you can stay at the **Inn at Duck Creeke,** a basic country clapboard under spreading trees in its own little park with a creek at its feet.

THE INN AT DUCK CREEKE
Main St.
Wellfleet, MA 02667
Tel. 508/349–9333

Wellfleet is a small, country town that the last 50 years mislaid. It has 200-year-old houses that accommodate you as restaurants and inns, a sportswear shop that still has Puritan brand clothing, and a rummage store on Main Street that sells 1940s dresses from its racks and has an old soda cooler from the same period; that it happens to be on the Cape is a bonus. Wellfleet is off down a slope from the highway, built around its port—an inlet off the bay—where many of the Cape's summer population take their small fry to see the boats come in. It still has a shellfishing fleet; Wellfleet's shellfish have the best reputation on the Cape.

Farther up the Cape, at its outer limit, is **Provincetown.** The place to stay is the **Asheton House,** a wood frame structure on the southern edge of town. It has six-over-six windows and flowers to compete with the fine sand that blows over everything.

ASHETON HOUSE
3 Cook St.
Provincetown, MA 02657
Tel. 508/487–9966

In the center of town a brick tower (a superb vantage point on the rest of the Cape) marks the spot where the Pilgrims first landed in 1620 and refreshed themselves before moving on to Plymouth. Provincetown has had its own peculiar character for several generations. First, it is the Greenwich Village of Cape Cod. This comes from its theatrical tradition, which began early in this century and drew a bohemian and gay population.

Second, it has a heavy concentration of Portuguese (recruited in the Azores to fill out the crews of the whaling ships that called there), who came in the 19th century and flourished in Massachusetts. The stripping and cutting up of as many as 50 whales at a time was once a common sight along Provincetown's beaches. The Portuguese have hung on to profoundly influence Provincetown's cuisine and fishing trade. Today they lead whaling expeditions of a more benign nature from the town's MacMillan wharf. The blessing of their fishing fleet, on the last Sunday of June, is something worth witnessing as a vestige of the Old World that has carried on in the New.

The third aspect of Provincetown culture that survives is the early American: This old whaling port has many charming, angled streets. Though the theater is gone, the gays still come to Provincetown for its fresh air of tolerance as much as for the sea. They live or stay in quaint old beach houses, eat in old Portuguese hangouts, and go out on Portuguese boats. The mixture seems to be to the advantage of everyone.

With the overall lie of the land sketched out, let's look at the fish that is unloaded at the docks; then we will go in search of restaurants that serve it. Most of the fishing fleets come in, at Chatham's, Wellfleet's, or Provincetown's

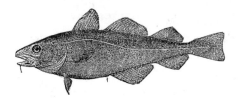

COD

wharves, about 4 PM. The sale of the catch is instantaneous and usually to the trade—restaurants and wholesalers. If you are renting a house, however, or wish to take home a fish to cook, or even to hang on the wall, a nod to the fisherman or a distributor is usually sufficient to have it set aside for you.

The Cod. The story of Cape Cod is the story of this particular fish. In 1602 its great numbers were discovered in nearby waters by Europeans, and the Cape was named and mapped. From an economic and historical point of view, codfish are among the most valuable food fish ever hunted in the world. Inadvertently they played an important role in the colonization of North America, and particularly New England. In the early days of Plymouth, as we have seen, the colonist was almost entirely dependent on this fish for survival. Fortunately, nature provided a fish with a powerful fecundity. A large female cod (weighing 75 pounds) lays more than 9 million eggs. Haddock is a subspecies of cod, and scrod is baby cod. Formerly salted, cod is best when baked or sautéed.

Blackfish. Now called tugtoe, this fish brings a smile to the faces of New England chefs. "A beautiful fish," they say. "Loaded with taste." But few have tugtoe on their menus, you notice. The reason is given unanimously: The blackfish (tugtoe) has bones; filleting them is not enough because blackfish fillets have bones. City people don't know what to do with bones or how to eat fish, goes the complaint, so the blackfish is saved for those times when most visitors have gone and the residents have returned to the Cape. Blackfish is best when cooked like sea bass.

Bluefish. A blue the color of neon: You must be in a boat when one is being brought to the side. Fishing them is often hit or miss, however, as they run in voracious schools, and there are either too many blues or none at all. They are protected by fish and game laws; only one netting permit is issued for the Provincetown fleet. Their rich, oily taste makes them a solid favorite with visitors to the Cape. Bluefish responds deliciously to smoking or grilling. Some chefs will do both.

Fluke and Flounder. Fluke is a giant of the flounder family; its meat is very savory and not at all too dry when the fish is fresh. Gray sole and yellowtail are also both flounders. Flounder hatch out of the mud in May, spawn in August, and are usually taken commercially in winter. Thus, gray sole is winter flounder dressed in another name (*see* Chapter 1, The White Hart Inn). Most people who say they like sole are really speaking of flounder. The flesh is very soft and has a tendency to fall apart; it is best when pan-seared.

Sea Bass. This is a slow-moving fish taken in very deep water; there are none at all on the upper Cape, but it is plentiful in Nantucket Sound, where it is taken in traps like lobster. Its flesh is sweet and flaky and is best when scored and served Asian-style in a soy sauce.

Snapper. The gray snapper is only an occasional wanderer as far north as Massachusetts (and the red fish not at all). If it is offered on the menu (as it frequently is), it has

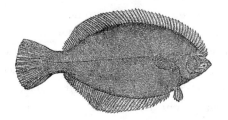

FLOUNDER

more than likely been frozen and shipped in from somewhere else. It tastes best when deep-fried.

Striped bass. Once the perennial menu favorite, the striped bass became a major casualty of overfishing and ocean pollution. It is banned for human consumption over some of its New York and Long Island range. On the Cape, however, it still may be taken in limited amounts. Its numbers are growing as it responds to protection. A count of the catch is kept by the National Marine Fisheries Service; when the quota is reached, no more fish may be taken that year. In 1992 the quota was filled by the first week in August. Plan accordingly. Striped bass is best when pan-seared and baked.

Tuna and Swordfish. The true giants of the Gulf Stream are caught 10 to 100 miles off the Cape. The latter cuts a swath through schools of cod, mackerel, and smaller fish, beating his bill like a scythe, mangling them, and returning to feed on them later. Both tuna and swordfish are so large that they are always served in fillets or steaks. Tuna is best grilled as rare as possible; the advice from a leading New England restaurateur on swordfish is "grilled; there is no other way."

Because the sea is dynamic, a cuisine based upon the contents of its market basket is not at all predictable. Attempts to stabilize it and its larder of crops always fail.

Year in, year out, fish move into ranges more compatible to their existence; some move out, and some are gone forever. Year by year some fishermen work harder just to make a living. The 60-odd-boat fin fishing fleet of Provincetown of 20 years ago is down to 23, and the bluefish no longer break nets with their weight. Even the eternal cod are running scarcer; haddock are petering out, and the boats must go farther and farther—up to 100 miles—to get them. As a result, the boats must be bigger, requiring major financing. Striped bass are also disappearing. In addition, commercial boats from Canada drop their catch on the U.S. market and depress the price of fish. Winter fishermen return from their icy work to find frozen flounder at their supermarkets at prices lower than they can sell it for. Conservation means that the government man appears at the dock to tell the fishermen that the mesh size of their nets must be increased again. The larger the holes, the more fish will get out; the smaller, the fewer. When they want the fishermen to bring back fewer fish or fewer of small size, they make the regulation mesh larger. But it is the fishermen who must buy the nets, which cost $5,000. What if they can't afford them, or have just bought one? Tough, the government says, and they are told to buy another, or they can't go out fishing. Meanwhile, other countries appear unwilling to regulate net sizes, and fish caught by their fishermen end up on the U.S. market.

You must come out to the Cape for real fishing as it is still practiced today, before it is gone: to Wellfleet, where they still have a shellfishing fleet; to Provincetown, for a harvest of the sea that wasn't raised on pellets; to see the fleets come in with what comes and goes in the ocean depths and feeds on its natural sauce, created by the cocktail of its open waters. You will see the natural way of harvesting real oceangoing

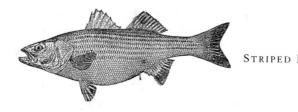

STRIPED BASS

fish when the boats come in on the first tide in the afternoon. It is a good thing, wherever you are on the Cape, to take a stroll down to the wharf in the late afternoon, to see what you can pick out for dinner, especially if you note what restaurants are there.

In Provincetown walk up to **Oceanic Seafood** (tel. 508/487–2441) on the MacMillan wharf. If you want to buy a fish for yourself, ask Raymond Duarte, who owns the place. He will probably pick out a nice red hake or a yellowtail, for they are plentiful just now, or a yard-long dogfish shark, which he might otherwise send to England, where they have become the heart and soul of the very British fish and chips. In the absence of Mr. Duarte, or in the meantime, here is a sample of what the local fishermen order at the eating places whose fish they have supplied.

Oyster Pie and **Clam Pie:** This is a rustic dish springing from a romantic time before the word cuisine was invented. If you went inside a fisherman's cottage, you would find this being prepared for the family. It is like chicken potpie, but it's made with oysters—a thick oyster stew simmering with onions, leeks, and crunched-up salt crackers, the whole contained in the flaky crust of a pie shell. When the shell is pierced with a fork a faint puff of steam escapes, and the pie is delicious.

Cape Cod cod fillets are sautéed amandine in a recipe currently making the rounds among most fishing villages; it is the way Cape Codders prefer the fish when they pay someone else to cook it. If cod is cooked too long, the flesh will start to flake and fall apart; sautéing it forces the chef's eye to stay on the pan. Amandine adds a nutty aroma to the sauce, as the cod's oil can smell quite strong on its own. That these and other cooking styles common in some of the restaurants began in the home shouldn't come as a great surprise. There is a cross-pollination among the fishing and restaurant communities on the Cape, as the same families are frequently found in both businesses.

Red eel (it has white meat) is among their more popular dishes, and not because it is cheap (which it is) but because it is very sweet. Try it here in a tomato sauce like the Breton fishermen brought from France. They made their *matelot* (first mate) version a triumph of Parisian bistros.

Finally, here are some restaurants where all these things we have mentioned come together. I have tried not to be fair. I have resisted every temptation to embrace the upper Cape impartially so that every postal zone and little village is represented with somewhere to go.

For **Chatham,** where the restaurants are often silver-sided, **Christian's** (443 Main St., tel. 508/946–3362), successfully turns the town's mild image into the laid-back. Go upstairs for the deck over Main Street and the piano bar. The dining on fresh soup, tuna steaks, and Cole Porter makes for an incomparable evening.

Pate's (Rte. 28, West Chatham, tel. 508/945–9777) has a charcoal grill for grilled swordfish and steaks; its prime ribs are the best. It is also a place on Cape Cod to try lobster. For drinks along near sundown, it is crowded and lively.

OYSTER

In **Wellfleet,** the **Wellfleet Oyster House** (E. Main St., tel. 508/349–2134) occupies a well-worn spot. Built in 1750, it is a favorite with generations of Cape Cod regulars as well as fishermen from Provincetown and their wholesalers. There is no more atmospheric place I know of to eat oysters in all Massachusetts. Most people take them plain with no cooking at all and just a squirt of lemon if that, though the giant Wellfleets are also offered fried. It is not for them the fishermen seem to come in, but for the taste of the big oceangoing fish, with codfish fillets being particularly well served in their amandine sauce. Although the Oyster House has always drawn the more seriously inclined in food, it is a place that welcomes you in at any time; you can eat as little or as much as you want and come as you are.

Should you want a place where you can put on some finer things, and experience far wider choices and finer desserts, try **Aesop's Tables.**

AESOP'S TABLES
Main St.
(next to the town hall)
Wellfleet, MA 02667
Tel. 508/349–6450

If you've been saving your money to spend it later, here's the place to do it. Aesop's Tables combines Cape Cod tradition and staples with a modern American food outlook and presentation. The five dining rooms range from one with a fireplace to a brick terrace circling an old oak that overlooks the port. The restaurant is a quarter-mile from the wharf; executive chef Fred Vanderschmidt puts in his orders by radiophone while the fishing boats are out to sea. Things don't get fresher than that. Striped bass comes to the table baked in an envelope of thinly sliced potatoes. The potatoes hold in the heat and steam and themselves cook to a golden brown. Sea scallops, lightly sautéed in oil with shallots, arrive accompanied with their long, cigar-shape roe, their flesh still quivering. Aesop's is a good place to eat the bluefish, as its oil is always very fresh, and still smelling of ocean. The tuna come out of the Gulf Stream in 100-pound sizes.

Another voyager of the Gulf Stream is the swordfish. The "stream," as every fisherman who spends his working life in it calls it, passes very close to Martha's Vineyard, sometimes close enough to almost touch it, and this is one of the best hunting grounds in the world for this big game fish. Swordfish are taken by harpoon by most fishermen off the Vineyard, but Vanderschmidt buys only those fished by hook and line, for they come in to his kitchen exhausted from the fight, their flesh pumped with adrenalin. The Wellfleets (oysters) are west side Wellfleets, that is, from the west side of Wellfleet Harbor, where the shells are thicker and the flesh in the shells heftier. The baked oyster on the menu changes nightly, going from dredged in cornmeal through Rockefeller to oyster in caviar butter. There is a heady wine list and a talented pastry chef; breads are made on premises, the chocolate cake is lecherous, and there is nothing missing at Aesop's that could be measured as a pleasure of the table. Ordering wisely from the larder of the sea visible from the

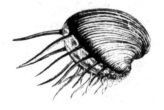

CLAM

doorstep can lead to a dining experience not to be duplicated by any restaurant in the world. Just try getting fresh-hooked swordfish in Paris.

Of raw bars there are plenty up and down the Cape. The main division is in their clams. There are long-necks and littlenecks, which have nothing to do with place names. The long-necks are soft-shelled steamers. The littlenecks include cherrystones, which are hard shell, and harder to deal with. Quahogs are the largest hard shells, with a diameter of over 3 inches; they have purple lined shells and are best used in stuffed clams and chowders. If you find the oyster pie hard to get, don't let anyone sell you clam pies prepared in Maine; instead, try **Fancy's Farm Stand** (Main St., East Orleans, tel. 508/255–1949). They also sell good clam chowder base (you add the rest so it's fresh), plus chicken and turkey potpies home-baked on the premises, and Cape-grown vegetables, wild blueberries, fresh cranberry pie, and the berries in season.

In Provincetown, at **Tips for Tops'n** (31 Bradford St., on the road to Herring Cove, tel. 508/487–1811), the Portuguese way to the sea through sauces shares the bill with the fish. Baked flounder is served up in a bed of sea clams under a dressing of tomatoes, onions, and seaweed. A special-ty of the house is Portuguese cold sauce. This is a recipe brought over from the Azores: a zesty marinade of onions, vinegar, saffron, and spices. Bluefish here is not quite grilled, but broiled in a double pan whose inner bottom is slotted so that the excess oil will drip off the fish, which is then sautéed in lemon butter. Mussels (little juicy ones) are steamed in a white sauce of white wine, olive oil, parsley, and garlic. The prices are low as the restaurant is out of the way, but the parking is easy, and a complimentary glass of *vinho verde* awaits those who come with this book.

Also on Bradford Street, at the last building on the way to the cove itself, is **The Moors** (5 Bradford St., tel. 508/487–0840). Here are all manner of Portuguese sauces and wines. Try them as a seafood smörgåsbord, a procession of appetizers, entrées, and delights to fill you up. They'll leave you with a tingle in the mouth and a gastronomic under-standing of the place that was named Cape Cod. Start with *caldeirada,* a Portuguese bouillabaisse made with simmerings of small fry, like hake (you must try this fish, as there is prob-ably a fishing hiatus coming on cod). In the soup with the fish are littleneck clams, tiny mussels, and maybe a crab or two. The sauce is fleshed out with tomatoes, herbs, and wine, and served with rice and sausage. Perhaps you should try *ameijoaf à bulhao pato* as well, steamed clams served in their broth with garlic, parsley, and coriander. *Atum de escabeche* is fresh tuna poached with vegetables and served over lettuce with capers on the side; if it's on special, it's $4.95. There are few bargains like these Portuguese restaurants on the end of the Cape. Try what is simply called Portuguese fish. These days it is probably red hake poached in olive oil, onions, basil and capers. Finally, for the history-conscious, there is *bacalhau à gomez de sà*. This is sun-dried cod, seasoned with sea salt. It is the original Portuguese salt cod, as hung up on the wooden racks of the 17th century on the beaches just beyond The Moors' door. It is the taste on which the Cape was settled as a European colony, drew its early sustenance, and was named. It is both the dish and the fish that founded Massachusetts.

Up in the main town, speaking of tradition, **The Mayflower** (300 Commercial St., tel. 508/487–0121) is a business that has been in the same family at the same address since 1929. It offers fresh fish done in simple ways so you can taste the flesh. There is swordfish fished off Nantucket every day and freshly broiled. (Would it be better grilled? Probably.) Two can dine here for $12. What else is fresh every day? "The scallops, the flounder, the scrod all come right from the pier," says owner Mike Janopolis. He goes on to recommend fresh calamari as a substitute for shrimp, which he says always comes from Thailand and is never fresh on the Cape.

At **The Lobster Pot** (321 Commercial St., tel. 508/487–0842), just off MacMillan Wharf, you can take a chance on potluck with Joy McNulty and her 1,200 diners every day. Her long-neck steamers are a joy in themselves, and Joy gets the palm for the best clam chowder on the Cape.

Provincetown is the best place on Cape Cod not only for café sitting (**Café Blasé**) but also for the sport of whale-watching. Here you are already 30 miles out to sea. Boats from other places have to chug along more than an hour just to get to where you already are; then they have to start back that much earlier to get to where they came from. But what has whale-watching got to do with food? you might ask. The answer is that while doing it you are looking at the top and the bottom of the food chain—which leaves the right amount of food for thought.

THE PORTUGUESE PRINCESS
MacMillan Wharf
Provincetown, MA 02657
Tel. 508/487–2651

Whales come into Massachusetts Bay in such great numbers because of the particular richness of plankton (minute or microscopic animal or vegetable sea organisms that drift in clouds, providing food for fish, seabirds, and whales) in its waters. In the complicated rhythm of the seas the plankton are rolled over from the Grand Banks, to the northeast, into Massachusetts Bay and penned up by the long arm of Cape Cod. The whales come in to get them. The plankton in the sea make the whale grow. When you see a whale, you will wonder how this is possible, considering you cannot see the plankton at all. It is as if the elephant could grow, attain his size, and prosper to old age from snatching flies out of the air. Plankton in the medium of the sea are infinitely smaller than flies in their medium of the air. The right whale pushes his head into a dive and its mammoth orifice opens. The in-rushing water pours through the sieve of whalebone and is exchanged with water already processed. The whale gulps 3 million gallons an hour, processing the 10 billion plankton in it. That they are there and available, growing out of seawater and light, is a creative miracle of the green machine that is our planet. It is a system that has been in place for 65 million years and still works for the 250,000 or so toothless whales that roam the seas of the world seeking to make a living for themselves as we seek the same for ourselves. Plankton are absolutely crucial to their life. Plankton are the basic form of all life on this planet.

When you are out whale-watching from Province-town, you cruise upon the sea of life of the Stellwagon Bank. This is one of the richest plankton pastures of the world. The whales who enter the watery corral between Provincetown and Gloucester to feed are only part of the oceangoing community. You can see dolphins, which don't eat plankton but often eat what does, but they are only what's on top; the rest is underneath, where you cannot see; plankton bloom on the bottom to come to the top, but you can be sure they are there as long as you can see the whales. Whenever the plankton disappear, there will be no more whales and nothing else that you do not see beneath the waves. The sea will be dead. As the sea gave all life to the planet through its exchange of water to plants, who will not be far behind? What we cannot see is as precious as what we can.

Out on the back of the sea, dappled green, gray, and blue as sun and clouds alternate, there is much that we can see. The whales turn up in twos and sometimes more; it is a rather safe bet that if you go out whale-watching from Provincetown, you will see them. Their breath hangs over their spout holes like great puffs of steam from a bicycle team racing by in December, just a puff of vapor over the heads. It is amazing with what joy people react. There are not many children on these boats, but that the people on hand behave like them is a compensation. There are no atheists aboard when a boat sights a whale. People display the most artful energy thundering to the rail. Faces you don't know smile at you and point to the creature blithely plowing the sea. There is not a thought of killing it. Whales are one of the most valuable resources of the New England coastline, a marquee attraction to all the people who go out to sea. It is amazing how the relationship between people and this animal has turned around in a hundred years. The universal instinct now is to draw just as close as possible to so majestic and peaceful a being. It is not only Melville who looked at the sea and saw in it the collective giant of creation. Day in and day out, and nights too, boatloads of people shuttle back and forth to the sea where the origins of their own human condition swell and vanish. It is as primal an experience of life as was once reserved only for the few explorers who went out on safari and those who worked a lifetime aboard ship. It is not for nothing that the whale has friends.

After a visit to the Cape, the ferry from Provincetown to Boston is a good way to go home. **Thrifty Car Rental** (tel. 508/487–9418) and **U-Save** (tel. 508/487–1539) are both in Provincetown and will take you to the slip on the wharf. In the three hours of clear sailing ahead your dreams will not be paved with macadam.

CHAPTER 10

MUNCHING, MARCHING, AND MARKET MARATHONS

Boston

Only 10 years after the *Mayflower* landed, John Winthrop led a party of 1,000 Puritans 100 miles up the coast from Plymouth and founded Boston. Not only was the harbor easier to get into, but the rivers ran down to the port. To say the place has changed since then is only partially correct. The first American city to claim parts of itself from the sea, the first to have a subway, and the first to hold a marathon run, Boston has consistently led the nation in renovation ideas and urban renewal projects. The recent revival of its center has left it standing as it was in the beginning: the nation's number-one market town. No, you cannot compare any other city marketplaces with those of Boston. They are stocked with live lobsters sold by live fishermen. Steamer clams come in from Maine, green fiddleheads are as fresh as Vermont, mâche and mesclun lettuce are trucked in from Pennsylvania farms overnight. In the crowded butcher stalls—beware of knives—hang oxtails and legs of goat. Out in the sun lies flaky dried cod; squid is in by the barrel, and so are Jersey tomatoes. There are Salinas crops from the West Coast, broccoli and such; shawarma sandwiches from the Middle East; okra and yucca from the Caribbean; and mortadella from Italy. Whatever can be led, flown, floated, or rolled comes into Boston and can be taken in hand to eat as you stroll through or sit in one of its pleasant gardens or bars. Some of these go back to Ben Franklin's time (he did come from here) and some people say this is where he still lives, but he was not what he is. (You'll see.)

HIGHLIGHTS:
- Happy landings on the Back Bay
- An uncommon green
- Puritans and General Hooker
- Faneuil Hall and its market
- Congas and cafés
- Eating through the marketplace
- A chowder's tale
- The city of scrod
- In search of steamers
- The French question
- The new food romantics
- Stalking the Haymarket
- The lobster corner
- Salmon at rock bottom
- What's cooking at the Ritz
- The game with a difference
- Cappuccino and espresso: two for the road

LENGTH OF LOOP: Less than a mile of walking
LENGTH OF STAY: Three days

Boston is a city of manageable size—a great walking town. You can fly in or park your car in any of the many downtown lots and forget it for the length of your stay. A weekend stay—two nights in a downtown hotel with Saturday morning on the scene—is required; you will see why (plan to arrive around Friday noon). With no car to rent, you can (and should) put everything into accommodations; plan on Boston Deluxe.

The right hotel here is the **Ritz-Carlton.** The site is perfect, the service is impeccable, and the sunsets on the Public Garden are sublime over drinks in your room. The hotel, one of the finest anywhere in America, sometimes runs a special cooking class: A visiting chef prepares a meal on Saturday morning and consumes it with his students while engaging in a roundtable critique (call the hotel for schedules). The weekend I chose to come, the chef was Gérard Pangaud. A morning and lunch with such a master of cuisine is a rare opportunity to flesh out and fill in any gaps in your kitchen technique.

The swan boats are just across the way on their lake in the Public Garden, bearing their cargo of kids and trailing convoys of ducks in their wakes. As you step out of the lobby of the Ritz into the park, the sophisticated, cosmopolitan Boston atmosphere of stone monuments and bronze soldiers under shade trees engulfs you.

On the other side of the garden, across Charles Street, is Boston Common. The park originally belonged to an old hermit who gave the land to the Puritans and then fled southward to Taunton, where he was killed by Indians. The first things the Puritans put in the green spaces were not benches in the shade or swan boats for the kids, but pillories and stocks for whipping and punishing people. The first person they put into the stocks was the carpenter who built them. He had been sacrilegious enough to charge too much, the Puritans said.

Over a hill and away from the traffic near a war memorial, the grass is worn through so that bare spots show from kids playing on it, and that is the best war memorial to have. Few dogs roam in this park; at last, coming out at

Beacon Hill (by the golden dome of the State House), I see a small golden retriever.

On the corner of Park Street is a mounted statue of a Union general, fighting Joe Hooker. How much fighting he did in the Civil War is still debated, but it was General Hooker who allowed so many prostitutes near his army that they still bear the name they took from him, hookers.

Down the Freedom Trail, a route tracing monuments to the Revolution, I plunge through slits of city streets and pass the site of the Boston Massacre (the old statehouse). The sound of distant drums comes through a narrow canyon, squeezing out a double beat. As I turn into a city square, a vast expanse opens up and I see a latter-day Ben Franklin doing a two-buckle shuffle to a banjo and two clarinets.

Benjamin Franklin left Boston because he found the Quakers of Philadelphia (who had fled there from Boston) more sympathetic than the Puritans. They didn't wake him with the whack of a ruler when he fell asleep at prayer meetings. But here he is back on the edge of Quincy Market near the same place where he lived as a young man. Judging from the steps he is putting down to the hot licks going up from the sticks, and the cheers coming from the lips of the crowd, he will be in the arms of Morpheus very soon.

QUINCY MARKET

All restaurants and shops
Faneuil Hall Marketplace
Boston, Massachusetts 02109
Tel.: See individual listings

Quincy Market is filled with a tremendous hubbub, like live steam from an enormous locomotive roundhouse. It is Boston's biggest tourist attraction and the favorite meeting place of its inhabitants. Some 200 yards wide by three football fields long, it is flooded by seas of people churning through assorted restaurants, boutiques, and food stalls seeking lunch. Four buildings make up the market square. A long one in the center has a dome on top and pubs and restaurants bulging like gunports on either side. It disappears, engulfed by the crowds. With the words QUINCY MARKET inscribed on the bow of its Greek Revival facade, it is faced at a distance of perhaps 40 yards by old **Faneuil Hall,** a Colonial building where the merits of the revolution were once preached and argued. Its steps form an architectural union, like a plaza within a plaza, with those going up to the Quincy Market building opposite. Across promenades on either side of the old market the long lines of facing buildings plunge to perspectives unseen. The smell of food is everywhere here. A Caribbean beat comes from a pair of conga drummers; a set of jugglers performs on the market steps. Flags and pennants wave above the trees; people eat at tables outside on the apron.

We've now had our little walk; our challenge is clear: We are going to eat our way around this market from one end to the other.

Because we are eating our way through the old, traditional market, it is here that we will seek out what is traditional in Boston food. The new and exotic will be picked up later, in other places, where newer, and perhaps international, tastes are served. In the marketplace we can find out what Boston tastes are like on their own home ground. Our marching menu includes the old New England standbys: New England clam chowder, Boston baked beans, Boston scrod, and steamers. This will also serve nicely as a budget buffer for the expensive taste in Boston hotels we enjoy. This market lunch, with all its moves and courses in different places (less drinks), will come in at under $25 per person, and it is a promise that you will love it. We reserve all rights, however, including the right to change our minds. The only question before we begin is, Where?

MARKETPLACE CAFÉ
North Market Building
Tel. 617/227-9660

Let's start at the north end of the market at the
Marketplace Café. With its outdoor garden in front, winter
garden inside, and milling crowd, the café is an enjoyable
place to visit in the spirit of the market. The Marketplace is
so big that finding a space in it no matter what the hour
shouldn't be a problem, but the bar seems more accessible as
there is no wait for a hostess. To begin with, then, served at
the bar, New England clam chowder: What could be more
New England?

"It's very spicy," the bartender warns about her chowder, and I consider whether I will have a cup or a bowl. The
bartender is a redhead. Her long locks are clasped under the
blue of a Boston Red Sox cap and held in the back by an elegant white chiffon bow. She's up to her elbows in glasses in
the sink and barely looks old enough to drink, but her opinions on Boston food seem very well informed. She has opinions not only on chowder but on where to go for steamer
clams that do not coincide with my itinerary. As it is a hot
day, I ask her to dry her hands and draw a cold one while I
consider what she has said. And what else should she draw in
a bar that affords the sight of Faneuil Hall through its bright
windows, but a Boston Samuel Adams Ale.

Something to consider, with respect to Boston's food, as
with all of New England's, is that the sea plays the most
important part in its tradition. Only after turning their backs
on the land, with its rocky soil and hard-packed density,
where barley did so poorly, and going to the sea for their
food, did the New England settlers become a viable colony
and begin to feed themselves. It is only natural that New
England clam chowder, their most successful staple, became
their standard dish. There is no precise recipe for it that is

official and handed down. Even those in cookbooks should not be considered immutable.

Chowder comes from the French *chaudière*. But even this is a word with as many vague meanings as chowder. The first five letters indicate that it comes from "hot." It has anything and everything to do with the home: It can mean a boiler pot that hangs in the fireplace; it can mean the rack on the back of the fireplace on which the pots are hung; it has also come to mean a housewarming, when it is applied to a party for newlyweds. The chaudière was probably the pot that Breton fishermen, who arrived off the New England coast in the 16th century, carried in their boats and cooked their vittles in. What these vittles were is anyone's guess, but they're likely to have included clams, salt pork (as everything did in those days), chunks of fish, and vegetables with simmerings of onions. What these vegetables were varied according to whim and taste, and also according to what the fishermen or colonist had on hand. Potatoes, onions, and whatever other vegetables could be stored were used, including corn. Also, as it was scarce—there were only three cows in the entire Plymouth colony eight years after its founding (*see* Chapter 9, Plimoth Plantation), milk was added to chowder for its fairer distribution. The Puritans' strong communal sense was symbolized and realized in chowder: It comes from everywhere—sea, seabeds, fields, cows—and feeds everyone.

What comes to the bar at the Marketplace Café is a chowder that smells of the sea and the dairy, too; fresh and steaming, the blend works. The heavy dose of spice may surprise you, but it is typical of New England home-style foods. The spice (here, cayenne pepper) cuts through the fat and starch of clams and potatoes and makes them sit up on the palate. The Marketplace chowder is particularly perky and good; if you take a cup ($3), you are more than likely to wind up wanting the bowl ($4).

I am sitting next to a French couple from Alsace on their way from New York to Montreal. Alsace has the most delicious beer in France; some of the best in Europe comes from there. The many different brews, each with its own personality and charm, all have character. The Frenchman tries to order a "blonde" beer (a national bland) from the redheaded bartender. I volunteer to translate and also volunteer that he doesn't want what he has ordered. But Frenchmen have personality, too. He counters that in summer he prefers a light beer to a dark one like I have. When his comes, he takes a sip and lowers his eyes. Without another taste he puts his glass down and tells me he'll have what I have; when he tastes it, he orders another for me for doing him a good turn. His wife has cranberry juice; she's doing the afternoon driving. We trade information on Maine and Paris; they'll sleep in Damariscotta that night (*see* Chapter 12).

The next eating stop is the wooden dining hall and old family restaurant known as **Durgin-Park.**

DURGIN-PARK
North Market Building
Tel. 617/227–2038 (call only for hours, see text)

Up the wooden flight of stairs you go, into a turn-of-the-century dining room that is no-frills plain. Fans rotate near the ceiling, and large, rosy-cheeked women tread the floors wearing starched white uniforms with black aprons, matching shoes, and white bobby socks. Their lipstick is bright, and most have straight black hair and sharp tongues: the kind of women who scared the wits out of our immigrant grandparents, but each has a heart of gold now. They make you feel at home and as though they're your sisters, the kind you never had. Durgin-Park is a place to visit without fail; it is more than a place to come to eat. It is a piece of history; people used to come here from boats before they went to new homes on trains. The women seat you at big, communal tables. This is a place for families, or to go to if you are hungry; prices are easy. They don't bat an eye when I say all I want are beans (less than $3).

Durgin-Park has the best baked beans in Boston. They smell of brown sugar; there is a sweet, cooked-onion aroma and plenty of chew in them. To get it right, Durgin-Park employs a "chief bean man." This is a more than century-old position. With it comes not only the awesome responsibility of

having selected the right sort of special bean to be cooked (the California pea) but also that of preparing these beans according to an undeviating ritual that will make them turn out to be Boston baked. It is an elusive miracle to say the least. And here you have the recipe according to Durgin-Park.

Boston Baked Beans. A 2-quart bean pot is used; beans in lots no bigger than that are cooked at Durgin-Park. No more need be made to serve even the biggest of families. Two pounds of beans (California pea) should be soaked overnight. On the morning of the day they are to be eaten the beans are boiled slowly for 10 minutes with a teaspoon of baking soda, then washed in a colander with cold running water. A half-pound of salt pork (have you noticed there is a lot of this in

New England cooking?) is diced into 1-inch squares (approximately—you don't have to be a maniac about this) and goes into the bottom of the pot along with a whole yellow onion. Next the beans go in; then another half-pound of diced salt pork goes on top of the beans. (You will need a whole pound of salt pork.) Meanwhile, on the side, two-thirds of a cup of black molasses, 8 tablespoons of sugar (many people use brown but white will do), 2 teaspoons of dry mustard, 4 teaspoons of salt, and a half-teaspoon of pepper are mixed in only enough hot water to almost (but not quite) rise to the top of the beans. Bake them in a 300° oven for six hours, leaving them uncovered. Enough water to keep them moist must be added to the beans as often as necessary—more than twice every hour. Don't be impatient and try to add all the water at once, or else you will wind up with gummy beans. One pot serves 10.

Durgin-Park is the ideal place to come for beans, especially if there are plenty of you. The tables are wide enough for a family feast, and the portions are generous. The waitresses walk around with signs pinned to their breast that say, "Specialty of the House—Prime Ribs of Beef." The ribs are as delicious and as big a bargain as the beans. Tables are only waited on and cleaned, never reserved or held. It's a food democracy at Durgin-Park; call them up, find out what the wait is like, and come over. Chances are good that on a weekday, noon service, always with a smile and a smart word, will be immediate.

Next door to Durgin's is **Donovan's** (North Market Building, tel. 617/523–9522), one of the oldest Irish bars in Boston. Its somber dimness harks back to a time when the neighborhood women, who were not allowed in, would try to peep through the windows to see if their husbands were there (or to see whose husbands were drinking). In the age of enlightenment, however, neighborhood women are welcome and find Donovan's sandwiches an excuse not to slave over a stove; the chowder and corned beef in the evening will serve nicely for a dinner for two. No plastic taken. And none given.

In the street outside Donovan's bar a bonsai tree cart beckons with the diminutive in the deciduous. Past this point, the North Market promenade starts to dissolve into a clutter of shirt, skirt, and gear shops. At the very end of the market, however, across the street, is the glass-and-cream facade of the bustling **Café Stella.** Here is pasta in most of its enticing forms and shapes, stuffed or plain. And here it is permitted to make "an espresso stop" for a cup of coffee as a sort of midmeal respite before going on. You can also mark the Stella for a return for the gelati, but there is no time for one now; there are miles of courses to come before the ice cream.

From here you won't have far to walk to the next course: Just around the horseshoe bend comes the South Market promenade, starting the journey back toward Faneuil Hall. In the far side of the turn, with its terrace set for outdoor summer dining, is the **Seaside Restaurant.**

SEASIDE RESTAURANT
188 South Market Building
Tel. 617/742–8728

Just as it was once hard to get bad saltwater taffy in Atlantic City, it is harder still to get bad scrod in Boston. Reason number one: They know what it is.

Scrod is a specific fish: It is baby cod. Portuguese travel huge distances and endure terrible hardships of homesickness and dangers of the sea cooped up in wooden ships on voyages of three months or more just to get cod, which is their national dish, often from waters just off Boston. An argument could be made that cod is also the national dish of Boston. Bostonians eat 11 tons of cod every day. They don't eat it heavily salted after it has spent three months in the hold of a ship because they get it from the bay at their doorstep fresh every day (*see* Chapter 9, Cape Cod).

Boston has many ways to serve its fresh scrod, but one of the best is the simplest way at the Seaside Restaurant, which is less than a mile from the fishing pier where scrod comes in on boats and is sold. Scrod is best to eat baked (unless you eat it every day and the change is just for changing). The pearly white flesh is firm and does not flake or fall apart in the oven. There is enough seasoning in its own oil to exude a thin, nutty flavor by itself; in a fresh young fish it does not take over the taste. There is no need to sear it or score it in one flash in a hot pan, or to dip it in bread crumbs or deep-fry it or add Oriental sauce or a layer of seasonings. When done correctly, scrod should come to the table like just what it is: plump, white, and juicy. All on its own it is one of the most delectable fish you can dine on in Boston, and has been since 1630. It should leave you feeling the way a nonalcoholic wine does—light and fresh and ready to continue your day; that is why scrod is such a good luncheon dish.

Moving from the table, we find in the South Market promenade a gauntlet of galleries, baggage, jewelry, and T-shirt shops. Among them are custard and candy-apple stands, but unless you dabble in these, and things like hot chocolate, mixed drinks, and ice-cream desserts from the '60s at **Serendipity 3,** or yuppie beers from Northern Europe and grilled fish at the **Salty Dog,** it's best to continue directly to the next stop, which is just outside the market.

Acting on a last-minute tip (from the bartender at the Marketplace), we are heading for the best steamers in Boston. As Boston must be the best steamer town in America—don't we want the best?—the tip has required of us a midcourse correction: We are going outside the Faneuil Hall Market to get to them. We cut in front of the Marketplace Café, cross the street on the far side, and hook around behind the next one to put ourselves on Union Street.

Across from the market the Boston skyline pokes above the low buildings in a delightful variety of pleasing shapes. Here a cupola, there a clock tower, then a bedecked and gold-leafed rhomboid. Around the corner, away from the hubbub of the market, the ancient precincts of Union Street lie behind the facade of the new city hall, and the contrast of the old with the new is not so pleasing. . . . The city hall comes off as a brick blockhouse so fashionable in institutional works after the 1960s, with a brick temple effect something like the Egyptian queen Hatsheput's; it would make a marvelous place for a riot. Along Union Street we walk on some of the oldest city pavement in downtown America and, if we are not careful, on some of the homeless. Franklin and Hancock lingered here, too, though not in so prone a position.

Soon we reach a storefront called Bosworth's Baked Beans. It is a cute *café à l'ancienne* with only three tables and bare brick walls. What they mainly do are beans. Although the condiments are excellent, the beans don't touch those of Durgin-Park.

For oysters and shellfish, the **Union Oyster House** next door has the best shellfish reputation in Boston. Until the young bartender spoke up, it had seemed like a good place to come for steamers; it still does no harm to look.

UNION OYSTER HOUSE
41 Union St.
Boston, MA 02108
Tel. 617/227–2750

The Union Oyster House inhabits the oldest restaurant building in America; when you go in, there reappears Ben Franklin (who lives—and lived—around the corner) sitting at the bar, his doublet a little soiled, his jowls pale and puffy. The bar is a semicircular wooden cutout hanging above plates and trays of oysters and clams on the half shell. It's a scene right out of the musical *1776*, with the players a bit mixed up. A bevy of laughing Italians are around Franklin hoisting a few; he's in the direct custody of a beautiful blonde Bostonian, and a crowd of Japanese are happily snapping pictures. I wonder if they will show that Ben's eyes are a little soft-boiled behind his bifocals.

The room is a visual feast. In the back are some of the oldest wooden booths and tables you will see in America, their rosy wax patina glowing in the dim light. A creaking staircase leads upstairs; beneath it a huge aquarium sprouting moss and seaweed sports some of the largest lobsters ever seen outside Maine. One is literally as long as an arm—the Italians have never seen anything like that. A group of three women comes bustling up from the back to pay their bill. The sight of Ben Franklin brings scowls to their otherwise friendly faces. "That Ben Franklin's always sponging drinks," complains one.

"Throw him out," demands another. "He's always hitting on the tourists."

"I'm going to call the Chamber of Commerce," says the third, who pays up, refusing to be mollified with samples from the big bowl of mints.

Meanwhile the oysters on the half shell are waiting for customers as the ice melts down underneath them, but not for me. But see the Oyster House for Ben Franklin, before the Puritans get him again.

Now we are ready to act on our tip, and this is where we will finish our lunch:

MARSHALL HOUSE
15 Union St.
Boston, MA 02108
Tel. 617/523–9396

It was once owned by John Hancock, and Benjamin Franklin took delivery of the 2 million silver crowns France gave to Revolutionary America in this building, but neither man is taking up space here now. Instead, it seems filled with all the residents of Boston, who have eschewed the empty city hall square. Why do they come?

For their three squares a day. The **Marshall House** is the place where the redheaded Marketplace Café bartender eats, and it is the best place for shellfish in or out of the market as the house with every seat filled will attest.

A big, lovely crowd of people from all over the city

MUSSEL

have their collective noses in what they are eating. There is one empty stool at the raw bar. I ask if it's taken, and the man who has his hat on it moves it from the seat and tells me the seat is mine. He is a fisherman. Here is what he is eating: two steamed lobsters (1 pound each)—price? $10.95; they are served with French fries or home fries and a salad; they were fished 20 miles from the door of the place. It's almost enough to make me change my mind on my order, but not quite. After all, I'll have my fill of lobsters in Maine (*see* Chapter 12), and I came here to eat steamers. I order steamers. The bartender himself goes to the back to put in the order. The fisherman's name is Frank. He has a headful of hair and red whiskers and says I've ordered wisely. "You'll get the best steamers in Boston here," he says. Boston eats 200,000 bushels of steamers a year. The bartender comes back and says it will take about 20 minutes to get my steamers; in the meantime I order a Sam Adams Ale. Frank says they do everything fresh at Marshall House, and that's why he comes here; so do most Bostonians who know their shellfish best. He tells me that if I went over to the Union Oyster House I'd probably see the place full of foreign tourists, with oysters open on the half shell before they were ordered, sitting on melting ice waiting for customers who wouldn't demand that they be opened fresh.

The steamers come, barely open, with steam coming out; their shells are very white and brittle to the touch. "Real soft shells," says my friend Frank. Are they sweet? Are they tender? These are the best clams I have ever tasted in the world. There are more than 30 on the plate, and I will hoard them all. It is equally important, as with all shellfish, that they be caught in a place without sand, as mud will come out of them but never all the sand; these are long-necked and sandless.

You use a small fork—optional—or you pull them out of the shell by the neck with your fingers. Or you can use the French technique, a little showy but effective. You manipulate a hinged and empty pair of shells between your fingers like chopsticks to pull out its mates from their shells and take them to your mouth. On the way you can dip them in melted butter, tartar sauce (supplied), or not. At any rate it's heaven. Until you have tasted steamers in Boston like this, you have not tasted the best in clams. I can honestly report I have never tasted the equal of these; not in France, not in Spain, not in Italy, Morocco, New York, or any other shellfish capital. Besides, these have had less than a half-day's boat ride to get from where they were caught to here. On the way they were hung over the side in a bag; this is the proper way to purge them.

Some of Frank's friends come in and sit across the bar. About the bar: It has a nice brass rail where your foot can feel friendly. One of the fisherman's friends is a woman; she smiles at me as I eat, or so I imagine. Frank says he is leaving the next morning for a vacation on a lake where he goes for calm summer days of bass fishing. The conversation turns to freshwater bass. "Taste like seaweed," say I who live on a lake and have tasted too many.

"Or the muddy bottom," says Frank.

"Or just mud," say we who have both grown tired of disguising their dishwater taste with butter or sorrel. Finished with his lobsters, Frank pays up and leaves. I linger a little longer over my clams and add up the bill my day's walking tour has accumulated—total—and it doesn't amount to $20, less the few beers.

On the way out, Frank's woman friend stops me at the door. She looks at me, and one easy question comes out of her lips as her eyes fill with hope. "I was thinking of ordering the steamers," she says. "I was trying to get your attention. Were they good?"

Many trees in the Boston Common are Scotch elms. They have replaced the American variety that were destroyed by the Dutch elm blight that hit this country a century ago through uncontrolled imports of plants, but they are in no way as great as their predecessors. A downtown park is one of the pleasantest ways for city dwellers to connect themselves through their walks to where they are going. The Common walks connect so many districts—the theater, Back Bay, Beacon Hill, downtown, the Freedom Trail—just as the Common connects Bostonians to the seasons through winter's snows, spring's flowers, fall colors, and the sighing of summer elms. But there is no time to dawdle, to watch for the first star in the sky from a park bench. At nightfall the staples of Boston simplicity will give way to measures of the city's culinary diversity.

For a Friday (or any night in Boston), here are two addresses to get your palate out of the museum and into new and exciting sources of inspiration. Boston has been a great port of entry for more than 350 years, and into all ports of entry comes the world.

You may notice the absence of a French restaurant in what follows in this chapter. This is not Boston's fault, but is due to conditions that are peculiar to French cuisine because it is French. Food comes from the ground and grows up, from the hands of the cook into the mouths of those who anticipate and await it, and there it succeeds or fails. When covering French food and wine for various magazines and newspapers while living in France, I noticed that there was a great gap between French food and what was served for French in American restaurants, so I began to harbor a question. It was a simple question that I would put to any wine or food professional who I considered knowledgeable on dining in America. Simply put, it was this: Aside from an occasional bistro, have you ever dined in a good French restaurant in America?

The answer, sometimes after a scratch on the nose, always came back, no. This was not out of chauvinism or ignorance. These were generous people, often purveyors of wines and liqueurs, who traveled, prospecting and visiting clients in every far corner of America. But one time, while dining with a major wine grower, I paused and thought to ask him a follow-up question:

Why?

The director of Moët & Chandon did not reflect long before he came back with the answer. "Have you ever heard good American jazz played in France?" (Though there are many who try.) "The good ones stay home." The exceptions seem to be those chefs who studied in France, apprenticed in France (it is not enough to have an idea; there must be an overview, for French cuisine is part of its civilization), began, at least, a career there, rose to recognition, and still hold forth in the kitchen created in this country. In addition, it helps to have relatives in France who maintain contact with French food professionals as a window to legitimate food supplies. Something else: As with theater, you can't have a good restaurant without a good public. The audience counts for keeping up the level of performance on the stage or in the kitchen. There are very few French living in their cultural swim in America (the exception is Louisiana, where the exceptional results speak for themselves). The French may travel, they love to visit, but the French always go home; Champlain, Radisson, and Lafayette died in Europe. John Winthrop did not.

Correspondingly, there are goodly numbers of Italians in America and in Boston, and this Mediterranean influence is felt in a variety of happy and far-reaching ways.

OLIVES

10 City Sq.
Charlestown, MA 02129
Tel. 617/242–1999

This is the hottest new restaurant in Boston, and it just might be the best Boston expression of a coming art in restaurants. The chef's name is English, but he cooks like an Italian. Todd and Olivia English do new things with American foods that Italians might do were they not inescapably Italian. **Olives** is not in the city's north end, known for its Italian restaurants, but it might be in the north end of Italy (try around Florence, or up in Montepulcino). On the oldest Main Street in America, Olives finds itself very much an American trattoria, Italian—or perhaps

Provençal—in tradition and feeling and in the style of its cooking; or a fusion of both places, as the two are often fused in the minds of their inhabitants. It lives in its own neighborhood like a neighborhood restaurant, making no concession to those who come across the Charles River to get there. When it recently moved to larger quarters, it kept to the same neighborhood and still takes no reservations for parties of less than six. The hundred or so seats make its setting somewhat less than very intimate (think bentwood and upholstered banquettes) and are on a first-come, first-served basis. Six is when they start filling up at night. Olives serves no lunch, but the tables turn at night—three times for dinner—so its's no place to linger.

Olives are the key to everything to eat at the restaurant. An enormous jar on the bar, which is a very good place to eat, is marked *Olio di Oliva,* and this is the cooking motif. Here Charlestown meets Tuscany. The jar is stuffed with grape and vine leaves; a plate of garlic-marinated olives rests at hand. You are encouraged to try them first, for this is the taste of the things that will come. You may especially appreciate the *lasagne al forno.* It is baked in a brick oven; the meat inside is rabbit. A word about the *forno* (oven): The restaurant is almost a kiln in itself. Wood fires burn constantly. One is in an oven, a second is in a grill, and a wood-fired rotisserie also slowly turns. What this does to the ambient summer temperature inside the restaurant shouldn't be told, but the selection of woods is exactly right to the taste of the meats. Apple, ash, oak, and sugar maple lend delectable sweet touches to meats. But the restaurant is capable of rising from the obvious to the sublime. For starters, there's warm Parmesan pudding, lushed with a creamed sweet-pea sauce—a trick Todd picked up in Tuscany from an ancient recipe—and this is hardly your standard trattoria fare; neither is charcoal-grilled octopus or squid, often seen along the Mediterranean coast where both animals are food staples.

Tuscan bean soup is done its classic way (who would ask to improve on it?) with gold globules dribbled down, like an extra-virgin oil slick, on top of the hot beans. Speaking of olives again, there is a tart of olives, with anchovies and onion; and very good with that, a salad with wood-smoked prosciutto. Special for all of us who love Thanksgiving for one particular delicacy is turkey osso bucco, which is what Todd calls his tail of the turkey. It is braised very slowly to keep its taste sweet like warm foie gras. Olives is a different

sort of place, even as it strikes its one thematic note. Aside from goat cheese, there is no dairy, and olive oil is used for butter in dishes such as salmon cakes with lentils (always wonderful with salmon) and aioli, or grilled tuna with garlic mashed potatoes. That American cooking is again relying on olives (*see* Chapter 9, Plimoth Plantation) may be an indication that it has come full circle. But with all its wit and popular appeal, Olives remains among the most reasonably priced restaurants in Boston, and the financial path to salvation may be the path that most American restaurants must consider.

One of the mightiest restaurants to come from Boston's past and speak to its future is **Biba.**

BIBA

272 Boylston St.
Boston, MA 02116
Tel. 617/426-7878

Is it an accident that inside the doors of this stunning palate palace the accents are Mediterranean, too? Here is a restaurant run by one of Boston's leading chefs and culinary lights, Lydia Shire. In Biba she has come up with something that, were it in literature, would not be considered new. She has had a long career in Boston, yet when she opened Biba in 1989, it astonished the city and nobody could figure it out. Biba has been called different, eclectic, and eccentric. Biba is all and yet none of these things. Biba is the first of the new food Romantics.

First, there is the unusual configuration of the place to consider. Biba, on one of the oldest corners of Boston, is a duplex of dining in a glass-and-steel mall. Its first floor has *tapas* (hors d'oeuvres in the Spanish style) and a splendid bar. Sherry is traditional, so you should try a fino or perhaps an amontillado. A mural on the wall depicts fat people. Are you about to become one of them? Is this what the chef has to say? Is it all inevitable and irresistible? Either way it's a daring argument from a chef, and you can cogitate on it until your table is ready and you're summoned upstairs.

The curving, open staircase gives glimpses of the glass-walled wine cellar, which is more a freestanding object of adoration than a cellar in the ground. Air-conditioning keeps it at the optimum temperature, so a cellar is superfluous. Besides, this way it gives you ideas.

Upstairs holds about 150 people in a room so serious about dining that the tables are wrapped in butcher paper. Oriental carpet patterns decorate the ceiling. The walls are bright yellow, and despite the fact that we know the immense solidity of Boston and Back Bay is all around us, we

have the distinct impression that we are about to break bread
under the canopy of an Arabian sheik. And some bread it is:
a different kind of Mediterranean, the kind that might come
on rose petals or grape leaves and goes "glumph" in the
mouth. You want linguine in parchment?—glumph. How
about some scallops and chili?—wham. And deviled pigs'
feet?—bang. Hot buttered chestnuts?—pow! Each course
comes on its separate plate in a concept of exquisite imagination. Each plate is a story of love. Undeniably. Quail grilled
on rosemary: puckerish. Ginger crab with pea-pod blossoms:
singing with flowers. Citrus salmon with parsley cakes: likewise. As though from a Piedmontese spectacular they come,
but with greater panache, size, and intensity. The customer
gets much more than a mouthful: The performance is bravu-
ra and fortissimo. There is nothing hidden yet everything is
tantalizing. Satisfaction explodes in an instant and is all-
embracing; then it is gone, and a new fascination comes on a
new plate. It is like dining with Salome, an original concept
in a modern venue. This restaurant is for anyone who likes
big-scene movies, the kind that aren't made anymore, for
television is too small and most restaurants too boring. Biba is
a place of epic tastes.

The individual frames—the dishes—are filigreed with
romantic fragrance. Smoked shad is offered with profligate
morels, asparagus, and onions, and comes wrapped in a pie.
Lamb is glazed with pomegranates and dressed with pearls
of onions, draped with leeks, and scented with garlic.

To say all this is not ultimately exquisite and pleasing
would be to succumb to the trap of damning the different, or
the generous, with the name of eccentric. But Biba and Lydia
Shire certainly give a pleasure that is copious and long-last-
ing. After a hiatus in California, where she started the
kitchen in the Four Seasons Hotel, that she and her new
restaurant would be found in a city of such old and carefully
established tastes as Boston is perhaps proof that she has

wisely picked her spot to be different, and noticed she is. After a generation of the minimalism of nouvelle cuisine, Boston is perhaps the logical place where a revolution of romantic excess should begin.

As intriguing as these prospects are, there is more to Boston food than is found in its restaurants. You should be about early on Saturday morning for two reasons: to visit the second great Boston market, and for our appointment after the market. Saturday morning early is exactly the right time for the invocation of the swells of people and the smells of foods in the antique and rustic **Haymarket.** It is held on Friday and Saturday mornings; Saturday is by far the best. This is where the New England Produce Market (*see* Chapter 3) in Boston's satellite town of Chelsea migrates on weekends. Adjacent to but in competition with the heavily promoted, admittedly lovely Quincy Market, but treated in a poor-relation, nonofficial way by the city of Boston (for reasons most often used by cities, mainly money), is this teeming, festering, and most interesting of markets. The Haymarket is a real market in the true sense of the word, a center for farm products, meat, specialty produce, and seafood that is second to none in North American big cities. It is the grazing ground and brokerage forum of the fruit and vegetable wholesaler, restaurant owner, and homemaker. Its dynamic is unofficial: It is the client of no public-relations agency, it appears in no glossy and colorful visitor's brochure and on no city maps, and those who work for the city, even for its mammoth tourist industry, will give you no information on it or city street markers to guide you. I don't want to say it is poor, but could we say it is a market of the unconnected and honest? As in honestly hard-working. Its values are the best in New England for so many things (wait till you see what they sell lobsters for). It is also unofficial because, after it has eked out an income for more than 200 years on the bleak granite of its city streets, the city is trying to destroy the market to make room for a superhighway project. Where would the city of Florence be today if it tore down its buildings every time a bureaucrat wanted a superhighway to go to the sea? Roads are no good without places to go to, and the Haymarket is certainly a place to go. In the last decade of the 20th century it is perhaps unique in our country: a place where a common farm heritage continues, where the small farmer or fisherman can come and prosper on what he grows or catches, and where the particular can find what they want. It has its defenders in the community, but outside of New England and Boston it is a place few tourists know, and that is why it is so excellent to visit.

THE HAYMARKET
Bounded by Blackstone,
Hanover, and North Sts.
Boston, MA 02116

Go a few paces toward the water from the Copley Square Hotel. Arrive a little after dawn on any Saturday of the year, and 222 licensed vendors will have set up their boxes, tailgates of vans and trucks, stands, and stalls, and opened shutters of timeworn shops in the wall of the vast area that is the most photographed spot in New England.

At first, as you come upon Blackstone Street, looming behind its tall hedges of trucks, you wander through stacks and mazes of cardboard-boxed fruit from California, celery stalks, broccoli from Salinas, oranges for export marked with Japanese characters and coated with resin and vegetable wax. But persist, for this is only the edge of the market. Penetrate and you will be rewarded. Even among the truckers' stands are things that are worthwhile: cartons of strawberries and blueberries from the Northwest; pick up one to drop in the trunk of your car, and you've got a whole winter of canned fruit to enjoy. At 90 Blackstone Street the shops in the building along the roadway start to become worthwhile with **Puritan Beef.** Here are many beautiful things to buy amid butchers wielding knives, whacking flesh at a huge block in the center of the shop. Keep back near the shelves that line the walls. There are fresh oxtails hanging, and beef, too. This is as colorful a market as you'd find in a souk. Fresh goat meat is 79¢ a pound—try that on your kebab. Goat meat is nutty in flavor with less fat than lamb, so it goes better with vegetables. Fresh-killed goat hangs in whole and half carcasses, unstripped, like rabbit. They will cut it up for you to go, as the clanging knives tell you. But there are literally bins of legs of goat already cleaved, and skinned skulls with their eyes still stuck in their heads; this is as comprehensive a goat market as exists to the public this side of Fez. Goat meat is a staple all over the North African edge of the Mediterranean, where they don't eat pigs and there isn't enough forage for cows.

Coming from the shop steps, we turn our back on the vendors lining the gutter as the tassels of their ears of corn show up limp and black or are cut off altogether. We keep to the line of brick buildings that are among the oldest in America; it is along this street that Franklin lived. Next door to the Puritan Market is 94 Blackstone Street (it will be hard to continue to be precise with numbers, for here and there they dissolve, or buildings have been removed or entrances have been bricked over or they have been incorporated into other addresses, or all of these things). Here a moblet is crammed inside, for the shop is small. A hanging sign advertises: Shawarma Sandwiches, Orders to Go, Middle Eastern Specialties, Falafel, Hummus, Tabbouli, Kafta, and Hamburgers. Everything is under $3! A little Lebanese man inside is fixing all of these things at once. He works hard while his customers stroll in and out on their way through the market. Some take home what he sells, as they have come from where he did—America is for everyone, he says.

We skip here and there, taking in only highlights, and no longer wander into the truckers' files at the curb unless we see something very special, for there is an important appointment that must be kept later this morning. At No. 96 is **The Blackstone Market.** Here are Syrian bread, jumbo eggs (a dozen for under $1), eggplant dip, "falafel from the

old country" (Lebanon), cow's feet (peeled), and oxtails and T-bone steak (at $3.25).

Is it bargains you want? Try No. 96A Blackstone, **Bargain Basement Beef.** You stoop and go down a flight of stairs from the street to an emporium that sells beef, in parts and its cuts, at $2 a pound. At No. 98 is **Harry's,** for cheeses and cold cuts. Outside, a smoking grill emits the savory smells of sausages, onions, and peppers. "Whenever the crowd calms down," says Harry, "we just throw some more peppers and sausages on the grill and watch them come in." Aside from what's hot, what are the best things for walking and eating? Brie is the best-seller (Arc de Triomphe brand); $2 gets a wedge big enough for two people. Gouda also sells well at $2. Inside are a host of cheeses, and what looks good at the right price? Roquefort Bee Brand is $4.50 a pound, and Italian gorgonzola, $4.49. Harry's customers won't spend much more than that, so there is where he stays. "French bread" is less than $1; it doesn't seem very French but seems a bargain nevertheless.

At No. 100 Blackstone is the **Haymarket Pizzeria.** This is in one of the oldest and most atmospheric places you're likely to find. Use even the slightest imagination, and there's no doubt that Ben Franklin (and not the one from around the corner) ate here. I doubt he paid much more, though what he ate was different. Now a whole pizza, a large one, goes for $5. You can get all you will need as a slice, and it's hot from the oven. "One dolla, pleese." I peel off the $1 (no tax) and step back from the counter into the dining room, which reeks with atmosphere. The tables are sawhorse. The floors are concrete. The captains' chairs are under big skylights. The hurly-burly of the market across the street comes freely in through the open facade, where the sun splashes across the vegetable and fruit stands. Beyond are the evil swirl of roadways that threaten to overrun this almost timeless historic legacy. The taste of fresh oregano in my pizza is the real southern Italian McCoy. It's a taste of pizza that brings back the first taste, and where it was taken. There is bargaining and movement of fresh fish and vegetables; I see a tailgate drop down a load of fresh figs. The Parisian market on the rue Levis has nothing on this.

At No. 114 Blackstone is **John's Market.** Here are more cold cuts and cheeses, with a particularly extensive selection among the meats. Outside are sacks of loose nuts—pistachios, cashews, pignoli, peanuts—and candy, too. Sausages sputter with peppers on the grill to pull passersby in by the nose. A crèche of cheeses offers a generous choice. Inside, the air-conditioning hums while loaves of meat sit behind cold glass. Bologna, several sorts of hams, pastrami—all sport neat, handwritten signs. Prosciutto, margaretta pepperoni,

Genova natural salami, and mortadella all keep the slicing machine spinning and the shop air heavy with spicy aromas. There are olives from Kalamata (Greece) and Sicily. Smoked mozzarella seems to be the people's choice to go with the sandwiches they take out.

At No. 118 Blackstone is the **Haymarket Bakery.** Now exotic fruits rule the stand and the weighing basket outside the store, as the clientele is heavily Caribbean. The fruits and tubers are essentially Central American: yucca, brown-skinned and waxy from Costa Rica; batatos, red-skinned and lumpy; cilantro; plantains from San Salvador; fresh basil; and green, pepper-shape okra of exceptional size. Eddos, brown and curly vegetables from Central America, are always on hand as well as mounds of spearmint to sweeten your meats. All are vital with health and of excellent quality. Here is the ideal place for a chef, a restaurateur, or a host to go looking for the rare, the exotic, and the strange to spice up a menu.

Coming to the corner of Hanover Street, we turn left and head up toward Union. Almost instantly we reach the **live lobster stand** run by Mike Anderson. He has been coming to this same spot in the Haymarket every Saturday for the last 10 years. Here Mike Anderson augments his lobsterman's income and finds human contact. He tends a line of 500 traps out of Rockport harbor and fishes on the swells five days every week. This one day, Saturday, he brings about 200 lobsters down to town. He sells them at $3.49 a pound: the best deal in Boston. The sale earns him the money to enjoy his Saturday night on the town; on Sunday he takes the day off. That is still the life of the New England fisherman, unyielding in its routine.

Mike is communicative and friendly; his stand is a good place to get a lab demonstration on lobsters. They are close up and very lively; he will show you how to pick them up by the carapace and squeeze them to tell a soft shell from a hard shell (*see* Chapter 12). His opinion is that the hard shells, with more meat, are the ones to take, so he differs from me. He also has Jonah crabs, like Florida stone crabs, and sells conch at $1 a pound. Many of his shoppers are Boston Asians, as well as Boston Italians, regular customers who will take nothing but the very best and come by to haggle with him at even these prices. It is part of the human exchange of the day, and each expects it.

If you are going to Rockport and want to see a fine old pier, try stopping at the wharf and asking for Anderson's boat, the *Judith Lee*. There you can direct your queries about lobster buying five days a week, or write:

MIKE ANDERSON
25 King St.
Rockport, MA 01966

Catty-corner to Anderson's stand is **Haymarket Fish** (in front of 389 Hanover St.). This is the place to come for what is fresh and running, at very, very low prices: 4 pounds of salmon for $5. Bluefish, cod, and blackfish, too, are on the ice shavings when they are running, and even local (Maine) shrimp are available around Christmas. Sea scallops are unusually fine and an exceptional buy. (Keep in mind that the Boston fish auction, which the public cannot attend, is held in the early predawn less than four blocks away.)

The next stand has salt cod in long, flaky shafts looking like splits of balsa wood. The market ends where Hanover Street meets Union. I feel like exploring the line of old pubs and restaurants going down the back of the old street, but there are many old streets in Boston, and they will have to wait for another time.

The special Saturday cooking class at the Ritz-Carlton gets underway at 10:30 AM. You meet a group of nice people with similar interests gathered in the little ballroom on the mezzanine. Coffee is served, and you have breakfast around several little tables (if you haven't already had a warm slice at the Haymarket Pizzeria). A hotel staff member gives a little welcome talk (the majority of the students come from Boston), a dietitian discourses on the value of nutrition (she's for it), and a tour of the kitchen begins. This first-rate professional site contains several valuable ideas: one, a kitchen shouldn't be an afterthought or a second-rate room—here it's flooded with light; two, good utensils and work surfaces are vital—stainless steel is everywhere; three, the division of the space into hot and cold sides by a center aisle seems to be a common denominator of most professional kitchens.

We then tour the dining room, which is marvelous. Czech chandeliers drip rings of cobalt-blue and white glass. The rug is blue and gold in a twisting vine Aubusson design. The ceilings are white and cream, picked out with gilded moldings. The blue-and-white curtained windows overlook the green glow of the park.

The door opens and our chef on hand for the day, Parisian Gèrard Pangaud, appears. His cuisine reflects northern French style and traditions. His reputation comes as a direct result of a talent that placed the restaurants he headed among the finest in France. He had a thirst for travel and guided a restaurant to the top of New York's lists when he came to that city. He is now opening his own restaurant in Washington, DC. With all that, he is still a young man whose love for golf is almost as ardent as his devotion to cooking; America is the right country for him to live in. Who should take classes with such an acknowledged master? Everyone.

Not only do you get your questions answered without waiting, but the essences, smells, and perfumes of a cooking class are are some things that don't come out in a video. For example: the difference between taste and flavor. "Taste is color, flavor is hue." Lemon taste comes from juice, flavor from zest. This observation emerges while he makes curried oysters with citrus vinaigrette. As we prepare a mousse of Roquefort: "There is too much attention paid these days to the visual. It's nice to have things look nice, but taste is still the king of the kitchen. There are four different tastes: sweet, sour, salt, and bitter. Rich taste will occur if all four tastes are in the same dish. Try to avoid this."

While making stock for a fish dish, he says, "My mother didn't have time to make stock every night, but she made good things for the family." He shows us a shortcut to stock for the home: water, thyme, garlic, butter, and shallots are gently heated in a pan for 5 minutes. The result soon fills the kitchen with fragrances of France.

On cooking oil: Grapeseed oil is the cooking oil with the highest temperature of fusion (temperature at which it breaks down)—600°F. It has no taste and is often mixed (in Italy) with olive oil to make a cheaper product. How to tell if your olive oil is pure? If it doesn't get runny and otherwise come apart when it is heated in the pan.

When finishing green tomato soup, Pangaud gives this interesting suggestion: The perfect accompaniment for caviar is tomato (instead of lemon), because of its acidity.

After a break, we return for the opulence of lunch with our cook and classmates. The chef comments on each dish. He finds one of the wines doesn't go so well with one of the courses, but everything else seems to have been done to expectations, and everyone is satisfied. The out-of-towners trade dining information with the Bostonians and addresses and telephone numbers are exchanged, with promises for a reunion dinner soon.

It is after three when a round of applause follows the chef through the door. From the windows I can see that Saturday traffic is light, and there will be no trouble exiting the city. But you can't go home yet, I am told. You can't go to Boston and miss **Jasper's,** say my new friends from the class.

And they are right. For more than 10 years Jasper White has been lighting up the Boston palate and putting smiles on its lips. It started at the Seasons restaurant in the Bostonian Hotel where he opened with Lydia Shire, and you know how she does what she does. Now both are in new restaurants (Jasper's was redone in 1991) and having the time of their lives.

JASPER'S

240 Commercial St.
Boston, MA 02109
Tel. 617/523–1126

The long slab of exposed brick wall is meant to suggest age, I suspect, but what Jasper White does is a new twist on regional cuisine. It might be called New England nouvelle, but with portions like Lydia Shire's (that go bang in the mouth). Sit down in any one of the red lacquered chairs. Right away, it starts with the breadsticks: They're flavored— sometimes subtly with cheese, perhaps Cheddar, but sometimes with spinach, sometimes spicy onion—a different flavor, if not for every table, then for every night. The cod cakes are classic, but they are supported by an unexpected cast of sizzling hot greens and bacon (remember the pork in the chowder) that give you a range of tastes to play with that go pop in the mouth. Styles come into fashion in restaurants as they do in clothes. After a while it's impossible to say where something begins, but rabbit (remember the lasagna at Olives?) is a taste (probably because of its Italians) Boston likes. Here the tortellini has a thumping rabbit sauce; it's made from the carcass and finished with the liver. The pasta is filled with milky ricotta with the sharp tang of Romano; the dish is layered over with thin shavings of the rabbit itself. There is the lucious élan of game about this place. It is packaged in the most outstanding dish of sautéed wild duck foie

gras with brandied peaches in its own crackling that we have
seen. The sweet and tart of the game, and the sugar and soft-
ness of the peaches, and their textures, tingle with each other.
It merits the icy bottle of Château Suidereau on Jasper's list.
What could be classified as almost as wild, for they are wild
to the taste and seldom seen even where they are plentiful,
are real Maine shrimp. They come to you floating on a
seafood platter, as beautiful and tasting of iodine and the
sweet-smelling Atlantic as any *cotriade* along the Brittany
coast. Jasper White has added flaky tempura mussels to his
platter; savory, buttery scallops; lobster sausages; and clumps
of sweet clams; with this it can truly be said, you haven't been
to Boston and tasted its watery delights if you've missed this
best that was saved for last.

But even with Jasper's it isn't over. I don't mean to rush
you, but there is one more thing we must get in. Who could
visit Boston without going to the North End? Currently
Boston's Italian section, it's crammed with cafés, candy stores,
gelaterias, pizzerias, and restaurants that strike an authentic
Italian note because the large Italian-American population
keeps them that way. There are all manner of interesting
food places for exploration in any amount of time you choose
to take. What is proposed, as an introduction (or a goodbye),
is one of the oldest.

VITTORIA CAFÉ
296 Hanover St.
Boston, MA 02113
Tel. 617/227–7606

Vittoria Café has been a landmark in the district for 70
years, since before the North End went Italian. Can you
imagine what American coffee tasted like to an Italian in
1920? The Vittoria Café became like a drop of water on the

parched plain. It is still an excellent place to have coffee in Boston. The sign on the window says it: Lavazza. Lavazza is one of the two great coffees of Italy (the other is Illy). When you go into Vittoria to have your espresso, or cappuccino, don't ask for a decaf. They don't have it, and you won't need it. Nobody in this world understands coffee as well as the Italians, or makes it so well. As a demonstration, Vittoria has the great, new Italian coffee-making machines produced by Bezzera. They have built-in pumps so powerful that they get

the coffee into the cup before the caffeine fraction in the grind has time to become part of the extraction. This is the safest and most healthful—and I might add delicious—way to make decaffeinated coffee. The caffeine fraction (and how to avoid it), was part of a study made by the director of Illy coffee, and the Bezzera machines were made to perform according to the same specifications. So, espresso or cappuccino, order what you like at Vittoria; sweet dreams are assured by Dr. Illy. Should you choose a cappuccino, however, it will be the best that you can have from Boston to Viareggio. Just watch Armando, who makes it, delicately put a head on a cup. It's the same sort of art as putting the head on a beer. Armando builds it. He gushes a little cappuccino into the cup. He adds cinnamon. He puts in more cappuccino. He taps in more cinnamon. More cappuccino, more cinnamon, until what he hands you is a white mound of sweet foam with coffee aroma and taste.

If you need a pastry with all this, Vittoria Café has them: cannoli, baba, *tiramisu* (*see* Chapter 2, Doc's). Then, if there's any room, to put you in true Italian hands, try a grappa. It's got the aroma of a bed of straw and the kick of a mule. Because this is not a salon, it's priced at only $3.

Which is the way it should be. *Arrivederci,* John Winthrop. We are much more than Puritans now.

CHAPTER 11

BLUE WATERS AND MUD CLAMS

York to Portland, Maine

The trail through the millionaire towns of York, Ogunquit, and Kennebunkport fetches up some tasty bargains in unexpected food exploration and leads to perhaps the most interesting town along the Maine coastline, Portland. Its port area, rejuvenated since the 1970s, makes Portland the San Francisco of the east, but smaller. Cleaned up and scrubbed up, with trellis-spangled walks and gaslit streets, Portland is the one city on the whole East Coast that is booming, but gently.

The metropolitan area contains 250,000 people. The city itself has only a comfortable 60,000. The parts to wander through are down-home-size, which makes visiting the tidy restaurant-lined warrens a manageable delight.

HIGHLIGHTS:
• A down-east clambake
• Stuffing for lobster
• A famous hot dog
• Maine's "most exotic" greens and herbs
• The freshest restaurant
• Windows over waters
• A fishing port and porpoises
• A walking tour of Portland
• A thumbnail guide to clams
LENGTH OF LOOP: 51 miles
LENGTH OF STAY: Three days

To get to Maine, take Interstate 95 north from Boston. Come off the interstate at Exit 4; the itinerary follows the general direction of U.S. Route 1.

All right, a word about billboards: You will see plenty of them along Maine highways. Some will be helpful. A plethora will invite you to the gauntlet of outlet malls along U.S. 1 where you are promised huge discounts. But after all, you are on vacation in the outdoor state of Maine. Is it worth it to stop and spend a day indoors?

Instead of shoe shopping (Bata is everywhere) on arriving in Maine, wouldn't it be better to head straight to a clambake? You can get in on one in York Harbor, just after you cross the state line from New Hampshire. There is singing and dancing, the country music is fresh as the air, and nowhere do they do a clambake as well and as thoroughly as they do it here.

FOSTER'S DOWN EAST CLAMBAKE

Box 486
Rte. 1A
York Harbor, ME 03911
Tel. 207/363-3255

Take Exit 4 off Interstate 95 north. Continuing on Route 1, turn left at the light in about a quarter of a mile; a left turn at the next traffic signal will put you on Route 1A. In about 1½ miles the low-lying buildings of **Foster's Down East Clambake** appear on the left.

As soon as you drive into the grounds the atmosphere is circuslike: Painted posts and portals are stuck in the ground; little signs point out the three major buildings and a host of other attractions. There are lobster ponds, clam pools, and horseshoe pits. Truly, this is an official place for clambakers. When former President George Bush and Barbara

Bush staged a clambake for Congress on the White House lawn, guess who they got to do it? Foster's Down East Clambake went to Washington with lobster crates, clams, corn, and seaweed. Over 1,000 members of Congress and their dates showed up. And they didn't get any better treatment than you'll get at the clambake facility in York Harbor.

The most important sign to notice is the one for the Clambake Pavilion. That is where you want to go. Clambakes are held noons and evenings, strictly by reserva-

tion. You must write or call ahead, a least from the road, to reserve places.

Because the pavilion is low and screened on all sides from the weather, clambakes can be held rain or shine, but not in the winter. (The Fin and Claw restaurant is on the premises; you can go there in winter or if you don't want to go to a clambake.) Even if you are a confirmed antisocial type, the clambake is an experience in village living and eating; it's the thing to do in New England. The pavilion holds a group the size of a small town, around 300, which gathers around an open hearth while the clambake goes on all day or far into the night. If you have no group to join for such gatherings, Foster's puts one together twice a day when they are busy. Try to arrive in the early evening. There is horseshoe pitching and volleyball outside, as well as places for kids to play: Foster's covers 7 acres. Teams choose up for softball and soccer, too, but at sundown everyone comes inside the pavilion. A cherub-faced giant in a straw hat and overalls plays on a guitar. He opens his mouth and out comes the sound of a frog, making even the sophisticates from Boston and Manhattan laugh. He wears red suspenders, croons washtub ballads, and on spoons plays tunes like "Jimmy Crack Corn." As the shadows descend an open fire offers warmth.

Paul Murphy, one of the two owners of Foster's, and Kevin Tacy, the other, slide an iron grill over the flames and heft a great wooden chest up on top. The chest is cedar, and that's for the flavor. What it's filled with is the ambrosia of the sea and of the fields: clambake. First, on the bottom of the chest, is a layer of weed, as in seaweed. It's wet with seawater—that's where the steam comes from— and it's salty. Then, working up from the bottom of the chest, is a layer of potatoes and onions. The potatoes are baby reds from the fields of Maine. The onions are little yellows and loaded with sweetness. Next comes a layer of what most people come to Maine for—lobsters. These are the kind locally called "chicken lobster," which means under 1¼ pounds. Some people declare this to be the sweetest, most succulent size. There is no doubt, however, that their taste has nothing to do with the limp, desiccated representatives of their race that decorate the supermarket shelves of America farther south. On top of the lobsters comes a heaping of corn. Few don't know how good this native American staple is boiled and buttered. Fewer know it's better roasted with steamers. Here's the place to find out.

Lastly, but not as an afterthought, come the steamers, the clams. It's not for nothing that despite all this goodness simmering, bubbling, and boiling in the great wooden box— think of the lobsters—this event is called a clambake. There must be something wonderfully special about these clams. Is there?

As the man who knows them says, Ha!

According to Murphy, only a fool or a poor man digs for clams in the sand. Once the sand is inside the shell, it only comes out in the mouth. Get your clams from a muddy bottom. It is important that the clams you eat down in this part of Maine, where the beaches are sandy, have been taken from the waters up around Brunswick, where the coast is rockbound. The "mud clam," as it is called by clammers and restaurant owners, is what you want. Fishermen get paid more for mud clams—also called soft shells—than for sand clams.

Despite the great heat and dramatic belch of flame, the temperature goes up very slowly in the steamer box because of all the water in the weeds and in the foods. While things are kept jumping with horseshoes and games outside the pavilion, and songs inside, it takes the better part of two hours for dinner to cook.

Once clams have been collected, there's the question of how to prepare them for the feast. To wash, or not to wash, and then with what? Even the mere washing of clams provokes a great deal of discussion. Some people say a saltwater mollusk should never be washed with fresh water, period. It's the taste of the sea you want; don't wash it away. Others, and they are just as insistent, though by no means as vocal, as if they wanted to keep it secret, say that oysters, clams, and mussels should not only be washed with fresh water, but that it should be barley water, with oatmeal in it, to purge the clams.

Murphy says it's an old wives' tale that oatmeal (although it's widely used, especially in city clam bars) gets foul water, not to mention sand, out of clams. His Down East Clambake does 50 bushels of clams every day in season, turning them over too fast for barley water to have any effect. Six days is about the minimum time for oatmeal to have any effect, but who would want to eat a clam held so long? At Down East, Murphy and Tacy spray their clams in fresh water and let it go at that.

The box opens and under a cloud of smoke the steamers, simmering in their own juices, appear. The shells are open and the flesh awaits.

These soft shells from Brunswick are a medium-size clam. Not big, but not as small as a cherrystone either. On the way from the plate to your throat they need no sauce. The mist of vapors of onions, potatoes, and iodine from the weed has gotten inside their shells. The wood of the box has added its flavor; there is one lobster per person, but everyone comes back for clams. As the feast becomes the entertainment, everyone concentrates on the food. The fire subsides and the evening passes with the cracking of shells and groans of contentment.

Little ones are carried to cars. You're not stuck in the middle of nowhere when you get out: Less than half a mile away, virtually on the same block, is a historic old harbor hotel.

There you will find four-poster beds, a Continental breakfast, and a view of a sandy beach when you get up.

YORK HARBOR INN
Box 573, Rte. 1A
York Harbor, ME 03911
Tel. 207/373-5119 or
800/343-3869 (outside ME only)

The heart of the **York Harbor Inn** is a 1637 fishing cabin (one of the oldest buildings on the east coast of North America) architecturally integrated into the multiwinged hotel, which perches its dormers and widow walks above the sea. From the tables in its dining room you can see the pink outlines of the Shoal Islands, where the cabin originally stood. The walk in the perennial garden around the inn is lupine-spiked in June and traced with lichens and shrubs that keep your socks free of sand. The York Harbor Inn is as happy a marriage of the antique and the comfortable as you are likely to find along a coast that delights in an architecture that nearly matches the sea in surprises.

Double rooms start at well under $100 and go up to about $125. Some are furnished with four-poster beds and some have brass beds; while all have antiques as accents, the honeymoon suite has a double Jacuzzi.

Leading from the inn, a scenic footpath along the cliffs is called the marginal way—a nice way of saying don't step over the edge. You should wear walking shoes and be covered up in case of a sudden breeze, but don't duck the walk, because it's a great way to get the feel of the Maine coastline. If you follow the path in a ring around the harbor, you find fishing boats and pleasure craft. You can take a cruise aboard a 50-foot sailboat, with cocktails served, or a sunset whale-watch voyage. Special evenings for guests of the inn are even arranged at Foster's Clambake Pavilion.

The trail away from the port blends into the hills, or you can discover the mini-Newport of York mansions by the sea. In all, paths trace four walks; pamphlets are available at the inn that describe even the plants, rocks, and lobster pot markings you will encounter. The inn has a gazebo, as well as 12-speed bikes ideal for exploring one of the loveliest mixes of scenery and hamlets that you'll see on the south coast. A stay at the York Harbor Inn will give you a taste of the benefits of living like a millionaire without needing to be one.

The restaurant is a place that takes chances. Its chef, Gerald Bonzi, has been on the scene for 11 years, long enough to give him the sense of security to make his own stocks and sauces. This is not your, "Hey Joe, steam one to go" lobster stand. Here is lobster for a Sunday palate; for example: Yorkshire lobster supreme. This is a whole lobster served in the shell, cracked and opened up; in the fissures, a tartare of shrimp and scallop meat is blended. Everything is under a thermidor sauce brought up with shallots, sherry, and Parmesan cheese. It is the most frequently ordered entrée at the York Harbor Inn, containing as it does, three of the chief attractions of Maine: lobster, shrimp, and scallops. The delicate and sophisticated thermidor sauce, blended with sherry instead of cognac, plays with three different tastes.

This is quite a risky concept along a coast where the supremacy of the lobster, plain and pure, and the public's demand for it, keeps many chefs from trying anything new. Bonzi's lobster-stuffed chicken is another example of his adventurousness. Lightly sautéed bread crumbs and Boursin cheese are added to the mixture. The two meats look the same, but they do not taste the same and they have different textures.

Back on the road, and moving from the sublime, a ridiculous value in food awaits you. Make sure to save a mealtime and room for a visit to **Flo's.** Flo's has no phone number or address; just a roadside stand on your right going north marks the spot where for 20 years a sign has said it all: **Flo's Hot Dogs,** and nothing more.

FLO'S HOT DOGS
Rte. 1
York, ME

But nothing is so simple as that: These are the best hot dogs in Maine. Pull in to the little parking depression and go inside to order.

While it may be correct to say all kinds of people stop at Flo's, not many tourists do. She's not in the phone book; the Chamber of Commerce will deny she exists. Her clientele is almost purely local or accidental trade, but once they come they keep on coming. Rolls-Royces and trucks line up equally; Flo's hot dogs are democratic but kept secret by mutual conspiracy. Most cars with out-of-state plates drive past, their occupants never suspecting what taste paradise might be harbored within a little roadside shack. Those who do stop, perhaps receiving a tip at a gas station, or to relieve a little traveling pressure on their wallets, get an object lesson in humility. There are no tables and chairs in Flo's, and just a few stools. The people come in and stand up, and the place is packed. Despite the interdiction on publicity, Flo's business is booming.

She has the best hot dogs in Maine, some say, because she cooks them best and has the best sauce. And it is as saucy and sharp as Flo herself. They don't use mustard up here— not enough bite. Flo's sauce takes after Flo, I'm sure you'll agree.

The hot dogs are deliciously hot steamed, and so are the rolls. That the spicy sauce is red and not catsup is the only clue to its mysteries I can give. It's no good to beg, bark, or flatter. Paul Bocuse once told me how to make his truffle soup, but Flo won't give up the secret of her sauce.

If you want one of these hot, crackly, fat sausages, you must come up and get 'em. Head toward Ogunquit on Route 1; Flo's is actually in Cape Neddick—keep your eye skinned. I cast my vote with the majority: They are the best hot dogs in Maine.

From Flo's door, Ogunquit is 5 miles farther up Route 1 North. It has antiques shops, a summer theater with a national reputation, fine homes parading down to the water on the Shore Road, an old and established economy, and some very expensive restaurants. If you go to one of these, you are likely to wind up not with the taste of Maine in your mouth, but of Soho, the right bank of Lyon, or some other food headquarters that happens to be trendy. Do you really want to eat pasta pesto here? Or vinaigrette with macadamia nuts?

Getting a look at real Maine food in Ogunquit means going out to the farm before stopping in town. The nicest farm of all is north on Route 1, across the bridge in the center of Ogunquit, and the first left turn onto Tatnick Road. Check your odometer: When 5.2 miles have clicked by, you should be in South Berwick. The road will be dirt, and if it is June through August, the 2½ acres on either side of the road will be waist-high in green leaves and pink and blue wild-flowers. You will have reached Arlis Sheffield's **Pain and Pleasure Farm,** where the smartest chefs in southern Maine come for produce.

PAIN AND PLEASURE FARM
Tatnick Rd.
South Berwick, ME 03908
Tel. 207/676–4072

This is a garden for a dream of summer, sun-drenched and vibrant with the singing of katydids and red-winged blackbirds. There is a house at the end of the road. What goes with it is a gardener for our times; and these may be renaissance times when it comes to farming.

Arlis Sheffield may be the renaissance farmer: He has anything but a farmer's background. Athlete and a suppressed chef in his school days; a graduate of Duke University with a master's degree in literature; raised in Texas, settled in Maine; Vietnam vet; five years a sous chef in Paris, where the food bug reemerged. He gave up being a chef when he got an idea: to grow foods for chefs alone, foods that were individual and different in taste. For seven years Arlis Sheffield has made his garden grow. The *Maine Organic Gardener and Farmer* writes that on his 2½ acres are raised "the most exotic varieties of herbs and produce in Maine, and possibly New England."

Along the path dividing the property in two he gives a tour and a feel of the garden that he laid out. Everything is grown for the table, to which it will go in a matter of hours after ripening.

There are edible flowers. Dwarf French marigolds and pinks thrive under the sun that drenches this field in the bright Maine summertime. Even at this short distance from the shore the moderating effect of the sea starts to lose its grip; the frosts of winter can last into June and return as early as the end of August. Still, there are the summer staples. The gay pink, yellow, and orange caps of nasturtiums last all season long spinning their flower chains, and according to Arlis they are the best-tasting flower. They have the attractive taste of pepper grass, he points out, and what a delightful way to add the zest of a different pepper to a salad. The leaves taste just as bright as the blossoms.

Arlis Sheffield takes as clients only local chefs who agree to accept a whole cycle of his seasonings, greens, and vegetables. They come out to Pain and Pleasure Farm (if you've ever gardened, you understand the name), where they walk the fields with Sheffield and talk about the results the chef is aiming for. They'll take and taste a stalk or a leaf of this or that, discussing and deciding what kind of food it would go with, just as they might with a wine. Gerald Bonzi from the York Harbor Inn is a client.

The seeds and plants come from all over the world. Arlis has had as many as 40 suppliers. He is particularly fond of his Japanese red shiso, which tastes like curry or cumin but brighter, as a living plant would be—just as fresh ginger is superior to dry. In Japan it is eaten as a garnish with sushi; it is also excellent with pasta. Red shiso looks like purple basil and grows waist-high until the first frosts.

In a separate garden plot no bigger than a few beach blankets, a three-year experiment in a planting green (a small bed given to trial plantings) is just bearing usable shoots. Sheffield has spent what amounts to a condensed month of his life on his knees over this little piece of ground, weeding out the unsuccessful from the successful greens, the weak from the strong, and now the bed is producing a lovely collection of greens that have adapted to conditions here: baby kale, baby collards, leeks, and greens for the salad plates of summer.

Loaded with eye appeal as well as taste, the Japanese mizuma is a mustard green stronger in taste than lettuce, but milder than most of its family. Saw-toothed and frilly, it is favored by chefs; greengrocers and vegetable sections of supermarkets never have it. Because it has a 40-day growing cycle, it can be grown in Maine.

Arlis's message to his chefs, as well as to others who adopt his approach and take the trouble to find him at his farm, is that the sensible way with vegetables and greens is seasonal. Eat what is locally grown; I won't get into the ecological argument for that here, except to simply and selfishly state that Arlis's products taste better, grown as they are for delectability—not for adaptation to mechanical picking and grading machines or for transport. In the spring, start eating dandelion greens, then go to young spinach. When there is no more spinach, rather than pay for some that has been shipped a long way and won't taste as good, go to Swiss chard.

Pain and Pleasure picks in the afternoon; its produce reaches a client restaurant in less than two hours. That is freshness.

(If you plan to visit the Pain and Pleasure Farm, I must tell you that Arlis Sheffield puts up his stand whenever he feels like it, usually around noon, but not necessarily every day. It is advisable to call ahead; again—as the fields call too—around noon.)

Where can you eat it?

Why, at the **Gypsy Sweethearts:** Once you've retraced the trail along Tatnick Road, Gypsy Sweethearts lies near the center of Ogunquit.

GYPSY SWEETHEARTS
10 Shore Rd.
Ogunquit, ME 10397
Tel. 207/646–7021

Like many eating places in town, this one is in a once-private home, circa 18th century, now restored as a restaurant. If you arrive early, you can sip your aperitif on a glassed-in wraparound porch while gazing out at the gardens. Judy Clayton, the chef, has not altogether suppressed the show business element in her restaurant. The name comes from a Victor Herbert song; many on the staff are theater hopefuls (don't forget, this is Ogunquit, home of summer theater), and Judy's mother was in the theater. What has come down from the mother is found in the daughter: The restaurant is incurably romantic. All Gypsy Sweethearts needs are Gypsy violins and cameo photos of stars on the tables, but understudies who play at the local theater come in live. There are even cubicles to hide and dine in. In cozy sofas and chairs before the fire in the lounge you can order dinner and eat your appetizer while you have a drink (they know how to make a Negroni). Pain and Pleasure vegetables come off very well on a canapé, as well as in a predinner salad. Should it be in season, the mozzarella salad comes with tomatoes from out on the farm; an antique tomato variety, the kind used before machines picked fruit, it's loaded with pulpy taste and has tender, fragile, thin skin. The basils are two separate strains, one very sweet, the other a little tart. The cheese is completely white and from local milk, although fruity with olive oil. If this isn't a Maine dish in conception, it certainly qualifies as one for most of the ingredients on your plate. Speaking of plates, the restaurant has completely resisted the patent platter boredom of Villeroy & Boch in favor of antique American dishes of period interest, shapes, and styles.

Bell peppers come out on a bed of mustard greens and little lettuce leaves. Pain and Pleasure gets an early start on the growing season by defeating the frost with mesh grills at night instead of plastic sheets, so the plants can breathe. Sheffield takes them off by day so the sunshine can warm the earth, encouraging the roots to spread. Pain and pleasure.

Among the many dining places in the big house is a spot in a little bay window. One candle is burning, and a lamp glows dimly. Sugar snap peas, lightly sautéed, arrive. Just a drop or two of oil is all they are turned in; the peas are so fresh and sweet, coming down from the farm within their allotted two hours (*see* Chapter 1, Dykeman's), that you eat them in the pod for the true taste of plant sugar. It is only during the first few days of their season that these peas have this intensely sweet taste. Rare miniature globe squashes also come down in perfect order from Arlis's field, where they have been pumping themselves up all day long in the sun;

they are now ready to give all the sweetness up. They might as well be little sausages, so neatly are they sliced into rondelles to be dredged in olive oil and sautéed. To say they go well with salmon that is pan-seared to luscious sweetness and caramelized with onions is to seriously understate their importance to the meal.

Then comes the meat—smoldering nuggets of tenderloin simply sautéed and tossed in a salad. The nuggets are hot from the pan, the salad fresh from the cooler. The leaves are slippery with vegetable oil, the tenderloin rich in animal oil.

It's green and rosy pink on the plate, hot meat and cold salad, each with its own taste.

Judy Clayton has been running the restaurant since 1980 with her husband, Frank Tarleton. She interprets Maine foods in a modern light. Her Maine crab cakes have more personality than the Maryland variety, for there is more sting to the bite. They come with aioli and are equally wonderful for starters or finishers with champagne.

Down on the same Shore Road, but farther along toward the sea—almost to Perkins Cove—there's a man in an old tavern who doesn't dream of aioli or garlic. Except for salads and to throw a bone to trends, he has about as much use for olive oil as for olives themselves. They're for putting in martinis. His name is Richard; what you go to see him for, and then sit around one of his eight fireplaces consuming, is traditional American food. Yankee pot roast, roast loin of pork, little roasted red potatoes in season, and chicken with apple and sage are the preferred bill of fare at **Poor Richard's.**

POOR RICHARD'S TAVERN
Shore Rd.
Box 984
Ogunquit, ME 03907
Tel. 207/646–4722

The tavern is an old Colonial, built during the Revolution. Poor Richard is Richard Perkins, whose family gave the cove its name. He grew up in a clutch of 10 children for whom he did the cooking with his grandmother, who came to live with the family when they were orphaned. Her recipes came out of her head; hanging at her apron was the only cooking school Richard Perkins would ever attend. Her native Maine food, which he has been promoting since 1960, is served in a traditional way and presented in an authentic Maine setting. These are foods and styles usually seen in old magazines. Going to Poor Richard's can be like taking a bite out of Yankee history.

The Yankee pot roast, a traditional chuck roast, is served with potatoes that have the buttered taste of gravy— real gravy, not simply reduced juices. It is seasoned with tomatoes and thickened with arrowroot. Promise yourself a mile's hike or a bike ride in the morning and dig right in. Speaking of the hot and buttered, there are old-fashioned pan biscuits on the sideboard. These are the baking-powder kind, made with lard, that rise hard on both ends but hold soft in the middle; where they are broken, steam rises. They are the sort that Edna Ferber had Joe and Julie swipe from

Queenie in *Showboat,* and no progress has been made in biscuits since then.

In days gone by, when pork was eaten by people who were hungry for meat, roast loin of pork was the best way to eat it. At Poor Richard's it is fixed as it was then, with drippings from the pan, stuffed with layers of sage, and served with an applesauce as hot and homey as what you find inside apple cobbler.

Ask yourself, what could come for dessert with any of these but apple bread pudding? For generations it was used on the farm to stretch out a food budget and give something sweet to the kids to get them to drink their milk. The custom still survives at Poor Richard's. To slices of stale bread milk-soaked in a baking dish are added slices of apples. Eggs and more milk are beaten together in a separate bowl and then go into the dish with cinnamon, nutmeg, and raisins. Sugar is sprinkled on top. The dish goes into a very hot oven, inside another dish of water, and what comes out is custard pudding crisp with apples and crunch.

Out of Ogunquit on Route 1 and ahead to Kennebunk we go, where a plethora of windows overlooks the sea.

WINDOWS ON THE WATER
12 Chase Hill Rd.
Kennebunk, ME 04043
Tel. 207/967–3313

Exit 3 off Interstate 95, the Maine turnpike, and a 10-mile ramble on Route 35 through down-east suburbia leads to a most engaging perch of tall windows over a town inlet with a pier and country views. **Windows on the Water** is a polished, timbered building. The walls, under cathedral wood ceilings, have high, wide windows, and the floors are shining wood. The food is another departure, into what we could call Maine Modern, or down-east nouvelle.

Down-east nouvelle should not be a term of disparagement. Nouvelle cuisine was a new term 20 years ago when French chefs started pairing purées of fruits, like raspberry, with traditional meats like roast duck. It became much more complicated, but what nouvelle cuisine grew into, on the eve of a boom in health and fitness in the public consciousness, were new ways of making old favorite dishes conform to new ideas, chiefly through a reduction in sauce, butter, and fat (and all too often, portions, too).

Maine nouvelle differs from New England nouvelle—which is all of the above, but with New England staples—in that it uses chiefly seafood. The dishes may make some concession to eliminating the rich, as in fattening, except that they often exploit products that are fads or food gimmicks. On the plus side, nouvelle has pioneered a cooking that depends on super-fresh and first-quality ingredients to deliver on taste, and the concepts it presents, like the dishes, are often simple to prepare and easy to digest.

For example, the most successful menu item at Windows on the Water is its both highly imaginative and prosaic "Lobster Stuffed Potato." It's a laugh to order and a real treat to eat. A baked Maine potato is brought to your table. Almost as big as a kid's football, it is packed with a generous portion of lobster meat, Jarlsberg (chosen with a nod toward its lower fat and calorie content), a large dollop of sweet cream, and a few scallions parked on top for greens. Health. It may not be what Michel Guérard had in mind when he worked out his nouvelle concepts, but who can deny the separate goodness of what's on the plate? Digging into the potato is like opening a present on your birthday. It is the thought that makes the meal.

In the same vein, at around the same price (about $10), is the baked Maine lasagna. The world knows what lasagna

is; in Maine nouvelle it's made with Maine shrimp and scallops layered where the beef and crushed tomatoes used to go.
As there is no stinting with the ricotta and mozzarella, their
cheesy textures are layered with cushions of spinach.

Windows on the Water may have aimed at nouvelle
and hit fast food. Whatever it is, it is resolutely American,
something that no European could imagine, and in a style
that many people want. It gets heavy traffic all weekend
long, and at Sunday brunch (another American concept), it's
impossible to get a table. All morning long fashionable locals
come to the light and airy place, where the decor is a match
for the dining. It's all such fun that as soon as you drive away
you want to come back again.

More of this sort of thing is the best of what you can
expect to find at popular prices as you work your way up the
coast from here. Attempts at the novel and different in food
frequently come out as mere novelty. You are likely to dine
better if you spend less and opt for Maine products (whichever you choose) simply done, because the products themselves
are nearly unique in their own taste. Attempts at the more
serious cuisine often come out as foreign or fad food. One of
the few places where the cuisine is new and different,
although local in choice of products, and mature in outlook is
in nearby Kennebunkport. **Seascapes** is at perhaps the nicest
lookout on the sea—and the nicest restaurant that looks out.

SEASCAPES
On the Pier
Kennebunkport, ME 04046
Tel. 207/967–8500

Here is a restaurant that has had lots of love. Nothing
is too good for its tables, which are certainly among the
warmest, with wicker chairs and original pottery and crystal.

Into Seascapes, Angela Leblanc has steeped the Mediterranean basin, covered with its wild thyme, tarragon, oregano, and olive trees. The limpid hue of the Aegean is matched by the blue of her tablecloths. In her tracing of these shores from Greece to Spain she has collected more than the pottery and glassware that decorate her tables, and she has collected more than recipes. She has been to restaurants and cafés, sat on windswept terraces where the haze of the mountains steps down into the blue of the sea; visited private homes; and shopped the great markets where they sell the swordfish head to tail with his bill on. What she has brought back is the taste for all this: the wild thyme covering the white, bauxite hills, the fruity and volcanic oils, of which no supermarket shelf in the world can give the slightest hint. To this she has married the sea fare from the cold waters of Maine. It is the best of all possible worlds.

Greek and Italian products are especially important in the kitchen where chef Ray Wieczerak holds forth—the Kalamata olives, the Tuscan oil. What? you ask, a Pole in a Mediterranean kitchen? There can be no doubting Wieczerak's talent with fish and Angela Leblanc's talent for ideas. Consider this: In Piraeus, restaurant goers have the habit of being served their hors d'oeuvres on the waterfront terrace, while the restaurants themselves sit across the way. The Greek waiters put the plates of sizzling stir-fried shrimp on platters and are across the street serving them while the shrimp are still hot. Seascapes puts feta, cilantro, and tomatoes with voluptuous oil into this shrimp experience it has recreated.

If they eat these shrimp looking out to sea in the Aegean, you can do no less at Seascapes. The lookout is across Cape Porpoise, where the sea mammals play, and it is the prettiest seascape—framed by painted pine and plant bedecked windows—this side of Portland.

The food of the Mediterranean can be at its best when it's disarmingly simple. Consider how veal and lobster are put together. The veal is lightly sautéed in a reduction of its juices; cream is stirred into a sauce, butter and cognac are added, and good-size chunks of lobster meat are glazed and laid on the plate. In so simple a dish everything must be perfection from the standpoint of the products: the veal, the cream, the butter, are all first-rate. In the Maine version, Maine lobster easily beats Mediterranean langouste.

Bouillabaisse, too, should be kept simple. The most sense I ever heard on bouillabaisse came from a friend in Marseille. "It is a fish soup," he said, "made with fish the fisherman cannot sell. So he brings them home, and they are so small his wife cannot make dinner for the family with them, so what she makes is soup." It is the little fish that have the most life and gelatin in their bones. At Seascapes the bouillabaisse is simple, with generous pieces of haddock floating in it, and especially, the mud clams and shellfish of Maine.

Also on the menu, the seared sea scallops are a good and simple idea, strongly tickled with cayenne and curry butter flavors. In some Mediterranean households, it is customary to eat shellfish, especially shrimp, so highly seasoned it has everyone at the table sneezing. At Seascapes the seared scallops won't make you reach for your napkin, but you'll get the idea. You will run no greater risk than to discover what they've known for 1,500 years in the Mediterranean: The natural affinity of shellfish and brine is stabilized through hot peppers or garlic, a delectable match.

The mushroom caps, stuffed with a duxelle of scallops and escargots, blend salt and sweet, carrying further the orchestration of tastes.

There is a medley of hot pastas: They come with lobster, shrimp, or scallops, in a range of seasonings from hot to tingling, piqued with tequila and jalapeño, swirled with peppers, and seared in hot cream. It was not so long ago that Italy gave us linguine with a pesto splashed with Polish bison-grass vodka. Why not? They went great together—one distilled from a green, one a pulverized green. Now Wieczerak gives us tequila with spinach linguine. At Seascapes we are offered a blend of old-world ideas improved by products and twists of the new world, forming a taste that binds both worlds together.

If you highball the Maine Turnpike (Interstate 95), deciding to stick to small towns, you may miss Portland. Prepare to give your accelerator some rest and do your legs some good: Stop. Portland is a vest-pocket town, one brightly cleaned up with a scrub of fresh air off the sea, one with old streets and hills and marvelous sea views. Leave the Maine Turnpike at Exit 7 and follow the signs to "Port." If you enjoy Manhattan's South Street Seaport, here is a whole, reclaimed city like that. Park your car. Go to the Visitor Information Center (305 Commercial St., tel. 207/772–5800), hang out, get a map, and walk around, for Portland is a walking town.

The compactness of the restored port makes it ideal for visiting: An area some eight blocks long forms a loose triangle roughly five blocks deep, not including seven public piers. The roofs of the buildings (mostly dating from the 19th century) are low—two or three stories; the sun shines down on the red bricks of the sidewalks and cobblestones of the street; and much vehicular traffic is blessedly banned. This is the way 19th-century cities ought to be, and maybe 21st-century ones will be again. (There are municipal lots just outside the pedestrian zone where you can leave a car, or you can drive up to the hotel where you're staying and park in its lot.)

Portland is the ideal town if you like old brick Federal buildings; skylights in roofs with light pouring down; trellis-lined walkways with flowers climbing up on the walls; flickering gas street lamps lighting up charming cul-de-sacs at night; antiques shops to browse in by day; marinas bobbing with sailboats and commercial sea craft; sports-fishing boats heading out to sea for tuna and shark; and good meals behind many doors.

If you think this is worth more than a brief afternoon's look (and it is) and you decide to stay in town, there are only two ways to do it. One is expensive. For this try the **Regency** (20 Milk St., Portland, ME 04101, tel. 207/774–4200 or 800/727–3436). It is an interesting converted brick armory right in the pedestrian zone with all the right touches, including the **Market Street Grill.** Its canopy and exclusive feel give you a sense of participation with the old town. Rooms, with taxes and charges, run to $110 plus a night, double. For much cheaper accommodations, try the **Everett Hotel** (51A Oak St., Portland 04101, tel. 207/773–7882). It's equally authentic; you'll have to climb a hill, but you can drive right up to the door and leave your car there. For about $35, and quarters for the parking meter, you'll have a place where the seagulls wheel around your windows all day and the sink is right in the room where you sleep. I predict you will dream of Bogart and San Francisco.

The center of Portland's old port is the Old Port Exchange. Here the masters of square-rigged sailing ships came in, posted their manifests, sat and sipped a pint, and entertained offers and bids for the cargo in their holds.

At the **Seamen's Club Restaurant** (1 Exchange St., corner of Fore St., tel. 207/772–7311), you enter the world of lobster stew: a thick, foamy chowder, with lobster simmered in the cream. Ask them to serve it family style; the whole family (at least the two of you) will be fishing the big chunks out of the creamy broth. Try the hearty rye or seven-grain bread with it; it's homemade. This is a nice, different, and economical crack at a lobster dinner, especially for more than two.

One block from the Seamen's Club—and leave the kids home for this—is **Three-Dollar Dewey's** (446 Fore St., tel. 207/772–3310), the best bar in town. Along a Maine waterfront a bar sometimes means beer, and the Three Dollar has hundreds of them. You can pick a beer from anywhere in the world (Belgium is very good). People sit on long wooden benches at common tables, and the conversation flows easily.

Fore Street becomes Pleasant Street farther down the block. **Alberta's Café** (21 Pleasant St., tel. 207/774–0076) is a few yards outside the pedestrian zone but animated with small-port atmosphere and an array of unusual things to eat. There is always something fresh and surprising for so small a kitchen: asparagus, summer squash, or eggplant go with specials such as grilled tuna. The big local favorite is "Pizza of the Day"; sometimes it's lobster. Try that on your tomato and cheese.

Middle Street is one block to the north, where we turn back toward the cobblestone road again. Here, in their little brick buildings, are two places to satisfy some very big cravings, for what amount to modest investments.

Carbur's Restaurant (123 Middle St., tel. 207/772–7794), might have the champion sandwich for Maine, at least for volume. The Down East Feast is a five-decker club; the layers of bread are all different, and so stuffed is it with ham, roast beef, seafood salad, tomatoes, onions, lettuce, and disgusting sauces, that every time anybody orders one, the kitchen staff come out of their lair and parade around the room singing and clanging pots and pans. It's the sort of place kids love; the hamburgers are excellent, and they're served with all sorts of deep-fried trimmings.

Just across the street, for a little romantic bistro in Portland, choose **Hugo's Bistro** (88 Middle St., tel. 207/774–8538). Hugo's in Paris would be just like this Hugo's if there were a Hugo's in Paris. The chairs creak, they have a nice wine list, the prices are low, and they have Maine crab cakes. Try them here if you've missed them at the pricier places. The service is unusually winning. They're open for dinner only, so plan ahead.

Off Middle Street is Market Street and a restaurant where Barbara and George Bush turn up when they're in town. **Raphael's** (36 Market St., tel 207/773–4500), tends toward fish and local seafood with an Italian accent. At least try it for an aperitif.

F. Parker Reidy's (83 Exchange St., tel. 207/773–4731) is in an old bank building. Area rugs and a bar behind the teller's window convey the distinct impression that you're eating in a Victorian savings and loan. At its popular prices, however, you needn't spend much to get the very best grilled steaks in town—top sirloin, 12 ounces, no fat, and no gristle. Bartender Ward Dudley knows how to make a Negroni.

From the port and wharves themselves at the end of the block you can ride out on the back of the sea. Try your hand at tuna and shark fishing in half-day bites. The *Indian II* (tel. 207/772–0727) takes 30 to 40 people out at reasonable prices. **Adventure Charters** takes only six and will find the specific fish you want to angle for aboard *Fishbusters* (tel. 207/284–4453).

Among the many more places that give pleasure and value, there's **DiMillo's Floating Restaurant** (tel. 207/772–2216), where you eat aboard a car ferry looking out from the port at DiMillo's Pier. If you insist on trying a "gourmet" style restaurant, where local people go when they are tired of the sea, there's **Back Bay Grill** (65 Portland St., tel 207/772–8833). More apropos of a sea hunt, the **Two Lights Lobster Shack** on the ocean in Cape Elizabeth, 2 miles to the east, has picnic tables; they call your number and you pick up your food. (If you can wait, a better one of these comes up next chapter.)

CHAPTER 12

LOBSTER POTS AND CLANGING BUOYS

Freeport to Bailey Island, Maine

North from Portland is where old-timers say Maine really begins. The beaches change from sand, and the coast goes to rock. The mists roll in and shroud the buoys that ring day and night in milky white billows of fog and sea. Northeaster is a feared word: The storms boil out of the North Atlantic to work their wonder on a coast where they have chiseled some of the most stunning seascapes in the world. Here is the lobster's real home. Here are the villages that harbor the lobster fishing fleets. Here are the piers extending from long peninsulas that point out into the sea. Here are the arms of the sea reaching inland. At the ends of these docks and the heads of these fjords are found those curious wooden structures where the boats come in to unload their catch and the world arrives wearing chinos and jeans to sit on rough benches—the lobster pound. For here on this coast is found in succulence the crustacean most likely to be candidate for any pot, the crowned king of American cuisine, Homardus americanus.

HIGHLIGHTS:
- Navigating the three Rs: roadsides, road stands, and restaurants
- Lobster rolls and lobster tales
- The quest for the perfect lobster
- Freeport, the Gucci of the North
- Fine wines and a cabin in the woods
- Beef values in tall grasses
- Newcastle and Damariscotta
- A festival
- Oyster barbecues and beds
- An inn on a millpond
- Lobsters hard and soft
- A pound, and Bailey Island, the thing found

LENGTH OF LOOP: 68 miles
LENGTH OF STAY: Three days

In this part of the trip the landscape lowers and the sky broadens. There are salt marshes and bays on both sides of the road. Also beside the road is an indigenous phenomenon: the Maine roadside stand—a great lesson in democracy in a country that could use one. Lobster rolls, which are to lobsters what Sloppy Joes are to beef, are found almost exclusively at Maine roadside stands from Memorial Day to Labor Day along the lobster coastline. Here, Americans bask in such a sea of plenty that they have turned the precious lobster into a hot meat on a roll—which is what the lobster roll is.

Would you like one, you ask?

Well, would you like a toasted hot bun stuffed with lobster meat oozing out of its sides? There are no shells to crack, remember, no need to pick through a leg for meat, no waste to pay for. These are luscious hot sandwiches, fixed with coleslaw and melted butter.

North from Portland, just into Freeport along Route 1, and marked with crossed red crustaceans on a sign before you actually get there, is a roadside stand where the lobster roll is rarely bettered. It is **Cindy's Fish and Fries.**

CINDY'S FISH AND FRIES
Rte. 1N
Freeport, ME 04032

Under the sign is a little park, with picnic tables, stands of trees at each end, and in between a ramble of lawn. Barbecue pits steam and smoke. Kettles simmer with hot lobsters in them, and there is a window to walk up to.

(*Note:* Route 1 is an excellent highway for shunpikers. If you take the Maine Turnpike throughout your trip to Maine, from exit to exit destinations, you'll miss things like this, which provide half the fun of traveling in Maine.)

The stand at Cindy's is even less glamorous than Flo's (*see* Chapter 11): You can't go inside. You walk up, nudge your way to the front, or wait your turn in line, whichever seems the more reasonable. If you've never seen a lobster roll before and don't know how to handle one, take your cue from those up front. Far from finger food, this is both-hands-on dining, and it does take technique. The roll is 10 inches of toasted bread, and the meat is stuffed in quite generously. Take a bite and it squishes out both sides. This creates a problem if you've used the condiments the way the regulars do. The coleslaw and melted butter are in squeeze bottles (very popular at Maine road stands), and the regulars use them both. When I went to Cindy's, I had on a new T-shirt, and I must confess I began to lose my appetite the closer I came to the stand. The lobster meat looked good and fresh, however, and I held my place in line. Inside the stand, open rolls were toasting on a grill; a boy was cracking dismembered pieces of lobster and putting the meat in a bowl. Cindy was doling out the meat on bread and handing out rolls as fast as she could make them. When I asked her how business was, she said, "Can't complain."

It was lunchtime. Pickups were piling into the parking lot and rocketing out again. No one was using the tables. The boy was kept extra busy because he had to refill the melted butter squeeze bottles as the customers poured on all they could. They walked away with melted butter dripping off the meat and down their chins. Most of them took no tissues back to their pickups but used their tongues as napkins. Can this be a healthy way to eat? I wondered. Wait till you see the size of Cindy's arms.

She handed down our lobster rolls, and we retired to a picnic table that we had to ourselves. There was a little stream running by, and despite the nearness of the road it was peaceful.

Cindy's stand (actually a trailer) is like many such worthwhile stands in Maine; it offers local Maine produce cooked in a homemade style that has survived. Because it has wheels, Cindy moves her stand around. The location I have given is where she has been handing out lobster rolls and otherwise pleasing customers since 1989. The little roadside park is 4 miles south of Freeport center. If not Cindy herself, someone else will be here.

About the lobster rolls themselves: The meat is so fresh and delicious, and it is such a good introduction to the lobsters of this northern zone (north of Portland), where the meat is sweeter to the taste, that you are sure any other way to serve it would be the way to spoil it. The four of us on this trip (two were from Europe) all went back for seconds and thought the rolls made every other lobster we had collectively tasted in different experiences and continents, up to then, and yes, even in Maine, come off like marzipan. Then we thought of it. If this place, which was so cheap and located so out of the way, had such delights to taste, what could we expect from the bright lights of Freeport? On the brink of civilization, then, in the heart of the world's greatest lobster grounds, the four of us dedicated our trip in this part (mid-Maine) of Maine to a single idea: the Hunt for the Perfect Lobster.

But nothing is as simple as that; there were four of us, with four different tastes. Some of us were sophisticated Europeans; lobster rolls were very delicious, but could lobsters be found in this part of Maine sautéed? "You know,"

reminisced a Parisian, "cut up and cooked with butter in the pan, and then put in the shell and served at the table?"

"Or stuffed with shallots," said another, "and basted with cream." A lawyer friend announced he would be happy to accept anything as long as it was the best, and I voted to hold out for the best simply boiled.

Four different lobsters then, and which would get the palm? This would be a difficult group to please.

Route 1 goes directly into Freeport's Main Street. Be prepared for crowds at almost any time you arrive. Freeport is home to the shops or factory outlets of some 120 retailers or manufacturers, such as Ralph Lauren, London Fog, Laura Ashley, and Banana Republic (*see* Chapter 11). The crowd—it often seems an omnipeded animal—goes from one corner

to the next, churning back and forth across the street seeking
bargains. Why anyone would waste time indoors when the
biggest bargain of Maine is outdoors is beyond me, but big-
time shopping seems to have replaced moose hunting as the
number-one sport in Maine.

The largest crowds of all are in front of **L.L. Bean,** the
Gucci of the North and internationally known outdoor-wear
purveyor, around which the other big names are grouped as
so many candles against the sun. Should you choose to stop,
and although it's slicked up and the floorboards no longer
creak under your feet, Bean's is a generic Maine attraction,
open 24 hours a day every day of the year. Park legally, however. If not, the police of Freeport will be sure to harass you.
The illegal spaces in front of the store are particularly well
scoured. Inside, despite the years of Guccification, men's chinos, camp pants for both sexes, Maine guide boots, shoes, and
buffalo-plaid wool shirts are still popular bargains and give
years of service.

Two miles north of town, past the entrance to the
Maine Turnpike, the forest returns; on the left is a courtyard
clearing and a motor hotel in the woods. As if out of an old
photo, the road to Americana and a legitimate Maine travel
bargain opens up under its sign and the boughs of its pines.

MAINE IDYLL INN MOTOR COURT

325 Rte. 1N
Freeport, ME 04032
Tel. 207/865-4201

The Maine Idyll can be your headquarters for exploring this part of Maine. Everyone has stayed in a place like
this, if not in a dream, at least in the movies. It's in the third
generation of ownership by the family that built the court in
1932. The trail from the manager's house leads down to individual cabins in the woods surrounded by forest. In the vir-

gin growth of trees you hear the wonderful spiral of the wood thrush. Behind the screen and wood doors there are three rooms, not counting the bath, and everything is in the homey style of a camp on Golden Pond. A party of four fits comfortably in one cabin. The charm is great, and the prices are short of $100 for four; half that before June 15. There are stone fireplaces and chimneys, right in the bedrooms; split wood is stacked on the porch. The fire crackles and shoots light on the ceilings and comforters on those surprisingly "cool" midsummer Maine nights. The fireplace is also dandy for grilling foods—steaks, or any fish you might have the good fortune to catch. This is good for at least one meal a day while you are stalking your own perfect lobster. For that, it is good to make your reservations immediately. The cabins have telephones, kitchens, and color TVs (this part of the country is one of the few where announcers hold onto their regional speech), and someone in the manager's cabin will be happy to secure restaurant reservations for you.

One of those you should select, **Ocean Farms,** is nearby. The restaurant is cool and comfortable in soft tones of gray and accents of maroon. Flowers on the tables add a touch of pink. The lighting is relaxing, street parking is easy, and so are the prices. Seven wines are always served by the glass; you can try something new and discuss it before committing to a bottle.

OCEAN FARMS
23 Main St.
Freeport, ME 04032
Tel. 207/865-3101

All of us order lobsters; we will have four opinions, then: two male and two female; two American and two Continental. What could be fairer? We all order them steamed in order to begin our test with a neutral palate: We are tasting for lobster and lobster alone—not the taste of butter poured on and not the taste of sauces dribbled on— nothing cute, just good and plain lobster. The wine we choose is one commonly selected with shellfish, for the French province of Brittany is not often surpassed for its muscadet. There is something disarmingly sweet in the lobsters; we discover that lobsters, depending on where they come from, can have many tastes after all. The sweetness suspected at the roadside stand in the afternoon was at that point chalked up to the melted butter. But these four, each one a pound and a half, with no melted butter at all, are the sweetest whole lobsters any of us have tasted.

We walk around after dinner enjoying Freeport's pleasant architecture in the long June dusk. Shortly we find something vital to our dinners back at the cabin, as indispensable to good dining as the flame of our fireside: a very good wine shop, called **The Wine Cellar.**

THE WINE CELLAR
2 Mechanic St.
Freeport, ME 04032
Tel. 207/865-3404

This could be your wine headquarters for your northern Maine holiday. If you are driving from home and don't take your own wine because of the jostling (very wise) or the midday heat in the trunk, or if you have come to Portland by air and rented a car, you should know that most lobster pounds will sell you something ghastly or let you bring your own; a wine shop is the obvious solution.

The Wine Cellar in Freeport is a surprisingly large store; it appears quite unexpectedly down Mechanic Street, off Main Street in the direction of the sea. Most major wine-producing areas of the world are represented on the well-lit shelves.

The French section is of special interest for its white burgundies, which go so well with what comes from the sea. Leading the group, and it would be a good stock for stores in the largest of cities, is a selection of Mersaults. No less than six producers are represented, ranging across as many as five different vintages; it includes Louis Latour and Olivier Leflaive. Four Puligny-Montrachets catch the eye, again including Latour, and there are four Chassagne-Montrachets from producers such as Drouhin and Morey. If you are a classicist, and shellfish make your thoughts turn toward Chablis, there are seven of those. Always a bargain with seafood is muscadet, with its clean taste that comes with acid balance; and the Wine Cellar has four. Among them is the Marquis de Goulaine.

The Wine Cellar also has a well-selected stock of chardonnays from California and Australia. The store is going into its ninth year of business; people come back to its shelves as often as they do to Maine for lobster or L.L. Bean's.

There is a lot to take up your free time in Freeport. (You can pick up a walking-tour map at the visitor kiosk on Middle Street run by the Freeport Merchants Association. Or write or call them at Box 452, Freeport, ME 04032, tel. 207/865–1212, for a visitor's kit.) Driving around in the car, you can enjoy New England architecture; try going out South Street and down the South Freeport Road. The clam cakes are good at the **South Harbor Fish Stand,** but as for the lobster, there's another deal coming up if you have the time to go farther north.

In addition to seafood and shopping, you can undertake an exercise in conversation and observation on one of two nature trails. The **Audubon Society** runs a sanctuary similar to their nature sites in other parts of New England. The second is a marine park, **Wolfe's Neck Woods Park,** a state park with a parking lot a few minutes' drive from the center of town. Behind the lot begins a nature trail leading through forest, wildflower sites, freshwater ponds, and tidal marshlands. Shorebirds can be viewed along inlets. In addition to the rare opportunity to observe close up the interdependent workings of a tidal estuary, Wolfe's Neck Park offers something else: Almost right smack in the middle of it is an organic farm, and its meat could be destined for your grill.

WOLFE'S NECK FARM
10 Burnett Rd.
Freeport, ME 04032
Tel. 207/865–4469

Wolfe's Neck Farm is a rare sort of organic farm these days because the crop it harvests is beef. Nine thousand acres of juicy natural grasses are at the heart of this park jutting out into the sea. Under the auspices of the University of Southern Maine, they form a biological proving ground for an experiment in beef cattle raised to fulfill the following criteria: lower body weight, less fat, and leaner but still flavorful meat. The installation is currently under the supervision of Guy Hutt, a specialist in the breeding of cattle. If in the unique setting of the park the farm seems far from the crash and boom of modern agriculture, it is because to achieve all this, the chief engine is the sun.

The fodder to feed the 300 head of cattle at Wolfe's Neck during the first two-thirds of their lives is home-grown on the same 9,000 acres as the beef. There is so much grass growing 3 feet high, crowding the fields and rolling in the wind, that it seems another sea beside the ocean. The cattle range across it in cinnamon, black, and brown-and-white hides, lost up to their hips in the tides. It is a picture that seems as right as it was when animals followed the crops from the south to north, or from lowland pastures to high (before they were all penned up), eating what the sun brought up. At Wolfe's Neck, as elsewhere, an animal that is visibly different is being developed to produce a leaner beef. It is smaller, with a greater muscle-to-weight ratio, and therefore less fat. Its maximum allowable weight is 1,200 pounds, compared with 1,500 pounds per animal in the recent past. This would be a reduction of nearly 20% in fat, but the loss is better than that because the original animal had a lower muscle density on the hoof (and muscle is heavier than fat).

The new animal at Wolfe's Neck Farm is a triple cross of older beef stock: the black Angus, the white-faced Hereford, and the Gelby. The last is a cinnamon-color, compact animal (popular in the West) considered a comer in breeding circles because of its smaller size (it uses feed more efficiently) and very high muscle-to-weight ratio.

In the genetic experiment being carried on by the University of Southern Maine and Guy Hutt, the Gelby is used to bring compactness to the animal; the Angus is used for the tenderness of its meat, and the Hereford for the tenderness of its disposition. Hereford mothers are outstanding among beef breeds, nurturing to the calves and very generous with their milk. But even successful experiments in genetics can come a cropper in the technique of feeding growing stock. It is this problem, cattle-feeding efficiency, that is attacked directly by the 9,000 acres of Wolfe's Neck grasses.

Some soils of the world, and this is one of them, are too dense to produce grain. America would have gone nowhere as a food power had it depended on New England for wheat. What is produced at Wolfe's Neck as cattle feed are the natural grasses—native fescues; perennial ryes; and Reed's canary grass, which as it matures develops yellow plumes that look like outstretched bird's wings. The grasses have taken over the fields, much as they did before there were farmers to plant them.

The results of this food experiment are in, and the taste is extraordinary—tender and amazingly sweet. Wolfe's Neck meats are dressed and packed at the farm and are for sale here, as the whole point of the Southern Maine experiment is to see if the public will buy a low-fat meat. The various cuts, including roasts, steaks, and whole tenderloins, can also be sent through the mail or by UPS like a basket of fruit from Florida. A brochure on prices and ordering will be sent on request.

A restaurant back in Portland, **The Pepperclub** (78 Middle St., Portland, ME 04101, tel. 207/772–0531), mostly vegetarian, makes an exception for Wolfe's Neck beef. If you want a taste of its tender sweetness, drop in.

Farther up the coast comes a string of stunning villages headed by **Wiscasset.** With its streets of perfect, sun-washed white houses, it is perhaps the jewel of the Maine coastline. The bridge just beyond it beckons you into a country that is a lacework of streams, lakes, rivers, and channels, all running toward the sea. The landscape is carved into ridges of green peninsulas with their tips in salt water.

Newcastle and **Damariscotta,** cheek by jowl on Route 1, are separated by the Damariscotta River. You see Newcastle first, from high up, as Route 1 traces a ridgeline. The green-foliage-backed white buildings of the towns are separated by blue water. Puffs of clouds below complete the pristine scene.

In this part of Maine, two words: Beware Cuisine. Nothing can be so unwholesome as a dining room full of Americans sitting around eating mediocre French food. Maine should be to America what Brittany is to France: a place we can go for the homey, the taste of the sea, and the authentic. Taste Maine. Leave expense behind or to locals who want a taste of the world.

On the 18-mile-long peninsula you are virtually out to sea. Know one peninsula well, and you will understand most of coastal Maine. We have chosen this one because of the lobsters, the lupine, and the oysters. With water on three sides, winters are no colder here than they are in Connecticut. In the second week of July there is joy. Each year in the Damariscotta region—Damariscotta Mills and neighboring Nobleboro—the second weekend of July is reserved for the **Oyster Festival.** This is the time to visit.

Never mind that this is a month without an R in it. Oysters are everywhere all the time. During the three days of festival, music and dancing fill parks and public squares. There are public events and oyster barbecues. It is a time when the life of the oystering community is hauled out of the water and celebrated, unfolding in the streets. Three dollars will buy you a button to the Oyster Festival. A big tent pitched down by the river in Damariscotta shelters food and events (like cooking and dog shows); with the button you can come and go and eat all you please. The Oyster Festival may be the best food bargain you will ever run into. The Damariscotta Chamber of Commerce (Box 13, Damariscotta, ME 04543, tel. 207/563–8340) even has a brochure about it.

Maine is a center of the oyster farming industry in America. It has been especially active in producing what is called the Maine belon. Belon is a place on the south coast of Brittany in France where the richness of the plankton in the water has given the taste of the oysters a worldwide reputation. People come from all over the world to eat the belon oyster in the cafés and brasseries of Paris. There was nothing like it on this side of the Atlantic, the native American oyster being of another species. Belons in France have such an oily, aggressive taste you'd swear your tongue was mugged. How to know if they're for you? If you like bluefish, they are; if you like flounder, they're not.

No exception to the laws of nature, however, an oyster is what it eats. The plankton in the sea give the oyster its taste and its shell, the gnarl and ripple of its appearance. France's belons are very pungent. Maine's are sweeter. They are especially succulent hailing from the waters of **Dodge Cove Farm;** its wharf at the municipal pier in Nobleboro is only minutes from Damariscotta Mills. Oyster farming is a form of animal husbandry in which the sea does the nurturing while the farmer does the seeding, the harvesting, and the hoping. Dick Clime farms Dodge Cove. He puts the belon seedlings down in the water on their beds when they are just a few millimeters (⅛ inch) in the palm of the hand and just weeks old. The seedling is called a spat and looks exactly like a mature oyster except that its shell is very thin, like a thumbnail. The bed is a tray of fiberglass mesh on which the spats rest. Through cilia around tiny ports in their shells they take in the nourishment of the seawater, while other ports expel waste. Breathing in the rhythm of the tides filled with plankton, the spats spend one growing season, the five or six months of spring and summer, on these beds. The spats are then transferred to beds with wider mesh to allow for greater circulation of water as they grow larger. Eventually they are planted in the gravel of the estuary bed itself, where great care is taken to place them so that enough water circulates to keep the plankton coming in to their cilia and expelled water going off their bed. At 18 months 35% of the spats reach maturity and are taken. By 28 months the rest of the class comes along, and the whole bed is harvested. Climes measures the glycogen (oyster fat—the more it contains, the sweeter the oyster) in his oysters before he takes up a crop. The Oyster Festival marks the end of such a cycle and the beginning of a new one. The oysters taken for the festival are not for export to restaurants. They are for local traditions and tables.

From the Route 1 exit marked 215, 129, and 130, take Route 215 for just over 2½ miles, to the sign for Damariscotta Mills. This will put you at the end of Lake Damariscotta, into which flows the saline Damariscotta River, where alewives swarm in spring to jump across the falls and into the freshwater lake to spawn. Almost at this juncture you will find an inn on its own pond, **The Mill Pond Inn.**

THE MILL POND INN
Rte. 215
Damariscotta Mills, ME 04553
Tel. 207/563–8014

Here you'll discover a cheerful couple of innkeepers, Sherry and Bobby Wheal, who take every delight in being where they are, as you will, too. Sherry Wheal routinely serves 3,000 of Dick Clime's superb and sweet belons at her oyster barbecues. (Climes also supplies New York's Grand Central Station Oyster Bar with their belons.) The barbecues are held the third Sunday in July, extending the festival. If you are a guest at her Mill Pond, or a reader of this book, Sherry invites you to come by to her lawn that third Sunday in July, where the odds are good you'll get to taste at least a few oysters.

Sherry serves these oysters so as not to remove, mask, or disturb what the sea has taken two years to put into them. They are offered on a 20-foot-long oyster bar by shuckers who perform their professional service on demand to ensure that the oysters stay fresh. They are not cooked in any way: "oyster barbecue" is a term for the whole feast. Most people do not use sauce: These oysters are a cocktail of the sea in themselves.

The feast at the Mill Pond Inn starts at noon. Some 350 people aged one to 91 come by canoe, foot, and car to the pond that wraps around the lawn and inn. There's no charge at all for this down-home country potluck. It's mostly neighbors who spread themselves out on the lawn—senators, bankers, wormers, and hotel guests. Farmers bring corn for the barbecue, townspeople come with cakes and rhubarb squares, and the Wheals themselves lay on 250 steaks. Along about 7 o'clock the party breaks up, and it is reason enough in itself to come to Maine.

Next, there are the lobsters. To reach them, drive out to **New Harbor,** 18 miles or so from the Mill Pond's door. Pemaquid Point reveals itself in hills rolling down to the sea and ends at Pemaquid Light. Pearched on its slippery scraggle of rocks, this is one of the most photographed lighthouses in Maine.

First, the lobster is a cold-water customer, and the colder the water it comes from the sweeter the meat, is the rule. The water around Pemaquid is numbing. Do not try to swim in it. If you think you're going north when you follow the coastline past mid-Maine, you're not. You're going east. Eastward lies the Gulf Stream and much warmer water. The Canadian coastline swings east to bridge the Gulf Stream east of mid-Maine. What lies in between is the Gulf of Maine. The Gulf of Maine is to the Gulf Stream what an ice cube is to a flame. Here the waters are at their coldest and the lobster is at its best. Canadian lobsters are sometimes loaded on trucks, driven through Maine, and sold farther south in New England as being from Maine. The Maine lobsterman cuts a V in the tail of the female lobster and throws her back when she has eggs, marking her as a brood female, guaranteeing that she can never be sold and ensuring the existence of a Maine fishery tomorrow. Meanwhile, the Canadian lobster fleet is state-subsidized; its lobster fisher-

men are paid by the government and are government workers. Gravid females are taken. Tails are not notched. Maine
fisheries have undersize and oversize rules and throw runts
back. The Canadians do not; their lobsters show up wholesale and puny-size in Europe.

How to know when you're getting a Maine lobster?
The best guarantee is to come to Maine. When you're in
Maine, go to Pemaquid Point. Lobstermen say it's the best;

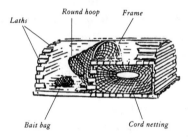

LOBSTER TRAP
CUTAWAY

scientists from the University of Maine do their lobstering
here. These are the best lobsters in the world.

SHAW'S PIER LOBSTER POUND
Rte. 130
New Harbor, ME 04554
Tel. 207/677–2200
Closed mid-Oct.–mid-May

Shaw's Pier (once known as Small's Pier) is a lobster
wharf right off a Maine postcard. The sun is setting at sup-
pertime, while the lobster fleet is just coming in. Traps are
stacked on the wharf; a dining deck thrusts out over the
water, half outside, half inside. Downstairs is an aquarium 20
yards long filled with live lobsters fresh from the traps. They

go bumbling and scuttling around, some enormous, some bellicose. The colors range from variegated to grungy blue-black to yellowy brown, almost ochre. Some have satiny finishes. The trick is to find and pick out the soft-shell lobster, the "shedder," as the lobstermen call it. The shedder is the lobster fresh out of the rocks after a molt. Its shell is soft and supple—not edible like a soft-shell crab's, though it peels like an orange. In the same way as crabs, lobsters need to shed their shells to grow. Depending on its size and growth rate, the lobster molts at least once a year—usually in summer when the water is warmest—and then it hides out in the rocks waiting for the new shell to harden. This molting and hardening process may take as much as six weeks. During that time the lobster may grow hungry and, if it leaves the rocks to search for food and stumbles into a trap and is caught, the lobsterman has his shedder and you have the chance for a particular delight.

The soft-shell's flesh is extremely juicy and tender. The "mud lobster," most commonly shipped from Maine, has a much thicker shell. Its meat is drier and impacted, more apt to be tough and stringy. Soft-shells are instantly recognized by fishermen. They are almost never shipped, so you have to go to Maine to get them.

The huge tank at Shaw's holds as many as 700 lobsters. How does a prospective diner pick out a shedder? First, you will almost never get one until mid-July from Muscongus Bay, where Shaw's lobsters come from. Next, the shell will feel soft. Should you squeeze it, it will bend. But remember, the claws of these lobsters are not pegged, and they are very frisky. A safer rule is just to look for lobsters with shells that are new, shiny, and unmarked, like a new car.

As long as you've come this far on your lobster quest, you might want to order at least a two-pounder. There's more meat on them. The tail is long like a hot dog; it tastes much better. After the lobster you select at the holding tank is weighed, you receive a number and can go upstairs to pick out a table and wait.

These lobsters are "ranched"; that is, they have been fished so long in these same waters they have taken to congregating at the traps for their food. They go scuttling in and out of the pots, not caught every time they enter and exit. As a result, their diet is bait, mostly porgie and redfish. The lobster young are in turn eaten by the codfish: Everything that swims is food for something else.

TRAPS ARE SET FROM 50 FEET TO MILES APART

Upstairs, when your number is called, you are handed the lobsters and a wooden mallet. There is hot buttered corn and fried onion rings, and everything is on paper plates. As everybody digs in, the room fills with the same enthusiasm as at a clambake. The experience is collective; it has nothing to do with eating at a restaurant. The shells zip away like so many orange peels, and no mallets are needed. Servers shove a garbage can up to where you're eating (it's for the shells, they say). But you close your eyes and blissfully chew. Yes, you agree, these must be the best lobsters in the world.

Gastronomically speaking, there is no reason to go farther up the coast. Lobster in Maine doesn't get any better than this. But there are other parts of you to nourish.

Go for your eyes. The white houses of Belfast will slip by in Greek Revival, Italianate, and Victorian styles. They sparkle like the white clouds above High Street as you cruise north on old Route 1.

Go for your spirit. The red granite coast of Acadia National Park awaits you at Bar Harbor. The sea is peacock-spangled here and frothed with green. The ospreys pirouette over the bays. On the way the fjords will perch you high above navy yards where toys of ships nestle in coves.

Everywhere along the coast run broken-finger peninsulas reaching into the sea and roller-coaster roads, happily hopscotching islets, often fringed with pounds and piers and restaurants of reasonable quality. You may be secure in thinking that lobsters anywhere don't get any better than the lobsters you've had.

And yet . . . Those were only boiled, the voices may bend your ear to say. What about sautéed? comes the unmerciful reminder. And Newburg, too, whispers another. Remember?

Outside Bath (Cook's Corners), the quest for lobster perfection continues. The perfect boiled one has been found, it has been mutually agreed, but can it be bettered? At dinnertime, the light dims and rain comes, and with the rain comes the fog. Looking through the windshield, you may despair of ever finding perfection or even your way. The road (Route 24) plays leapfrog with islets. Without a map you may have no idea what you'll find at the end of the point, but past experience by now indicates that there could be a restaurant.

If you come this way at night, keep your eyes skinned for a road sign that reads Bailey Island. Once you pass it, you will cross a bridge into a gloomy obscurity where the fog rolls over the road and headlights have no effect. Finally, atop a pier in a long building with cedar shake sides appears **Cook's** restaurant.

COOK'S LOBSTER HOUSE
Garrison Cove Rd.
Bailey Island, ME 04003
Tel. 207/833–2818

Within the immense dining space, despite the racket of whatever storm may blow outside, calm greets you when you cross the threshold. The enormous Adirondack-style lodge has high cathedral ceilings. Timbers are stripped down to

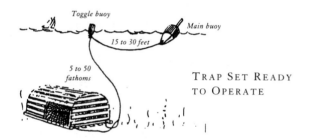

TRAP SET READY
TO OPERATE

their smooth white sides, and the place has the wholesome smell of wood. Ringed with picture windows, the room brings you into both sky and sea—on our visit here, menaced with electrical pulses. A pleasant-looking woman faces us with menus. "Menus?" I murmur, vaguely remembering. "But where are your mallets," I ask, "your garbage cans?"

"Do you have reservations?" she asks.

That word sounds strangely foreign to us after so rough an adventure of road stands and lobster pounds, but it seems we have reached an oasis of understanding. The storm has forced some opportune cancellations.

While we mull our menu choices, we get out of wet moods and into dry martinis. In no time we are convivial and once more pick up the challenge of our hunt, knowing somehow that this time we'll be satisfied. We become convinced that the storm that is crashing and flashing outside has been staged for our benefit.

There is sautéed lobster—and it is served mouth-wateringly, sizzling on a bed of Ritz cracker crumbs in a hot casserole. The casserole and its baked crumbs have come out of a hot oven at the same time as the lobster—three whole sets of claws and two tails. Sweet and bubbling in a clarified butter, the lobster is eaten out of the casserole with mouthfuls of crunch that comes from the crackers. Hot buttered Maine it tastes like, and Paris loves that.

Fished off the foot of Cook's wharf, the lobsters are fresh today and of the same quality you might find in Freeport but never in New York. The baked stuffed lobster is split in two and stuffed with cracker crumbs before it goes into the oven. The crumbs bake together and form a crust that holds in the juices. This simple dish is excellent—perhaps (but only perhaps) the choice of the evening. A muscadet on the wine list forms the clear crisp background that the sweetness of the lobster deserves.

With the lobster Newburg, the sauce has been prepared separately. A reduction of the broth that comes from lobster stew, which is used in lobster chowder, is combined with milk and butter and heated with a sherry and stirred until thick and creamy. Then, dribbled over the boiled meat of three lobster tails, it is served piping hot in a casserole; the result approaches perfection.

So well do we dine and feel that the weather seems eventually to agree. The rain parts and we cross the parking lot under a full moon. The next day is our last in Maine; so good are our feelings from the night before that we retrace our path back to Cook's. We all order the same thing for lunch and end our hunt toasting the lucky ill wind that blew our hunt to what we agree is its perfect conclusion.

LOBSTERS ENTER
TRAP THROUGH
HOOPS IN NETS

Clearing the
Table

It can be argued that civilization began when people sat down and ate together. Dining is the very essence of companionship; it demands trust. The Celtic chief who sat down by the fire of his enemy did so at his peril. He might be poisoned; he might be taken by his enemies, who came out of the shadows to carve him up; or he could get a bad sauce. Why then did he risk the doubtful companionship of the table?

I have a friend who confided to me after a divorce that she never ate alone. Being alone is bad enough, she said, but when you eat alone, you are really alone. This desire for companionship at dinnertime harks back to the deepest and most profound feelings within the human family. To be alone at such times provokes the stress of isolation. Dining and celebrating with food form the very foundation of the human family. The consumption of food through the act of communal dining paved the way for communal food gathering, food cultivation, and even the creation of sciences through acts—and later, arts—of cooperation. All this was thoroughly understood by a 19th-century German poet living in Paris. A friend from his hometown came to visit him, and the two men went out to dinner. They dined very well in one of the leading restaurants of the city; when the cheese tray came, it was laden with what seemed the full array of France's 365 cheeses. Instantly recognizing the awesome agricultural achievement that was represented on the cart, the poet pointed to the cheeses and exclaimed to his friend, "That is civilization."

It is estimated it takes 700 years to produce a good topsoil. Yet what it takes the earth so long to create and render beneficial to the species that share its surface can be destroyed by one of them in a few of his lifetimes. The cycles of soluble fertilizers used in intensive agribusinesses pull enormous yields out of the soil at the expense of leaving chemical salts in the earth that won't wash out or dissolve. Each treatment of fertilizers, as this goes on through successive growing seasons, raises the level of salts in the ground until they become so concentrated that they burn the roots of plants; then the land is no good for even sensible farming, and 700 years of topsoil have been destroyed in a few generations. Much of California's Imperial Valley is now threatened in this way. We have come in many parts of this country to the point where the act of modern farming itself destroys usable land and with it, dining. We don't need a German poet to tell us what will happen if we allow this to continue.

If we savor local produce, the very tastefullness of that produce could save us. There is information for us in taste. Goodness will save our farms. It is farmers dedicated to the land who grow produce for taste. The way to protect our food and lands is to protect the families that live upon them and draw life from them, for families tend to grow what they can live on and leave to their children. It is in their self-interest to protect it and not fill the land up with salt and then move away and leave behind a barren place and bitter pools.

As important as it is to sound an alarm, however, it is also important to celebrate the changes for the good. There are new generations of farmers in New England whose produce is superior to what comes in boxes in supermarket chains and is available at places like Guido's near Pittsfield, Massachusetts, and Hobson's Choice in Wilmington, Vermont, and the

Haymarket in Boston. As well as decrying what's happening to the land in this country, we should support the good that does come from it. There is a renaissance coming in produce that can survive and continue only if those who want it will go out and find it, and this must be both the heart and the soul of food exploration. It means taking the car up the coast road to Maine on Sundays in winter and finding $2-a-pound stands for local shrimp, in support of the people who go out in boats and freeze their knuckles off for them. There should be similar support for local fishermen selling their winter flounder— pay no attention to sole from Dover and red snapper from Chile. It means discovering, too, that the most delicious fish soup can be made from squid bits and shrimp shells (for a recipe write the West Street Grill, *see* Chapter 2). We should also get used to eating kale in its season and learn to love the turnip. Above all it should profit us to learn that food is best in its local season; it is the nearness to the source that makes food best; and the far better produce is the produce not grown to travel far. When you are in the adorable restaurant in the north of France, the chicken served to you came from a barnyard no more than a half-mile from where you are sitting. The turnip served with it is from a field you could walk to, and neither had a negative impact on the earth, where people have been farming for 5,000 years. What the earth still gives is rich and tasting of youth.

The pleasures that come from dining and drinking have been enhanced by what made these more comfortable. Yet we seem to have forgotten today how important meals were to the development of the crafts and the arts that grew up around dining. It is time to take a look. The first thing that man drew pictures of was his food—upon the walls of his cave. Tables and chairs were created around the feast on the floor, and then came plates and glasses so that what was eaten and drunk could be seen and admired.

HITCHCOCK FURNITURE COMPANY

Rte. 20
Riverton, CT 06065
Tel. 203/379–4826

Farmington, Connecticut, is a wonderful old spot at the end of a lovely drive in the country on Route 20. At the **Hitchcock Furniture** factory they make tables and chairs in the early American tradition. The chairs are of the same recognizable shapes and slat-back forms that were one of America's earliest trademarks. There is no tour of the works, but the furniture can be seen in the venerable factory store. The trestle tables and spindle and rush-seated chairs show the stages of the art of wood turning in this country, as well as of design and wood-drying techniques. Although they look the way they do, they are not antiques and are offered at outstanding prices shipped from here.

The nearby **Old Riverton Inn** (Box 6, Riverton, CT 06065, tel. 203/379–8678), on the same Route 20, offers dinner on examples of what you are coming to see. The gentle Farmington River is just out the door. People's State Forest is 4 miles down the road, and the inn makes a nice overnight stop for a full day to follow.

The work of Richard Bennett in Housatonic, Massachusetts (*see* Chapter 3), has been mentioned for its artistry in pottery and plates to go with the tables and chairs.

In the same vein of what arts brought to the table, if you go to the studios of Simon Pierce in Vermont, it is certain you will appreciate glassware more. Simon Pierce is a glassblower as well as a man whose restaurant bears his name. Here you can enjoy his lunches and dinners, entertainment, and artisanal glassblowing.

SIMON PIERCE
The Mill
Queechie, VT 05059
Tel. 802/295-1470

The windows of the snug and cozy dining room in an old stone mill on the Queechie River look out on a mad tumble of foam over falls. The cuisine shows a special talent for ways to tickle different flavors out of fish and lamb. The service and soda breads are what you might expect at a country Irish bed-and-breakfast, but it is downstairs that the spectacle can truly be said to begin.

The glassblowing operation is vast; there are open flame pits where glass is blown from red-hot globules into crystal clear curves of glasses and bowls while you lunch. There is a precise chemistry in the mass of material that is heated; the temperature of the flame must also be precise. All this invention is purely to produce a bend in a glass for a clear surface to eat or drink out of, just as many of our arts owe their existence to the one art of dining.

Some poisons were known to cloud the drink to which they were added. When glasses were made clear, they became the skin of the beverage they contained. What was inside was exposed with its flaws to the scrutiny of the eye. If it was murky, it could be dangerous, so what was to be drunk had to be made forthright to stand up to inspection. That a good part of the history of drinking is the history of glass should not be overlooked.

In all these explorations we have seen that food in New England came up from the beach. With the quahog in its ebb pools and cod in its tides, the sea was the giver of life to the New England colony. Without it there would have been no subsequent branching out, no pathfinders' canoes coming up the rivers from harbors into forests. What then was worked was no miracle of nature but a cooperation of the human family. Corn taken from the Indians; ham smoked over corncobs; sugar taken from trees; the miracle of heat and ideas, too, where glass was blown in open-flame pits into curved goblets for the enjoyment of drink; and ovens, such as those we have seen along the way of this story: These are the elements of New England's creativity inspired by our need for food.

Cooking differs everywhere on this earth; what is a feast for one is taboo for another. Among the most intimate and fundamental laws dealing with human behavior and culture are the laws we make for our foods and our diets. The basic and final test of any civilization is what it puts into its mouths. Food is more than what we eat.

It is who we are.

INDEX

5

Personal Itinerary

Departure *Date*

Time

Transportation .

Arrival *Date*   *Time*

Departure *Date*   *Time*

Transportation

Accommodations

Arrival *Date*   *Time*

Departure *Date*   *Time*

Transportation

Accommodations

Arrival *Date*   *Time*

Departure *Date*   *Time*

Transportation

Accommodations

Personal Itinerary

Arrival *Date*   *Time*

Departure *Date*   *Time*

Transportation

Accommodations

Arrival *Date*   *Time*

Departure *Date*   *Time*

Transportation

Accommodations

Arrival *Date*   *Time*

Departure *Date*   *Time*

Transportation

Accommodations

Arrival *Date*   *Time*

Departure *Date*   *Time*

Transportation

Accommodations

Personal Itinerary

Arrival *Date*   *Time*

Departure *Date*   *Time*

Transportation

Accommodations

Arrival *Date*   *Time*

Departure *Date*   *Time*

Transportation

Accommodations

Arrival *Date*   *Time*

Departure *Date*   *Time*

Transportation

Accommodations

Arrival *Date*   *Time*

Departure *Date*   *Time*

Transportation

Accommodations

Addresses

Name _____   Name _____

Address _____   Address _____

Telephone _____   Telephone _____

Name _____   Name _____

Address _____   Address _____

Telephone _____   Telephone _____

Name _____   Name _____

Address _____   Address _____

Telephone _____   Telephone _____

Name _____   Name _____

Address _____   Address _____

Telephone _____   Telephone _____

Name _____   Name _____

Address _____   Address _____

Telephone _____   Telephone _____

Name _____   Name _____

Address _____   Address _____

Telephone _____   Telephone _____

Name _____   Name _____

Address _____   Address _____

Telephone _____   Telephone _____

Name _____   Name _____

Address _____   Address _____

Telephone _____   Telephone _____

Personal Itinerary

Arrival *Date*   *Time*

Departure *Date*   *Time*

Transportation

Accommodations

Arrival *Date*   *Time*

Departure *Date*   *Time*

Transportation

Accommodations

Arrival *Date*   *Time*

Departure *Date*   *Time*

Transportation

Accommodations

Arrival *Date*   *Time*

Departure *Date*   *Time*

Transportation

Accommodations

Discover New England all over again this year

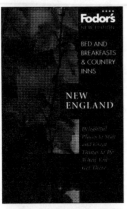

Fodor's Travel Guides

Available at bookstores everywhere, or call 1–800–533–6478, 24 hours a day.

U.S. Guides

Alaska

Arizona

Boston

California

Cape Cod, Martha's Vineyard, Nantucket

The Carolinas & the Georgia Coast

Chicago

Colorado

Florida

Hawaii

Las Vegas, Reno, Tahoe

Los Angeles

Maine, Vermont, New Hampshire

Maui

Miami & the Keys

New England

New Orleans

New York City

Pacific North Coast

Philadelphia & the Pennsylvania Dutch Country

The Rockies

San Diego

San Francisco

Santa Fe, Taos, Albuquerque

Seattle & Vancouver

The South

The U.S. & British Virgin Islands

The Upper Great Lakes Region

USA

Vacations in New York State

Vacations on the Jersey Shore

Virginia & Maryland

Waikiki

Walt Disney World and the Orlando Area

Washington, D.C.

Foreign Guides

Acapulco, Ixtapa, Zihuatanejo

Australia & New Zealand

Austria

The Bahamas

Baja & Mexico's Pacific Coast Resorts

Barbados

Berlin

Bermuda

Brazil

Brittany & Normandy

Budapest

Canada

Cancun, Cozumel, Yucatan Peninsula

Caribbean

China

Costa Rica, Belize, Guatemala

The Czech Republic & Slovakia

Eastern Europe

Egypt

Euro Disney

Europe

Europe's Great Cities

Florence & Tuscany

France

Germany

Great Britain

Greece

The Himalayan Countries

Hong Kong

India

Ireland

Israel

Italy

Japan

Kenya & Tanzania

Korea

London

Madrid & Barcelona

Mexico

Montreal & Quebec City

Morocco

Moscow & St. Petersburg

The Netherlands, Belgium & Luxembourg

New Zealand

Norway

Nova Scotia, Prince Edward Island & New Brunswick

Paris

Portugal

Provence & the Riviera

Rome

Russia & the Baltic Countries

Scandinavia

Scotland

Singapore

South America

Southeast Asia

Spain

Sweden

Switzerland

Thailand

Tokyo

Toronto

Turkey

Vienna & the Danube Valley

Yugoslavia

Fodor's Travel Guides

Available at bookstores everywhere, or call 1–800–533–6478, 24 hours a day.

Special Series

Fodor's Affordables

Caribbean

Europe

Florida

France

Germany

Great Britain

London

Italy

Paris

Fodor's Bed & Breakfast and Country Inns Guides

Canada's Great Country Inns

California

Cottages, B&Bs and Country Inns of England and Wales

Mid-Atlantic Region

New England

The Pacific Northwest

The South

The Southwest

The Upper Great Lakes Region

The West Coast

The Berkeley Guides

California

Central America

Eastern Europe

France

Germany

Great Britain & Ireland

Mexico

Pacific Northwest & Alaska

San Francisco

Fodor's Exploring Guides

Australia

Britain

California

The Caribbean

Florida

France

Germany

Ireland

Italy

London

New York City

Paris

Rome

Singapore & Malaysia

Spain

Thailand

Fodor's Flashmaps

New York

Washington, D.C.

Fodor's Pocket Guides

Bahamas

Barbados

Jamaica

London

New York City

Paris

Puerto Rico

San Francisco

Washington, D.C.

Fodor's Sports

Cycling

Hiking

Running

Sailing

The Insider's Guide to the Best Canadian Skiing

Skiing in the USA & Canada

Fodor's Three-In-Ones (guidebook, language cassette, and phrase book)

France

Germany

Italy

Mexico

Spain

Fodor's Special-Interest Guides

Accessible USA

Cruises and Ports of Call

Euro Disney

Halliday's New England Food Explorer

Healthy Escapes

London Companion

Shadow Traffic's New York Shortcuts and Traffic Tips

Sunday in New York

Walt Disney World and the Orlando Area

Walt Disney World for Adults

Fodor's Touring Guides

Touring Europe

Touring USA: Eastern Edition

Fodor's Vacation Planners

Great American Vacations

National Parks of the East

National Parks of the West

The Wall Street Journal Guides to Business Travel

Europe

International Cities

Pacific Rim

USA & Canada